HITLER'S SECRET WAR

HITLER'S SECRET WAR

THE NAZI ESPIONAGE CAMPAIGN AGAINST THE ALLIES

'This was a secret war whose battles were lost or won unknown to the public. . . . No such battle has ever been waged by mortal man.'

Winston Churchill

by

CHARLES WHITING

LEO COOPER

First published in Great Britain in 2000 by
LEO COOPER
an imprint of
Pen & Sword Books Ltd
47 Church Street
Barnsley
South Yorkshire
S70 2AS

ISBN 0 85052 744 9

A catalogue record for this book is
available from the British Library

Typeset in 11/13pt Candida
by Phoenix Typesetting, Ilkley, West Yorkshire

Printed in England by Redwood Books, Trowbridge, Wiltshire

ACKNOWLEDGEMENTS

My thanks are due to ex-US Senator de Amato, to Tom Dickinson and Professor H. Morris in the United States; to Carl Shillitoe and my son Julian in Great Britain; and to Dr H. Friderichs, Professor Pohl, Heinz Hohne, Dr Sareyko and Wolfgang Trees in Germany.

CONTENTS

AUTHOR'S NOTE

I met my first spy when I was seventeen. He stood out in that echoing Belgian barrackroom, heavy with the stink of the 'piss-buckets', amid a couple of hundred men waiting to be sent to the front as reinforcements. Most of us were green teenagers, though the word had hardly been invented in those days. A few were veterans, 21- and 22-year olds who had been wounded in the fighting in Normandy and were returning for their 'second bash', as the phrase had it.

The spy was different. He was an old man, perhaps all of thirty. He was strong-looking and surly and he'd obviously been an officer until quite recently. You could see the lighter marks where his pips had once been. Otherwise his battledress blouse was devoid of all unit insignia or medal ribbons, save for one thing left from his, to us, unknown past. They were upturned white-and-blue wings on his chest, complete with a parachute. I'd never seen the device before, but I recognized it for what it was. It indicated that he had jumped behind enemy lines three times.

He kept himself to himself. He smoked a pipe much of the time, clenched tightly between his teeth, as if somehow by this means he was forceably restraining himself from talking. Why and about what I could only guess. Once, however, before the 'big flap' when we all disappeared to our various dates with destiny, he got drunk.

Perhaps it was pay day. Perhaps he'd taken up with one of the tarts who haunted the cafés-cum-brothels around that Belgian cavalry barracks and had conned her into buying him drinks. Tough they were, but soft-hearted in a way, if your face and attitude were right. At all events, he staggered in, helped to fill the giant piss bucket near the door – it took three men to lift it – and took up an aggressive stance at the sagging wooden bunk, still adorned with the eagle stamp of the *Wehrmacht* who had occupied this same barracks a couple of months earlier, leaving behind their bedbugs as souvenirs.

There he shot off his mouth: 'Why *us* – fer Chrissake?' I wasn't particularly sensitive in those days, but I guessed that he wasn't really addressing us, but his former masters and an unjust world which had dumped him here, from whence he would probably go to his death sooner or later.

He had been in the SOE or the SAS; the initials meant nothing to me in those days. He'd worked with the Dutch underground. Finally he'd been parachuted behind the lines to the Dutch, taking with him a small fortune in gold coins for the Resistance. But he hadn't delivered. Like others of his kind I was to meet later, he felt he was beyond the normal laws of military discipline and accountability. Perhaps he felt he deserved a reward for the dangers he had incurred. Anyway he'd gone on the run, holed up in some big city, right under the *Moppens'* noses (he'd used the slang Dutch word for the Germans) and spent the money on wine, women and song before the authorities caught up with him. They always do.

When the 'big flap' came a couple of weeks later he disappeared. Naturally I never saw him again, but over the next half-century or so to come, whenever I met others of his kind, it seemed to me that that vaguely remembered spy was somehow typical of them all.

Spies, at least the ones I've met, always seemed to believe that they were in control of the situation, when, manifestly, they were not. It led to a sense of grievance that their admittedly dangerous activities were never properly rewarded. Fred Winterbotham, the guardian of the Ultra Secret, complained, 'Not even a good gong.' Even as an 80-year-old, who was soon to become more famous than ever he had been as a spy, Group-Captain Winterbotham was bitter and resentful.

Spies appear always to think that their acts of espionage resulted in earth-shaking changes. 'When I was told to defect by the CIA contact, I smuggled out four hundred key documents, welded into the chassis of my Skoda,' Major Frolik, of the Czech Secret Service, proclaimed proudly. 'That opened Washington's eyes!' Two or three years later nobody cared. Major Frolik had served his purpose.

Colonel Giskes and Major Ritter, Germany's wartime spy-masters who directed espionage operations against Britain and America, were cast in the same mould. Thirty years on, when this author had dealings with them, they were still boasting about how they had hoodwinked the Allies and how they had had spies, perhaps even assassins, in close proximity to Churchill and Roosevelt. Little did they understand that they had already been relegated to the status of minor footnotes in the history of the Second World War. The real threats to the security of those leaders during the war were still alive, kicking and unmasked, thanks to the machinations of the KGB.

With a finger on the trigger of his 'special' and a beautiful, nearly naked, blonde on his other arm, Ian Fleming's creation, James Bond, looks like these real spies might have imagined themselves in that sleazy underworld of betrayal and counter-betrayal.* In fact they were nothing like that, never were since they first made their appearance in Chinese accounts five centuries before the birth of Christ. As Montesquieu remarked in the 18th century, 'Spying might perhaps be tolerable if it were done by men of honour.'

But the real spies weren't 'men of honour'. Neither were they 'gentlemen' in the older English sense of the word. The real James Bond, if he ever lived outside of the novels of John Buchan, is dead.

But what of the man who controlled the destinies of those Second World War spies, Admiral Wilhelm Franz Canaris, who led the campaign against Britain and America and whose agents ranged the world from Afghanistan to Arkansas? 'Father Christmas' his enemies called him. 'High C'** was another

---

* Ian Fleming was in Naval Intelligence during the Second World War, desk-bound virtually all the time, but it was during this period in 'Room 39' that he conceived his ideas for the globe-ranging super British gentleman-spy, defending what was left of the Empire and bedding exotic beauties everywhere in the course of proudly being a member of 'Her Majesty's Secret Service'.
** Pun on the first letter of Canaris' name and a well-known German vitamin drink, containing vitamin C.

mocking name given to him by some of his more malicious agents, such as Giskes. But for most of those who knew him when he had 3,000 full-time agents, and thrice that number of part-time ones, under his control Admiral Canaris remained an enigma. As William Shirer, who knew him, remarked in his book *The Third Reich*, 'He was so shadowy a figure that no two writers agree as to what kind of man he was, or believed in, if anything much.'

'He always tried to maintain his distance,' Colonel Ritter, the virtual US citizen who returned to his homeland to spy against his new country, told the author, 'when he came to visit our branch in Hamburg. When he invited us all to dinner after his inspection, the Admiral was always close, unlike those Germans who tell you their life story within five minutes of meeting them, we never got anything out of *him*!'

American writer Ladislas Farago met Canaris, or so he said, in 1935. As he wrote in his *Game of Foxes*, 'I could not believe that this rumpled, tongue-tied, absent-minded little man was the new chief of the *Abwehr*. . . . I had anticipated eager curiosity that sparkled in the eyes. . . . [Instead] he impressed me as an honest dullard.'

So he remained a mystery not only to his most intimate colleagues but also to the huge Nazi police *apparat* led by sharp young men out to get him. As hatchet-faced Dr Kaltenbrunner, the last head of the Nazi police organization, wrote after the Nazis arrested him in late 1944, '[Canaris] managed to throw sand in all their eyes – Heydrich, Himmler, Keitel, Ribbentrop, even the Führer.'

Heydrich, the sharpest of them all, who had known Canaris the longest of those out to bring him down – he'd been a naval cadet under Canaris back in the late '20s – told his wife Lina that Canaris needed careful watching because he was 'a cunning old fox'. *

The motives of Canaris are very hard to fathom. How are we to explain that, although he worked for years to undermine the Weimar Republic (1919–1933) because it was 'not German or nationalist enough', he immediately set about doing the same to

* Frau Heydrich to the author.

the Third Reich, led by the greatest German nationalist of them all? What can we say of a man who harboured a major anti-Hitler plotter in his office (Major-General Oster, his Chief-of-Staff) and even helped the Resistance to place their first bomb in Hitler's plane? When he first heard of the July 1944 attempt on Hitler's life Canaris cried, '*Dead*? Good God! Who did it? The Russians?'

So many questions, so few answers.

Dreamer and realist, patriot and traitor, genius at deception and hopeless fool, cunning conspirator and genuine self-sacrificing friend, family man and predatory homosexual – all these were part of Canaris' complicated make-up. How different he was from the simple souls who spied and sometimes died for him.

Compared to Canaris those other two great spymasters involved in that dirty war in the shadows between 1939 and 1945 seem innocents abroad. Allen Dulles, the American, convinced that he was changing the world in the name of the United States of America, was an amateurish bungler who, unwittingly it seems, was directed by Canaris' *Abwehr* and Stalin's KGB. Even the chief assistant of Dulles's boss, General Donovan, was a Soviet spy.*

'C', for his part, head of the SIS, an intelligence service that didn't exist as far as the British Government was concerned, but was praised and admired by no less a person than Adolf Hitler, was also the victim of a Russian spy** and hampered by the fact that he represented a dying empire.

In the end it appeared that Dulles and 'C' had won the war in the shadows. But now, half a century later, it is clear that Canaris cast a longer shadow. That Swiss connection, which he protected and which ensured that Germany had the financial means to continue the war long after it had been predicted that the country would be hopelessly bankrupt by 1940, occupies German Chancellors and American Presidents to this very day. Forgotten in name, Canaris is still with us in that continuing war in the shadows right into the New Millennium.

* Duncan Lee.
** Kim Philby, the greatest British traitor of the 20th century, a double agent who might well have become 'C' himself if he had not been found out in time.

BOOK ONE

THE BATTLE BEGINS

'I can't tell you what sort [of job] it would be. All I can say is that if you join us you mustn't be afraid of forgery and you mustn't be afraid of murder.'

Secret Intelligence Service recruiting officer to Colonel Sweet-Escott, London, 1940.

THE MAKING OF A SPYMASTER
1917–1937

'The Secret Service is a service of gentlemen',

Admiral Canaris (1939)

Now the 'Bunker' was quiet again. But Danish Colonel Lunding couldn't sleep. He tossed and turned on his hard, narrow prison bunk. Overhead the harsh cell light glared down on him from the concrete ceiling.

This wakefulness was nothing new for the former head of Denmark's Military Intelligence. For ten months now he had been imprisoned in Flossenburg Concentration Camp not far from Nazi Germany's border with what had once been Czechoslovakia. Here in Cell 21 of the Bunker, which housed the special prisoners of a dozen different nationalities, he had rarely spent a good night. Even when his emaciated body screamed out for sleep, his agile mind continued to work. His daily task of darning old German Army socks and sweaters, heavy with the odours of their dead former owners, certainly did not act as a soporific.

Lunding lay awake night after night, listening to the stamp of the SS guards' heavy boots in the courtyard below and the snores of the prisoners around him. All of them were special for one reason or another and all were fated to end on one of the six nooses waiting in that courtyard.

But on this particular night in April 1945 he was burdened by the knowledge of what must soon happen to the elderly German in the next cell. The thought wouldn't let him sleep. Even though the German had been Lunding's most formidable enemy before the Gestapo had arrested him, the Dane's mind was full of concern for the man they called 'Father Christmas'.

Just after two in the morning on that April night, four weeks before the end of the Second World War, SS Sergeants Wolf and Weihe dragged the German back to his cell. Lunding had been awakened from a fitful doze by the sound of their heavy boots clumping down the stone corridor and the rattle of the prisoner's chains as they had flung him back into his cell, more dead than alive. Then they had marched away. As always the two torturers were in step, as if they were on a parade ground. For a while there had been silence. There always was after an interrogation. While he waited, the Dane could imagine the elderly German sprawled, beaten and bloody, on his straw-filled bunk, counting the steps until his SS torturers were out of earshot. And by now he too knew how many steps there were. Like all the *Prominenten* in the Bunker, that number was seemingly engraved on his mind.

Lunding was right. Almost immediately after their steps had died away and all was silent again in the death house, there came the first hesitant taps on the cell wall. The Dane hurried to the door. He peered through the crack. No one in sight. He moved in his stocking feet to the wall and tapped out the acknowledgement with his chipped tin mug.

Then the message began. It gathered speed and it seemed to the Dane that the German was regaining his confidence. It was as if he was strengthened by the knowledge that someone in this Nazi hell-on-earth could share with him his last hopes and fears. 'It was my last interrogation,' Lunding recorded the message years later. 'They beat me up again. I believe they have broken my nose.'

There was a pause. It was as if the German on the other side, his ear pressed to the rough concrete of the cell wall, expected some sort of comment. But the Dane remained silent. He could offer no relief. He knew *Scharführer* Stawinsky. He always beat up his prisoners. It was part of the routine. If Canaris survived this time the SS would beat him up again later.

Canaris started to tap on the wall again. 'Now I shall die for my Fatherland. I have a clear conscience. You'll understand that, as

4

an officer, I did my duty when I tried to oppose the criminal stupidity with which Hitler led Germany to its ruin.'

Lunding could have commented, but he refrained. The German was as good as dead anyway. Why reproach him? Finally he tapped out a few words of encouragement, but even as he did so he knew they were worthless. He had glimpsed Stawinsky's face through the gap in the cell door when they had come to fetch Canaris. He knew what the spiral motion the SS man had made with his right forefinger to the other guard meant. The German was 'going up the chimney'. First he'd be strangled, as Hitler had ordered should be the fate of all these high-ranking traitors. After that he'd be despatched to the ovens and the smoke of his funeral pyre would ascend through the chimney.

Canaris started tapping on the cell wall once more. Lunding pressed his face to it. Now the sound was fainter. Obviously the German was weakening. Thus, as recorded by Colonel Lunding, his last message came through. It read: *'It was all in vain. I knew Germany was finished in 1942. All in vain.'*

Admiral Wilhelm Canaris had just a few hours to live.

Nearly three decades before, in the summer of 1917, Wilhelm Canaris, First Lieutenant in the Imperial German Navy, had completed three very adventurous years of war in the service of his Imperial Majesty Kaiser Wilhelm II. Surprisingly enough, none of them had been spent in the activity for which he had been trained since he had joined the Navy at the age of eighteen in 1905 as a member of the crew of an Imperial dreadnought. Instead his war had been spent fighting on the secret front of espionage. Virtually from the start of his long military career Canaris would do battle in that murky world of treachery and counter-treachery, the 'War in the Shadows'.

Back in October 1914 he had been serving on the German cruiser *Dresden*. Under the command of Admiral Graf von Spee, the *Dresden* had been part of the German fleet which had sunk the British Pacific Fleet. For nearly three months thereafter the Germans had been masters of the South Pacific until the Royal Navy had caught up with them. Smarting from the disgrace, the Admiralty in London had hastily assembled a powerful fleet, which it had despatched to the Falkland Islands. The fleet's orders had been simple in their brutality: *Wipe out the Germans*.

On 8 December 1914 the cruisers *Inflexible* and *Invincible*, under the command of the aptly named British Admiral Sturdee, had met the Germans. Trapped, Graf von Spee fought back bravely, but to no avail. Badly outnumbered, the German fleet was sent to the bottom. Only the *Dresden* escaped, due to her superior speed.

Four months later, however, the *Dresden*, too, met her end. Coaling in Chilean waters off Mas a Tierra on 9 March 1915, she was surprised by a salvo from the British cruiser *Glasgow*. The *Dresden's* captain, *Kapitanleutnant* Luedecke, sent Canaris under a white flag to the *Glasgow*. Canaris' assignment was to explain that the *Dresden* didn't want to fight; after all she was in neutral waters.

The *Glasgow's* skipper wouldn't buy it. He snapped back, 'I have my orders to sink the *Dresden* wherever I find her. All the rest can be solved by British and Chilean diplomats.' And that was the end of the one-sided conversation.

A little later Canaris reported back to his own skipper who knew he was in a fix. He couldn't escape to sea. Even if he could, he hadn't yet taken on board enough fuel. If he stayed where he was and tried to fight it out with the *Glasgow* he would suffer severe casualties. But he was determined not to let his ship fall into the hands of the enemy as an easy prize. He'd rather scuttle her. Thus, as the first salvoes from the *Glasgow* shattered the morning stillness, the Germans opened their seacocks and the seawater began to flood in.

The sinking of the *Dresden* was, with the exception of a few months as a U-boat skipper in 1918, the end of Canaris' career as a fighting sailor. Although in the end he would reach the rank of Admiral, he would now start his new unorthodox career which would earn him the contempt of his former naval comrades, that of an agent, spy and finally spymaster.

For a while Canaris endured the dull existence in the Chilean internment camp where the survivors of the sunken *Dresden* were held by the pro-British Chilean authorities, but not for long. He spoke excellent Spanish as a result of his previous tours of duty in Spanish-America and he felt he could escape from the camp and reach Germany if Luedecke would give him permission. In the end, after a lot of pleading, Luedecke gave way. He would be allowed to escape.

Eager to get back to the fighting, and in the hope of rapid promotion due to losses in Europe, Canaris wasted no time. Stealing a boat, he rowed himself to the mainland from the island where the internment camp was. By dawn he had stolen a horse and started on his long and dangerous journey through Chile to pro-German Argentina.

The journey took him several months. He hid by day and travelled by night. He skirted all towns. What supplies he needed he stole or bought from the Indians. Time and again he was struck down by malaria for which he possessed no quinine, or any other medicine for that matter. But his iron determination to get back in the war kept him going. In the end he crossed the Andes in a three-day-long snowstorm, reached the plain and celebrated Christmas 1915 at the hacienda of a rich and aristocratic German settler, Herr von Buelow.

The German, a patriot with dual nationality, wanted Canaris to rest up for a while. *'Mensch, Canaris,'* he said, *'Sie sehen aus wie der lebendige Tod'* (You look like death warmed up). But Canaris, burned black by the sun, emaciated and still plagued by malaria, was impatient. In spite of his host's protests, he bought false papers and booked passage on the neutral Dutch ship *SS Frisia*, bound for Rotterdam, the great Dutch port which he would help to conquer a quarter of a century later.

His cover story was complicated but clever. Under the identity of Reed Rosas, a combination of both a Spanish and English name, a Chilean with a British mother, he was on his way to Holland to claim a fortune left to him by a suddenly deceased female relative. Thus he was a neutral heading for a neutral country. Yet he deserved the assistance and respect of the British sailors who would surely help him because he was half-British, had suffered a personal loss and might well join the British forces in due course. Indeed Canaris went out of his way to cultivate the other Britons on the ship, 'to brush up my English which I learned from my mother', as he told them. They were contacts which were going to turn out useful.

As he had expected, their steamer was stopped off Plymouth by a four-funnelled destroyer with zigzag wartime camouflage and ordered to heave to. Wearily the Dutch skipper, who had been through it all before, protested against this breach of the freedom of the open seas. The British destroyer captain ignored the Dutchman's protest and the ship was ordered into Plymouth, where the crew and passengers were interrogated by suspicious civilians and by naval officers of British Admiral 'Blinker' Hall's Naval Intelligence. By using this illegal method of stopping neutral ships on the high seas they had caught many German spies. It was something that Canaris would bear in mind as he watched them go to work on the apprehensive passengers.

However, he sailed through the grilling with flying colours. His new British friends spoke up for him as a 'nice helpful young man of British stock'. Indeed, in the end one of the interrogators who didn't speak Latin-American Spanish actually asked him if he could verify that a fellow passenger who claimed to be a *Chileno* from Valparaiso really spoke with a genuine Chilean accent. Canaris obliged. He verified that the man was from his 'native' country. One wonders what thoughts must have been going through his mind at that moment, but his diary reveals nothing of such matters.

Next day the *SS Frisia* sailed on, leaving several of Canaris' fellow passengers languishing in the cells of the naval barracks at Plymouth. A few days later he arrived by train in Hamburg so exhausted and ill, both physically and mentally, that his hands trembled uncontrollably. Yet, despite the demands the long escape had made on his health and nerves, he had had his first taste of undercover work – and he had liked it. He had been infected by the exciting sickness of the war in the shadows. He never would be cured.

In the summer of 1916 Canaris appeared abruptly in Madrid. No one knows how he managed to avoid the British sea blockade of Germany and it would have been very difficult for him to reach Spain through the Allied countries of France and Italy. At all events, somehow he got there and was set to work immediately on an undercover assignment under the command of the German naval attaché *Kapitain zur See* von Krohn, based at the legation.

His task was to raise a force of coastwatchers from Spanish fishermen and the like, whose job it would be to report the movement of Allied naval and merchant shipping through the Straits of

Gibraltar. Three decades later the sons of those Spaniards would be working for the same master who, on occasion when the fancy took him, would don an apron and a chef's hat and cook them a meal.

Canaris then had a more important assignment. Since 1915, when Italy had entered the war against Germany on the Anglo-French side, German U-boats had been operating in the Mediterranean. Now it was his job to ensure they were supplied with oil and food by bribing local Spanish merchants. At the dead of night they would sail out to the waiting U-boats with essential supplies. Naturally the Spaniards had to be well paid as it was a dangerous game. As the 'factional' accounts of First World War writer-agents such as Compton Mackenzie and Somerset Maugham reveal, the British Secret Service did not stop at murder.

Canaris ignored the danger. He liked the Spaniards, their language, their style of living and, possibly, their lax sexual *mores* with regard to homosexuality. And in Berlin and Kiel his chiefs liked his work. He was thorough. Despite his youth and inexperience, he gained the confidence of his superiors.

But not only German intelligence was interested in Canaris' work in Spain; so also was French Intelligence. They knew from their own agents in the Spanish Mediterranean ports what was going on, but as long as Canaris remained in neutral Spain there was little that the French *Deuxième Bureau* could do, save have some hired assassin stab him in the back one dark night. But as yet the French were patient, waiting for the day when he would have to cross the frontier into France en route for Germany.

The months passed. The man who had been called *'der Kieker'* (North German dialect for 'peeper') by his parents because as a boy he loved to peer through keyholes, became a very different man from the career naval officer who had first appeared in Madrid. His nature became more secretive, as if he felt he was being watched all the time (which he was, whether he knew it or not). He was still superficially charming. He clicked his heels and kissed women's hands in a most winning manner. He brought flowers when visiting people, being careful to take off their wrapping paper before handing them over, as German *etiquette* demanded. In short he was the perfect gentleman.

But underneath he had become introspective and was given to bouts of melancholy. For no apparent reason he began to weave a new and romantic legend about himself. He told those who asked about his un-German name that he was descended from a famous naval hero in Greece's 19th century War of Independence, Konstantinos Kanaris, who later became the new Greece's prime minister. No one now knows why this change took place. He was beginning to play his cards close to his chest, as he would continue to do when he became Germany's chief spymaster; already he was learning that one survived by half-truths and deceit. Only fools told the truth. *

Towards the end of 1917,however, he felt the need for a change. He knew that he was well regarded in Berlin, but if he wanted a real future in the *Kaiserliche Marine*, he knew that he needed active sea-going experience. Von Krohn, the naval attaché, was loth to see his subordinate go, but Canaris used his malaria, which had returned, as an excuse to return to the cooler climes of Northern Germany. So the naval attaché let him go. But how was he to return? Spain was hemmed in by Allied countries. As an agent known to French Intelligence, he would have to risk the dangers of the Allied blockade once more.

The train came to a halt at the Mediterranean border station of Port Bou, the main railway crossing into France. First the fourth-class Spanish peasants descended, laden with live chickens, bunches of onions, fruit and the like which they would sell to the local French for a good profit in this third year of war. Even in the rich agricultural south, goods in France were in short supply; everything was destined for the front in the north.

The passengers sat in the stifling heat behind drawn curtains, closed so that they couldn't see the French frontier defences. Finally grumpy French gendarmes started to pass down the corridors, checking passports and baggage.

Most of them were too old for service at the front. Others were younger men who had been badly wounded. But both were sharp-eyed; the front awaited all those who slipped up and they knew it. They touched their *kepis* politely enough, but their gaze

* In fact Canaris was descended from an Italian, Thomas Canaris, who moved to Germany from Italy in the 17th century.

was suspicious. They were on the lookout for *passeurs* and spies.

The emaciated young man handed over his battered Chilean passport and coughed, his whole body racked by the movement. A priest with a shovel hat looked up at the policeman sadly, as if to imply that the young man next to him hadn't long to live.

The cop didn't seem to notice. 'Reed Rosas.' He read the name on the passport aloud. 'Where are you bound for?' The young man explained that he was going to Davos for the 'cure'.

'What cure?' the policeman asked.

Canaris lowered his gaze and said huskily, 'For consumption.'

The Frenchman handed back the passport as if it might well transmit the disease to himself. He saluted and went on his way. Obviously he was heading for the WC to wash his hands.

Five minutes later the train started to pull out from Port Bou. In their compartment the priest and the 'dying' *Chileno* looked at each other. Then they burst out laughing. Canaris had cleared his first frontier.

The tuberculosis trick, to which Canaris' malaria-ridden frame lent verisimilitude, worked on the Franco-Italian frontier as well. Safely, he and his friend, a real Spanish priest, passed into Italy and rattled on to their destination in Switzerland. The Italian coastal plain gave way to hills. Mountains followed as they neared the Swiss frontier. Then their luck ran out. French Intelligence caught up with Canaris at the border station of Domodossola where the train halted and both the priest and Canaris were arrested. Escorted by two Italian soldiers armed with fixed bayonets, they were taken off to prison.

For the next few days Canaris was grilled around the clock. He stuck to his TB story, although he knew the French had obviously informed the Italians of his true identity. Time and again his interrogators attempted to trick him into telling the truth. But Canaris refused to be fooled. He saw through all their ruses. He knew he was fighting for his life. If he failed, they'd stand him up against the nearest wall and shoot him without compunction.

But he knew, too, that it would only be a matter of time before the French passed on to the Italian authorities all they knew of his activities in Spain. His last remaining hope was to convince the Italians that he really *was* Reed Rosas, a Chilean, on his way to Switzerland to be admitted to a sanatorium.

11

As ever he was very resourceful. Secretly he bit his lips till the blood flowed. When the guard posted outside his cell door wasn't looking, he spat in his food bowl and tin chamberpot in an attempt to convince the former that he really had a bad case of TB, but it didn't work.

For a week he kept up his masquerade. Then one day the guard entered with an evil smirk on his face. He put down the daily ration of soup and sour red wine, but, instead of leaving, he stayed and stared at Canaris. The look on his face boded no good for the prisoner.

Finally the guard's face broke into a malicious grin. Twisting his dirty hands as if he were putting a noose around Canaris' neck, he pointed at the latter and uttered the word *'Dopodomani'*. He followed this with an imitation of someone being slowly garrotted to death. Thereupon he departed, leaving the prisoner to ponder on the meaning of the Italian word *dopodomani* – the day after tomorrow.

But, although Canaris recorded the incident in his diary, he never expressed his feelings about that eventful moment. Perhaps the memories were too traumatic; the day after tomorrow the Italians intended to hang him.

It would be nearly thirty years before that dreadful prophecy came true. Canaris did not die on the day after tomorrow. Amazingly he escaped with his life. But how? That has remained a mystery to this day.

German writer and agent Karl Heinz Abshagen, who first got to know Canaris in 1938 and worked with him till the end of the war, explains his miraculous and mysterious escape thus: 'The news of his arrest had been received by his friends in Madrid who organized help. Influential connections were used. The Italian Government was informed by both official and un-official means that, in spite of everything, Reed Rosas was what he claimed to be. Whether Italian counter-intelligence was convinced is a matter of doubt. At all events, Rome thought it opportune to let him go. However, he was not allowed to continue his journey to Switzerland. He was put aboard a Spanish freighter with the priest, which, sailing from Genoa via Marseilles, was bound for Cartagena in Spain. Perhaps the Italians thought thus they would be absolved from the unpleasant affair, leaving it to their French colleagues in Marseilles.

'At all events Canaris read the situation like that. He went to the Spanish captain and explained that he was not Reed Rosas, but a German officer. He put his fate in the captain's hands.'

The Spaniard didn't let him down.

'He set course directly for Cartagena. If the French had been informed by the Italians and had been waiting for their "catch", they waited in vain. Canaris appeared in the von Krohn house like a ghost, pale and worn.'*

Ladislas Farago, who met Canaris in Berlin in the same year as Abshagen, has a different and more dramatic version of how Canaris escaped. He wrote of the episode: 'He made his way out of jail by killing the prison padre (whom he had coaxed into his cell), donned his garb and walked out before the body of the murdered priest could be discovered.'** It was a rumour that clung to Canaris for the rest of his life. Was it a figment of Canaris' imagination like the account of his supposed Greek ancestor, or was it the truth? Certainly we know that in the years to come Canaris would be involved in two major political murders.

Like so much else in Canaris' life the manner of his escape remains a mystery. Was he not only a traitor to his country, as many would say after the Second World War, but also a man who could kill a priest in cold blood? Many questions, but few answers.

One year later, on 8 November, 1918, the U-boat flotilla to which Canaris' submarine belonged sailed into Kiel harbour in close formation. At the mast they flew the black skull and cross-bones, plus the banner of the Imperial German Navy. They had done well in the Mediterranean. Now they hoped their victories would be recognized by the people on the home front.

But the new Lieutenant Commander Canaris and his crew, who had sunk three British ships, were in for a surprise. The war was nearly over. The next day the half-British Emperor, Kaiser

---

* Karl Heinz Abshagen, *Canaris: Patriot und Weltbuerger*, Union Deutsche Verlags-Gesellschaft.
** L. Farago, *The Game of Foxes*, Hodder & Stoughton.

Wilhelm,* whom they had served so loyally for four years, would flee to neutral Holland. He would abandon his forces and leave the sailors and soldiers to the revenge of the victorious Allies and the rebellious German citizens.

But the weary U-boat men did not know that yet. All the news from the *Heimat* they had received while in the Med had been rigorously censored. It was only when they came closer to the capital ships of the Imperial Fleet, most of which had not sailed since the Battle of Jutland in 1916, that they spotted a different flag fluttering at the battleships' masts from the one they flew. It was the red flag of the communist revolution. The German Fleet had mutinied.

In many cases the mutineers had formed 'soldiers, sailors and workers' revolutionary councils' (*Soldatenrate*). Officers had had their epaulettes torn off and their dirks broken. Some had been tossed overboard by the ships' crews. A few had been murdered. Overnight, it seemed to the homecomers, Germany had changed, and for the officer class of the German Imperial Navy it had been for the worse.

For Canaris, who had won the Iron Cross, First Class, during his brief combat career in the Mediterranean, the red flags fluttering over the home of the 'U-Boat Weapon' (*U-Bootwaffe*) that November day meant the end of the first phase in his life. Gone now was the comfortable old world of the monarchy in which he had grown up as the spoiled son of a wealthy North German industrialist. The monarchy was dead. Now he was confronted by a new Germany, governed by the 'reds', whom he hated and saw as the men who had stabbed the German military in the back and brought about her defeat.

Eight years later, in 1926, in Canaris' only recorded comment on the events of that November, he stated categorically, 'The Navy was healthy. The germ of the disaster came from outside. To the bitter end the relationship between man and officer in the Imperial Navy was of the best.'

Naturally, in 1918 Canaris, who had served throughout the war

* He was the grandson of Queen Victoria and the son of her namesake, the Queen's eldest daughter.

outside the Homeland and who had lived strictly for his profession, could not accept the new situation. The Navy had been the apple of the Kaiser's eye, the proud expression of the Emperor's love–hate relationship with Britain. For Canaris, too, it had been the only life he had known since he had been a teenager, an integral part of that man's world that went deeper than just normal male comradeship.

Almost immediately he joined the secret society of German naval, and later army, officers who were plotting to overthrow their new 'red' masters. He volunteered to go to Berlin as a staff officer with the reactionary and aristocratic Guards Cavalry Division to stamp out communist agitation on behalf of the new Social Democratic Government under Chancellor Ebert. *

In Berlin revolution was in the air. Together with mutinous sailors, the two Sparticist revolutionaries, Rosa Luxemburg and Karl Liebknecht (their group was to be the forerunner of the German Communist Party), had taken over a working class area of the city. There they defied all attempts by troops loyal to the new government to dislodge them. Now the Guards Cavalry went into action. Not for the first time in this turbulent post-war period, and certainly not for the last, German fought German on the streets of the capital. No quarter was given or expected. Finally both Rosa Luxemburg and Karl Liebknecht were captured. Later their barely recognizable bodies were discovered in a canal. They had both suffered severe beatings. The Polish Jewess and the bearded German agitator had been murdered.

Once the fighting was over and the revolt put down, the Socialist government decided to trim the wings of the right-wing officers who had stood by them at the time. An inquiry was ordered into the murders. It opened on 1 May, 1919. The traditional workers' May Day was obviously intended to send a signal.

Not for Canaris, however. He allowed himself to be selected as a member of the court; it was the height of cynical mockery,

---

* Surprisingly enough, Canaris was one of the first of the old Imperial officers to swear an oath of allegiance to the new Weimar Republic, governed by the men he was purported to hate – the socialists and liberals who had 'stabbed Germany in the back'.

15

especially as he had just arranged for a fake passport to be produced for one of the accused. If the latter were found guilty, he could use the passport to flee abroad.

The man in question, 1st Lieutenant Vogel, who had 'found' Rosa Luxemburg's body in the Spree Canal, was duly convicted. Naturally, before he could be sentenced, he fled the country. The German left-wing press raised an outcry and in due course Canaris, one of Vogel's 'judges', also found himself in the cells. Thus, for the third time in his 32 years, he ended up behind bars.

But not for long. His comrades of the Guards Cavalry and the Navy raised such a fuss that the government, threatened by yet another 'red' revolution in Bavaria, had to release him and no further enquiries were made into his role in the Vogel affair.

In 1920, having for a time toyed with the idea of leaving the Navy (his parents were still rich and he had married a wealthy heiress in what was really a marriage of convenience), he was promoted. He became the executive officer of the pre-war cruiser *Berlin*, anchored off Kiel, one of the few allowed to Germany by the Treaty of Versailles.* The post, however, was a blind. As usual Canaris was up to his neck in clandestine operations. In reality he worked as a secret aide to Rear-Admiral Baron von Gagern, monarchist commander of the Baltic Naval Station, who wanted to overthrow the Berlin socialist government and re-arm the German Navy, emasculated by the *Versaillesdiktat*, as the Germans called what they believed was a peace dictated to them by the victorious allies.

Today what Canaris did in the early 1920s is hard to determine, but for a relatively low-ranking officer in a tiny Navy plagued by money shortages and galloping inflation he did a good deal of travelling. He went to Holland, Finland, Spain, Switzerland and even as far afield as Japan, sailing there on the cargo ship *Rheinland*, on what was officially supposed to be a training voyage.

During those years it is more than probable that he was a member of the *Geheime Reichswehr*, the German Secret Army.

---

* Most of Germany's major ships had scuttled themselves off Scapa Flow, Scotland, rather than surrender to the British.

Everywhere in Occupied and Unoccupied Germany there were Allied controllers checking that the post-war German Army did not exceed the 100,000-man limit imposed on it by the Versailles Treaty and that they did not obtain weapons forbidden to the German military by the same agreement.

As a result the *Geheime Reichswehr** trained outside Germany, in the end even in the country of their arch-enemy, Soviet Russia. Picked officers of right-wing inclination were despatched to foreign countries such as Sweden, Spain and Switzerland, which were prepared to supply the castrated German Army with illegal planes and tanks. As General Kurt Student, the father of the German paratroops and later associate of Canaris in the Second World War, told the author, 'I served clandestinely in Communist Russia during this period, preparing for the day when Germany would have an air force once more. . . . I was responsible for 800 products connected with the manufacture and employment of aircraft.' He ended with a wry grin of secret triumph on his face, 'And I had them developed so that they could have been put into production on a mass scale within twenty-four hours.'

As the twenties passed, Canaris developed an almost feverish restlessness. He never seemed able to stay in one place for more than a few days, travelling all over Germany and Europe under a variety of false names and disguises. He showed little concern for his new wife and the two daughters she bore him. Indeed it was said that he held more affection for his two dachshunds than for his girls.

Even Christmas found him on the road without any real reason for his journey except his restlessness. His associates in Berlin and Kiel joked that he had no *Sitzfleisch* (literally 'sitting flesh') and one of his performance reports characterized him as 'a restless spirit provoked to great performance by extraordinary and difficult challenges in the handling of confidential and complicated military-political assignments on his frequent missions abroad.'

In 1928 Canaris was taken off his mainly clandestine duties and

* Also known as the *Schwarze Reichswehr*, the Black Army.

appointed first officer on the ancient battleship *Schlesien*, based in the backwater of Wilhelmshaven.* It was a responsible job which should have occupied him fully, looking after the training and welfare of 800 men. Yet he continued his secret activities, for it was the war in the shadows that now interested him, not the boring daily routine of a conventional naval posting. Indeed for a time he actively considered resigning his commission while he was young enough to start another career. However, he did not know what that career might be and he intensely disliked the thought of having to live with his wife and family. So he stayed on, encountering in this period another loner like himself, a tall blond cadet named Reinhard Heydrich.

As the twenties gave way to the thirties Germany plunged into the Depression. Soon six million Germans were out of work. In Wilhelmshaven, which, like most north German ports, was traditionally left-wing, Communists and Nazis fought openly in the back streets.

Canaris did not seem to take much notice, save to remark to his comrades that he did not like the new people 'with the lumber-jack chins'; he meant the brown-shirted Nazis. However, he remained staunchly right-wing, opposed to the policies of 'the reds', who had ruined the old Imperial Navy and who were still attempting to run a chaotic Germany in the form of a Social Democratic Government.

In January, 1933, Germany underwent a dramatic change. A new man became head of state – a former Austrian citizen who had only recently, in 1928, become a German national. His name, of course, was Adolf Hitler. The appointment of a new chancellor didn't change Canaris' career, but he was beginning to notice the State's new attitude to the Armed Services. More money was flooding into the Navy's coffers.

In 1934 he was transferred from the *Schlesien* to become fortress commandant at Schweinemunde on the Baltic. It was a fancy-sounding title, but Canaris knew that it meant little. The

* As far as the author can ascertain, the *Schlesien* was the first German Navy vessel to go into action in the Second World War when it pounded the Polish defences off Danzig in September 1939.

18

'fortress' of Schweinemunde consisted of a couple of batteries of antiquated coastal artillery and a small naval garrison, more concerned with summer flirtations with the middle-aged ladies who flocked to the coastal resort for the season. Once again it seemed that he had landed in a backwater, where, as a 45-year-old four-ringer, he could serve out his time. Then he could retire as a rear-admiral. But he was mistaken.

After almost thirty years of service, the last and most dramatic phase of his life was about to begin. For the new National Socialist bosses in Berlin had plans for him. When they came to power they had brought with them their own rudimentary Secret Service under the indirect command of one-time chicken-farmer SS Führer Heinrich Himmler. He looked like a harmless schoolmaster, with his pasty face, receding chin and pince-nez, but he was later to become known as the 'most feared man in Occupied Europe'.

With him from Munich Himmler had brought Reinhard Heydrich, the one-time naval cadet whom Canaris had befriended in the '20s. Heydrich had been cashiered from the *Kriegsmarine*, as the Navy was now called, on account of an unsavoury affair with the daughter of a high-ranking official and friend of Admiral Raeder, the old-school head of the Navy.

Born with an outsized chip on his shoulder, Heydrich was obsessed by the fear that he was half-Jewish. His schoolmates had mocked him with the supposed Jewish nickname of 'Issy' and he never forgot or forgave a slight. The Navy, from which he had been cashiered, and its officers were for him a constant source of resentment and feeling of injustice.

Now as the new head of the German SD, the SS's own intelligence service under Himmler, Heydrich was forced to work with the military's intelligence *apparat*, the *Abwehr*. Starved of funds for many years, the *Abwehr* was still Germany's only international intelligence service, combining in itself both intelligence-gathering and counter-intelligence.*

In charge of the *Abwehr*, just as with the British MI6 or SIS, was

* Unlike the British system of MI6, which operated outside the UK, and MI5, which was restricted to counter-intelligence within the United Kingdom.

a sailor. He was an old hand at the game named Patzig, Captain Conrad Patzig; and as soon as Heydrich arrived in Berlin it became clear that Patzig's days were numbered. To Heydrich Patzig represented the naval establishment, especially Admiral Raeder, who had brought the court-martial charges against him.

Naturally Patzig, who enjoyed intelligence work, tried to hold on to his job, although he was growing pretty long in the tooth. Unfortunately, however, he not only alienated Himmler and Heydrich, but also War Minister Werner von Blomberg. The latter, who would soon be removed from his post due to the machinations of Himmler and Heydrich, demanded that Patzig should be transferred.*

Raeder wanted to keep the head of the *Abwehr* appointment in the hands of the Navy. So, as preparations were being made to get rid of Patzig, he ordered a review of the records and fitness reports of all naval captains who might be suitable for the *Abwehr* post. Thus he came to read Canaris' reports, in particular the one prepared on the fortress commander by an Admiral Bastian in 1934.

Bastian, who had been Canaris' superior officer on board the *Schlesien*, had pulled out all the stops, for he had not wanted his subordinate and friend to be relegated to the backwater of Schweinemunde. So he gave a glowing assessment of Canaris. Raeder's eye was caught by the final heading on the official report which read: 'For what special position would this officer qualify?' Bastian then listed a whole series of possible posts: 'naval attaché', 'head of Hamburg Naval District', 'Inspector General', etc. But it was the final recommendation which took the old Admiral's fancy. It was 'Chief, *Abwehr* Department in the *Reichswehr* Ministry.' That did it. The Admiral picked up the phone and asked for the *Reichswehr* number.

Wilhelm Canaris' orders to report as the new chief of German Intelligence at the War Ministry on 1 January 1935 arrived as a

---

* Late in life von Blomberg married a lady of easy virtue, who, known to Heydrich and Himmler, had made money by selling pornographic pictures of herself in the shady dives of the capital. Himmler and Goering, the Prussian President at that time, demanded his dismissal on account of the fact that he was a security risk and had insulted the Führer, who had attended the wedding.

surprise Christmas present at Schweinemunde. He knew that Raeder didn't particularly like him. He thought Canaris too secretive and difficult to work with. Privately he suspected him of 'unnatural practices', according to the dictates of Paragraph 175 of the German Legal Code (homosexuality).

But Canaris didn't hesitate. It was the chance he had been waiting for and he grasped it with both hands. At eight o'clock on the morning of New Year's Day he knocked the snow off his highly polished shoes and walked for the first time through the portals of Number 72–76 Tirpitzufer, the home of the *Abwehr*.

Despite the early hour and the fact it was a holiday for most people, Captain Patzig, veteran of the war in the shadows, was waiting for him. He escorted his new Chief into the gloomy entrance hall of the *Fuchsbau* (the Fox's Lair) as the *Abwehr* HQ was called. 'To be frank,' Patzig said, 'I didn't expect you this morning, but I'm glad you came.'

Patzig made no attempt to conceal the fact that, although he loved his job, he was glad to go; Himmler and Heydrich were making too much trouble for him. Canaris said that he felt he'd be able to get along with the two upstarts.

Patzig shook his head. 'I'm sorry for you, Captain. You don't seem to realize what a mess you're getting into.'

'Please don't worry about me,' Canaris answered. 'I'm an incurable optimist.'

Patzig shrugged. Let Canaris get on with it. Then he said, 'I'm sorry to say that this day is the beginning of your end.'

GOD BLESS AMERICA (1937–40)

'The tales and descriptions of that time speak
only of self-sacrifice, patriotic devotion, despair,
grief, heroism. But it was not really so. Most of
the people at that time paid no attention to the
general progress of events, but were guided only
by their private interests.'

Leo Tolstoy.

On Sunday, 8 September 1935 Canaris got off the train at the one-
time country station of Berchtesgaden in the Bavarian Alps,
walked down the tunnel under the tracks and entered the brand-
new VIP lounge.* There he was met by one of the Führer's aides,
all braid and dangling lanyards, and taken out to the waiting
open black tourer.

Immediately they were seated the driver set off up the steep
road to the Führer's modest mountain chalet. Unlike his pre-
decessor, Canaris was about to meet the Führer to 'report'.

Half an hour later he was seated in an easy chair in the large
sitting-room, spartan in many ways, bourgeois and middle-class
in others, facing the new master of Germany, Adolf Hitler himself.
Unlike Churchill, Hitler professed little interest in intelligence
work. All he apparently seemed to know was that both the
Soviets and the British were far superior to Germany in that field.
Like Roosevelt, who didn't even possess a real secret service, if

* The station is still there, but it is a great deal shabbier than it was then. Today
the kiosk sells soft porn and Turkish newspapers for the local 'guest-workers' and
the one-time VIP lounge is a run-down tourist office, mostly closed.

one overlooked the FBI, he was more interested in what the *Abwehr* could offer by way of insider gossip: who was sleeping with whom; the particular type of perversion enjoyed by this or that leading European politician; who took bribes from industry and newspaper owners, and the like. It was said that the Führer had never been known to shake the hand of a spy, and never would, however important his services to the Reich.

So Canaris indulged the leader. He gave him what Hitler wanted to hear: details of the Prince of Wales's liaisons with married women; how Reynaud of the French Government was dominated by his mistress, as was King Carol of Rumania, and the like. Canaris also 'crawled' a little. He told the Führer, 'I have asked for this meeting, *mein Führer*, to give you my first full progress report and especially to ask you to instruct me about any plans for which you may need the loyal assistance of the *Abwehr*.'

It was the kind of opening that gave Hitler pleasure. He loved to dominate the conversation. His hour-long lectures constantly bored the pants off his staff, especially at night when they sat and listened, longing to go to bed or get on with their private flirtations, of which there were many on 'the Mountain', as they called the Hitler cantonment.

Hitler mentioned his problems in the east with the Poles, Czechs and Russians. In Poland and Czechoslovakia, he said, Germany had agents enough; there were sizeable German minorities in both countries. Soviet Russia was another kettle of fish, a very difficult country to penetrate. He told Canaris what the German military attaché at the Moscow Legation, General Kostring, had told him recently about the Soviet capital: 'An Arab on a white horse in a white flowing robe could pass through Berlin unnoticed easier than a foreign agent in Russia.'

Canaris laughed dutifully and asked what the Führer thought of intelligence operations in the Anglo-Saxon countries. The Führer reacted sharply. He didn't want any German spying to be carried out in England. He was getting on well with the English, a Germanic people like his own. If they busied themselves with their Empire and kept their noses out of Europe's affairs, he'd be perfectly content. Besides, he was conducting long-term diplomatic negotiations with that country. Any British discovery that he was spying on them might prejudice those talks.

Canaris, who, like the Führer, was mainly concerned with European operations, asked if the Leader had any intelligence plans for that 'land of unlimited possibilities', as the Germans liked to call the USA in the '30s, when some still regarded New York as a place where gold lay on the streets, conveniently forgetting the Depression.

Hitler shrugged. With his typical Central European outlook, America seemed a very long way off. Besides the Americans had problems of their own and were too constrained by their isolationist policy to want to interfere in the affairs of Europe. After all, didn't America rank militarily at about the same level as Bolivia?

Canaris allowed himself an inward chuckle, but his devious mind was beginning to race. He had recently learned that his organization already had full-blown spy *apparat* inside the USA, but he kept that information to himself. He didn't want Hitler interfering in any of his plans, for he knew that Admiral Raeder expected him to pull something out of the hat. The Navy had to have some success and, as he was the naval intelligence representative at the Berlin War Ministry, it was up to him to do it. *

In postwar years it was often claimed by both Germans and non-Germans that Canaris was an opponent of the Nazi régime, but on this peaceful Sunday afternoon, four years before the outbreak of war, Canaris heard some of Hitler's intentions straight from the Führer's own mouth and he was experienced enough to realize that his plans for a new *Drang nach Osten* could only lead to war.

In the mid-1930s the United States was isolationist, concerned with its own economic problems, which Roosevelt, the new President and his 'New Dealers' were trying, but not managing, to solve. Those few interested in Europe, including a sizeable number of German-Americans, were predominantly anti-British and pro-German. The British had got them into the First World

---

* Hitler was not very fond of the Navy. Central European that he was, he didn't feel easy at sea. Indeed, he tended to suffer from sea-sickness even when he travelled to the north German harbours just to launch a new ship for his *Kriegsmarine*. In the end, half-way through the war, he would have Raeder mothball his capital ships and concentrate on Admiral Doenitz's U-boats.

War, they reasoned, and then welshed on paying back their war debts. As for the Germans, they'd had a raw deal at Versailles in 1919 and were now doing wonders with their own battered economy, thanks to Adolf Hitler and his Brownshirts.

American Big Business seemed, on the whole, to take the same attitude, but for different reasons. American corporate business-men felt, rightly, that Roosevelt and the liberal New Dealers were anti-business and probably pro-communist. Again they were right, for as the recent 'Venona' decodes have shown, such supposed victims of McCarthyism as Harry Dexter White, Assistant Secretary of State for the Treasury, and Hiss, of the State Department, were active communist agents. * Possibly there were more, still to be discovered. At all events, US businessmen often felt that Hitler's anti-communist, anti-Jewish policies were the right ones. More importantly, post-First World War Germany seemed an ideal place to invest money at a very good return.

Allen and John Foster Dulles, respectively the future head of the CIA and the future Secretary of State for Foreign Affairs under Eisenhower and Kennedy, then lawyers with the New York firm of Sullivan and Cromwell, were instrumental in using their contacts with German industry (Foster Dulles had once been on the board of the *IG Farben* Group, which was to manufacture Zyklon B, used in the concentration camps' gas chambers) to contravene US government restrictions and invest in Germany. Many of their clients made excellent deals with German industry, paying a much lower rate of income tax. What these investors didn't know, or didn't want to know, was that the Germans were using their honest greenbacks to pay off Germany's reparations to the Allies, including the USA. Indeed, thanks to anti-New Dealers like the Dulles brothers, seventy per cent of the money flowing into an impoverished Germany, with its worthless mark and no foreign currency to speak of for purchases outside the Reich, was coming from major US investors.

By the time Hitler came to power these investments had

* The Venona decodes were started in 1943 and continued into the '50s. They were decodes of messages sent to Russia by prominent US traitors. Only recently have they been declassified.

25

become an open scandal on Wall Street, and, indeed, in the City of London, for Montague Norman, the Governor of the Bank of England, was exceedingly pro-German and encouraged similar investments. The USA, in the throes of the worst depression ever recorded, was crying out for domestic investment. Instead it was being short-changed by its bankers and businessmen. Fearing 'that Jew and cripple' Roosevelt on Capitol Hill and his bunch of liberal 'dollar-a-day' men, they preferred to invest in 'anti-Red' and 'anti-Kike' National Socialist Germany.

Henry Ford, the founder of the great automobile company, was one such. He was virulently anti-semitic and anti-communist. While Hitler was still an obscure right-wing fanatic in Munich Ford had published his book *The International Jew* (1927). It was still being distributed in Latin America and the Arab Middle East as late as 1946. In 1931 Hitler told an American journalist, 'I regard Henry Ford as my inspiration.' Later he would keep a picture of him in his office, boast that Ford was the inspiration for the Volkswagen, the People's Car, and in 1937 bestow upon him the highest award Nazi Germany could give a foreigner, the Grand Cross of the German Eagle.

That year the senior executive of the German branch of General Motors received the same reward, for both Ford and GM invested heavily in Germany. Ford had built its first factory in Berlin in 1925 and four years later, in 1929, GM bought up the old German automobile firm of Opel AG at Russelheim. By then GM was virtually owned by the Du Pont Corporation, dominated by Irene du Pont, a fervent anti-semite and racist.

For Ford and GM these investments were now paying off handsomely. With the Reich beginning to re-arm, the two companies would be in an excellent position to supply the *Wehrmacht* with new trucks and half-tracks. Indeed, by the middle of the coming war the two US-owned firms would be supplying Germany with nearly three-quarters of its trucks and, by one of those bitter ironies of war, Edsel Ford would continue to receive dividends from the German Ford Company right up to 1943. *

---

* Both Ford and GM had the gall to demand compensation for damage to their factories in Germany, incurred during wartime bombing raids by the Allies – and they got it.

As for GM, an American writer, Bradford Snell, who had spent twenty years researching GM's involvement in Nazi Germany, told a major Holocaust conference in Washington in 1998 that 'General Motors was far more important to the Nazi war machine than Switzerland. . . . Switzerland was just a repository of looted funds [from Jews and occupied countries], while GM was an integral part of the German war effort.'

The US car giants were not the only members of US Big Business to invest heavily in Nazi Germany in the thirties. Standard Oil of New Jersey (today Exxon) had linked up with the German petro-chemical giant, IG Farben. The aim of both was to create a major monopoly in synthetic oil and rubber. In any future war, the investors in Standard Oil and its company officials reasoned, the lack of European oil and rubber, to be replaced by synthetic products, would greatly increase the value of a company like Standard Oil which knew how to produce synthetic versions.

There were a dozen other major US companies, such as ITT, under its chief executive Colonel Sosthenes Behn, who were also doing major business deals with the Nazis in one form or another at the time that Canaris had his first meeting with the Führer. The morality of these dealings with a fascist country that was a potential enemy of democratic America didn't seem to worry US Big Business a bit. Of course the US businessmen and their scientists knew that the synthetic products which they were helping to provide for the Germans would be vital to any wartime economy and would undoubtedly help to keep the Nazi war machine going, for Germany itself could only produce a minimal amount. If, for instance, Germany's major European source of oil, Rumania, were cut off in a war, the Reich would have to depend upon synthetic fuels almost exclusively. The same applied to Germany's source of rubber. Without it, what would happen to the Reich's mechanized steamroller, the Blitzkrieg?

But although the US industrial giants co-operated willingly with Germany in both the production of planes and trucks (Ford offered the German Army rights to the first commercial four-wheel-drive vehicles, for instance, which later would be vital to the *Wehrmacht* in the mud and ice of Soviet Russia in 1941), they were only prepared to sell some of their secrets for dollars and by the late '30s Nazi Germany was running out of foreign currency.*

Here it was that Canaris' *Abwehr* came to the fore. If Germany couldn't afford to buy the US patents and secrets, then Canaris' agents would have to steal them, just as the successors to the Soviet Union do from the West today.** In particular, the emerging German *Luftwaffe*, under the enormously fat Hermann Goering, needed the latest US technology in the field of aeronautics. The Germans wanted gyroscopes and automatic bomb-sights – most bombers in Europe were still unable to hit their targets, hence the invention of the frighteningly accurate Stuka dive-bomber which could be *aimed* at its target – retractable landing gear, four-blade propellors, flight indicators and the like. So the *Abwehr* used a host of volunteer German-American agents, who, having been pariahs in the US after the First World War, had now become proud of their German heritage. After all, as Hitler once stated, two-thirds of all American engineers were of German origin and 'the people who were originally responsible for the development of the USA were nearly all of German stock'. Later, the Führer was thrilled when he was told that German had nearly become the language of the USA when the Americans had voted on whether German or English should become their official tongue. It was these new agents who were going to rob their host country blind.

By September, 1935, when Canaris met the Führer in Berchtesgaden, one group of *Abwehr* agents alone, under the leadership of a German-American aeronautical engineer named William Lonkowski, had obtained details of every plane being built at the Sikorsky plant at Farmingdale, the specifications of the Boeing bomber and the SBU-I carrier-based bomber Vought Aviation was making for the American Navy.

The method of delivering the information gathered by his sub-

---

* The illegal export of large sums of foreign currency from Nazi Germany carried with it the death penalty at that time. In the end skilled forgers in concentration camps provided large sums of counterfeit US dollars and British pounds, and the wartime looting of European gold did the rest, thanks to Switzerland.
** In Germany today it is rumoured that the CIA does the same thing for US industry as well.

agents and transmitted to Lonkowski's home on Long Island had been prescribed for him by Canaris' naval spymaster at Wilhelmshaven, Dr Pheiffer. Information from the USA was taken to the New York docks where picked sailors from the German Blue Riband holder *Bremen* or the *Europa* smuggled it through any possible customs or FBI checks for delivery to the *Abwehr* in Hamburg or Bremen. By this means the Lonkowski group didn't run the risk of radio transmissions being picked up or letters using the newly developed microdot system of conveying secret information being detected.

For the time, in that relatively unsophisticated age, it was an almost foolproof system. Indeed, as Dr Pheiffer revealed to one of his key agents, whom he entertained in New York's Cafe Astoria that year: 'At every strategic point in the United States, we have at least one of our operatives. In every armament factory, in every shipyard . . . we have a spy, several of them in key positions. The United States cannot plan a warship, design an airplane, develop a new device that we do not know of at once. . . . [It was] the most elaborate and effective penetration of a major power in the whole history of espionage.'

It was indeed a damning indictment of a country which would soon become the powerhouse of the Free World and emerge from the conflict to become *the* superpower. It was as if that vast nation was completely unprotected against Canaris' spies who, out of patriotism and for minimal reward, seemed to be able to steal secrets to order. Yet there was one thing which Canaris and his *Abwehr* operatives didn't take into consideration, and never would throughout the real shooting war. It was the vagaries of human nature, the foibles and little weaknesses of humankind, which can undermine and destroy even the seemingly most perfect of plans. The Germans were never able to make an accurate assessment of the people they employed. Agents who had been apparently attracted to the *Abwehr* for financial reasons suddenly turned out to have stubborn characters, not responsive to bribes. Loyal patriots, seemingly overnight, became traitors, betraying fellow Germans without a second thought. Intelligent, responsible men of the world fell for the crudest of 'honeypots', selling all they knew for a night in bed with a cheap whore. It was as if the character of the average German was flawed, unable to

29

distinguish shades and nuances in their agents. For Canaris' *Abwehr* spymasters the people they employed always appeared to be seen in terms of black and white.

On 25 September 1935 the pride of the German passenger fleet, the *Bremen*, was preparing to sail once again from Pier 86 on the Hudson River for Bremerhaven. In those days such departures were occasions for protracted celebrations with jazz bands, cocktail parties, press receptions, much drinking, flag-waving and last-minute stateroom naughtiness, which usually ended in tears.

That September day, amid the noise, a lean bespectacled man stopped to talk to one of the German stewards in his white bum-freezer. The man caught the eye of one of New York's customs officials, a certain Morris Josephs, who snapped, 'What kinda violin you got in that case?' and pointed to the violin case the man was carrying.

The man answered, 'Just an ordinary fiddle.'

'Is that so? Well, I'm interested in violins. Let me have a look at it,' Josephs said. Like many New Yorkers, especially those of Jewish origin, he didn't like the Nazi *Bremen* and her crew, who were all supposed to be fervent Nazis, and stormtroopers to boot.

The man opened the case nervously. Josephs peered in. Beneath the violin, resting there on the blue velvet lining, there was a collection of drawings of pursuit planes. Josephs didn't know what they signified, but it didn't seem right to him to have such drawings in a violin case. He beckoned the man to follow him to his boss, a Mr John Roberts. Together they searched the foreigner and in his pockets they found four rolls of film and several letters in German.

A day later the customs people had had the films developed. They showed parts of aeroplanes, while the letters, signed *'Sex'*, contained telling phrases such as 'Of interest is the single strut . . . the fully streamlined shape is also. . . .' Roberts knew they'd caught a strange fish and needed to call in someone more knowledgeable. He called a military intelligence officer he knew at Governor's Island. Fortunately for the man with the violin he was out, but a Major Dalton took up the matter and declared, 'I don't see anything wrong with these pictures. Anyone might have them. Let him go for now, but tell him to come back tomorrow when Major Grogan will talk to him. Incidentally what did you say his name was?'

Roberts turned to the suspect and repeated the request. The civilian hesitated, then answered, 'William Lonkowski, sir.'

'All right, Mr Lonkowski,' Roberts said. 'You can go now. But be back at this office tomorrow morning at ten. We'll have a few more questions to ask.'

Naturally, as Roberts admitted later, 'I never set eyes on him again.' The incident was indicative of just how unprepared the US authorities were for what was soon to come.

That night Lonkowski crossed the border into Canada. From there he was directed by Dr Pheiffer to the port of Rivière du Loup on the St Lawrence River where a German freighter was waiting for him. On 28 September the freighter sailed for the Reich, taking with it the fugitive who then disappeared, a 'blown' agent destined to become a footnote in the murky history of the war in the shadows.

Still, he had played his role. With other German-American agents, his ability to dig out the American aviation industry's secrets had an almost historic significance. They had made it possible for the new *Luftwaffe* to reach peak fighting pitch at a tremendous rate. Even as late as 1944 the *Luftwaffe*'s fighter planes were, in many cases, superior to those produced by the Allies. Stolen American ideas and techniques had been applied more quickly in Germany and had been refined in the light of combat experience in the years since 1939. As one writer on the subject has remarked, 'Without this aid from the United States, it would have taken considerably longer [for the *Luftwaffe* to develop so rapidly] and the Germans could not have gone to war as soon as they did.'*

But there was still one major piece of American aeronautical equipment which the *Luftwaffe* lacked, as did all other European air forces, including the RAF for that matter. This was an accurate bomb-sight. For years the RAF, whose chiefs believed that 'the bomber will always get through', had been using bombers on operations throughout the British Empire in order to keep

* L. Farago, *Game of Foxes.*

'restless natives' under control. Currently the RAF officer soon to be known as 'Bomber' Harris was serving in the Middle East and taking part in just such a bombing campaign. RAF bomber squadrons such as his would miss their targets not just by metres but by miles! Skill and experience didn't really count; an accurate bomb-sight did.

Now it had come to the notice of the *Luftwaffe* chiefs that the Allies were developing just such a sight, referred to by America's uncensored press as 'this country's most jealously guarded air defense weapon' which gave 'the United States a headstart in precision bombing'. This was the so-called 'Norden Bomb-Sight' developed by Carl T. Norden, in association with Theodore H. Barth, with additional work by Elmer Sperry.

The device was so secret that in wartime when a US navigator used it over the target he would lock the door of the compartment in which it was placed, whereupon the sight took over control of the Flying Fortress or Liberator until the bombs were released. Indeed, *officially*, the Norden bomb-sight and its secrets were not sold to the RAF until one year *after* the war had ended.

Naturally, in those pre-war years when inventors had to develop and sell their products without US government aid and the press didn't know what government censorship was, nothing remained secret in the United States. Thus by 1936/37, when a customs official had inadvertently blown a major *Abwehr* spy ring, the Germans already knew something about this exciting new invention.

Goering's friend and First World War fighter ace, Ernst Udet, now the chief of the *Luftwaffe's* air ordnance, personally asked for Canaris' help in obtaining details of the Norden bomb-sight in June 1937 and again the following August. Canaris did his best. A set of drawings reached Berlin from a new espionage source in Brooklyn. But *Luftwaffe* experts could make little of them. They had been forwarded via the *Bremen* without notes or explanations. However, one piece of information from the source in Brooklyn did interest Canaris: the man who had made the drawings for him, which now turned out to be useless as far as Goering's experts were concerned, worked at the Norden plant on New York's Lafayette Street. With Goering and Udet breathing down his neck, Canaris decided to make a new approach.

32

He would go round the old German-American volunteer spy ring to which Lonkowski had belonged. For all Canaris knew, compromised as it was, it was already being watched by the FBI. Instead he would use a new man on the case. He was a complete novice as far as Intelligence was concerned. However, the new agent was a native-born German who had fought the Americans at Château-Thierry back in 1918 and had worked in the States for ten years as a businessman, so he spoke fluent English.* Indeed he had taken out his initial American citizenship papers and had married an American wife. His cover was excellent and he knew America and its customs. These two factors would make up for his lack of experience.

The new agent used many names in the half-decade he worked for Canaris. In Holland he was known as 'Dr Jansen' or 'Dr Reinhardt'. In his homeland and the Middle East he favoured 'Dr Renken'. German bourgeois that he was and a bit of a middle-class snob, he dearly loved academic titles. But in his clandestine battle against the United Sates, and later the UK, he used the name of 'Mr Alfred Landing'.

A decade later that same Mr Landing would be working indirectly for the emerging CIA against America's enemies in Europe. Now, however, he had as his 'Target Number One' the United States of America.

Captain Nikolaus Ritter, the agent's real name, had first met Admiral Canaris in 1937, soon after his return from a ten-year stint in the USA. An infantry officer in the First World War, he had gone to the States in the twenties where he had prospered in the textile business. He married an American girl and fathered two children, but in the middle thirties the Depression had hit the textile business, so he decided that the 'New Germany' might provide him with a better future and he applied for an assisted passage back to his native country.

To his surprise he had been summoned to meet the German

* Surprisingly enough, in his several conversations with the author at his home in post-war Hamburg he never spoke a word of English and his correspondence was always in German.

Military Attaché in Washington, General von Boetticher, who had suggested, to Ritter's complete amazement, that, at the age of 40, he should rejoin the German Army. But Ritter who felt himself a bit long in the tooth for the infantry, was not destined for a fighting arm of the newly created *Wehrmacht*, which was rapidly expanding beyond the 100,000 men stipulated by the *Versaillesdiktat*. Instead he was assigned to the *Luftwaffe*, in particular to the *Abwehr*'s air intelligence unit in Hamburg. 'Not the best of postings,' Ritter remarked years later, 'especially as I knew nothing of flying or intelligence work.'

In due course he was seen by Canaris in Berlin, who chatted with him for a while before passing him on to his subordinate, Colonel Peickbrock, in charge of Group I, Secret Intelligence. Ritter was not impressed by his new boss. 'Actually, he was colourless,' he said afterwards. 'His gestures were considered. He spoke carefully and softly. His eyes were an undefinable blue; his face was regular but in no way remarkable. In short he was hard to describe.'*

Nor was Ritter impressed by his new office in Hamburg's Gerhofstrasse. It contained only a couple of chairs, a bare desk and an empty safe. Not a file nor a piece of paper to be seen, nor indeed any information about his supposed target country, Britain.

But for the time being Britain had to be forgotten, for almost as soon as he took up residence in Hamburg, a city new to him, he received a signal from Canaris ordering him to extend his 'intelligence work . . . at once, to cover the air force and aviation industry of the United States.' Ritter didn't know it then, but he had become involved in the secret of the Norden bomb-sight.

In later years Ritter made out that he took the decision to go back to the USA to acquire the sight for patriotic reasons. In fact, he was not too pleased by his new assignment. He had become a spymaster without spies and had no inkling of how to find any.

Anyway, he took the train from Hamburg's *Hauptbahnhof* to Berlin and presented his rough-and-ready plan to Canaris personally. Canaris didn't like it one bit. He told Ritter how badly

---

* In an interview with the author.

the Reich needed the Norden bomb-sight. 'This is a very important assignment and the mission is fraught with danger. We should not jeopardize it unnecessarily by exposing you in the process.'

Ritter protested politely, 'Herr Admiral,' he answered, 'I realize that this is a delicate mission. That is why I propose to go myself.' He explained that he knew the country well and spoke 'American English'. 'I know how to conduct myself and am confident that I can carry off the mission without mishap.'

In the end Canaris gave way and allowed Ritter to go, but he gave him some parting advice. 'Stay clear of all official Germans, especially your friend the Military Attaché. General von Boetticher has no understanding of our work. He thinks he can do it better than we can. Under no circumstances go near him or any other German official stationed over there.' Whether Canaris was jealous of the General and was trying to protect his own fiefdom, or whether he had other reasons for warning Ritter that day, the latter never found out. But that interview taught him one thing about Intelligence and his new masters in Germany – never trust anyone. 'They were all out to feather their own little nests. First came their own personal prestige and then the interests of the Reich. In fact, before my cover was finally blown and I had to leave the *Abwehr* for the regular *Luftwaffe*, I'd come to the conclusion that the New Germany was no different from the Old Germany, a bureaucratic country full of office-seekers out for personal privilege and acclaim.'

On the second Sunday after his arrival in New York, 21 October, 1937, Ritter drove from the Hotel Taft to see the man he had come so far to meet at 248 Monitor Street, Brooklyn. (The Taft could almost have been the American *Abwehr* HQ for so many of its spies seemed to have stayed there, including one who was apparently assassinated under mysterious circumstances.)* He

---

* The last time the author stayed there to meet yet another spy of the postwar version of the war in the shadows, the Taft lived up to its reputation. Waiting for his taxi outside the hotel, he was witness of a shoot-out to the death between the police and a robber who had shot an off-duty member of New York's finest. As a Vietnam veteran lying on the ground next to the author remarked, 'Hell, this is worse than Nam!'

was a broad-faced man of 35, Hermann Lang, who, after ten years, was still waiting to become an American citizen. Lang worked in the factory at 80 Lafayette Street in Manhatten that was now producing the Norden sight.

Lang, code-named 'Paul' by the *Abwehr*, had achieved the rank of inspector at the factory by dint of hard work, punctuality and the thoroughness of his German vocational education. How such a man – a good father, a loyal husband and excellent provider – had ever become a spy Ritter didn't ask himself. Such questions did not concern him.

The blueprints of the Norden apparatus were supposed to be returned to the safe after production was finished for the day. But not all of them were and Lang was in the habit of taking some of them home. There he had begun to study them and after a while he started copying them.

He explained the situation to Ritter, saying that he was going to give him the copies, not for money, but for the sake of the old *Heimat*, now recovered at last from its terrible defeat of 1918. If the possession of this US secret helped to make Germany stronger that would be reward enough for him.

According to Lang, it would be impossible to obtain the complete plans because, as he explained, 'The *Amis* are so secretive that they have it assembled at different plants, like the Mergenthaler Linotype Company on Ryerson Street here in Brooklyn.' Lang, however, thought that 'your engineers will be able to reconstruct the missing sections from the prints I'm able to give you.'*

The drawings in question presented a problem, however. Like other secret documents stolen by the *Abwehr*, they would have to be smuggled back to the Reich in the *Bremen*. But Ritter didn't want another fiasco with the now doubly-suspicious US customs. He had to be careful. For a while he was tempted to take them

---

* It is one of those minor ironies of the Second World War that Mergenthaler, also German, sent his grandson to fight in Europe as an ordinary GI. He was to die in battle in the Ardennes in 1944. Today his death is commemorated by a large slab of local stone on the road between Diekirch in Luxembourg and Bastogne in Belgium, symbolic of those many German-Americans who didn't betray their new country, but fought – and died – for it.

aboard in his briefcase, but it turned out to be too small for the large-scale drawings. So the aid of another steward was enlisted to take the plans aboard the liner.

He was a fat Berliner named Herbert Jaenichen, who, like all Berliners, was renowned for his quick thinking and cocky manner. Ritter arranged to meet him at a drugstore in the Times Building. With him he carried the stolen documents wrapped inside a cane umbrella. But Jaenichen objected to taking over the umbrella. He said he had passed through US customs on his afternoon shore leave without one and what would happen if the eagle-eyed customsmen spotted the fact? Naturally they'd stop him and ask to have a look at it, as they had done with the violin case previously. However, he'd return on the following day with an umbrella of his own, which he'd display conspicuously to the customsmen.

Ritter agreed to the new scheme and, returning to his hotel, prepared for the meeting on the morrow. Unfortunately, it turned out to be a beautiful sunny day, certainly not the kind of day when one would need an umbrella. Ritter wondered how the steward was going to manage. He need not have worried.

With a cheeky grin on his face, Jaenichen appeared, leaning heavily on a battered brolly. 'I had to have a reason for carrying this damned thing on such a beautiful sunny day,' he explained, 'so I told them that I had sprained my ankle and had only this umbrella to help me in walking.'

In this fashion the drawings of the world's most efficient bombsight were carried on board the *Bremen* on 31 October 1937!

In the end nothing much came of the affair. A delighted Goering invited Lang to Germany, where he was feted and shown the German *Adler-Geraet* (Eagle Apparatus), a bombsight developed by a certain Professor Fuchs of the University of Göttingen. When he saw it, Lang's face fell. 'You already had it,' he exclaimed. 'All my work was unnecessary then!'

Hastily they reassured the hero of the hour, 'That model would not be on that table without your valuable contribution, Herr Lang.' But Lang was eventually forced to pay the price for his 'valuable contribution' and, naturally, for his betrayal of the country which had taken him in in 1927. In 1941 he was brought to trial before a US Federal court, together with several other members of a German-American *Abwehr* spy ring. The trial caused a minor sensation. For the first time the average American realized that the Germans were actively spying on their country, although the USA was still neutral. As for Lang, he was sentenced to a term in prison and disappeared into obscurity.

As did the *Adler-Geraet*, based on the famed Norden bomb-sight. The RAF had already seen to that. In the winter of 1940/41 RAF Fighter Command had destroyed most of Goering's bomber fleet over the British Isles and by the time the Lang trial was held there was no need for German precision bomb-sights. In the new war over Soviet Russia there was little demand for the kind of pinpoint bombing that the Norden and Adler sights had promised. Russia, Germany, and soon Britain would concentrate on so-called 'area bombing', which meant taking out whole towns without any scruples as to whether they were legitimate war targets. Indiscriminate bombing was the name of the game, or, as Professor Lindemann, Churchill's German-born scientific adviser, put it more primly, 'de-housing the civilian workforce'.

Four years later, as Patton's triumphant Third Army raced through Bavaria heading for Czechoslovakia, his troops stumbled across what the British called a 'shadow factory', a war production plant hidden in a rural area far from Allied bombers. Immediately the scientific soldiers, the 'T-Teams', attached to most Allied armies at the end of the war, thought they had struck gold. In that last mad rush before the Russians took over the East they were eager to spirit away any German secret inventions before the Russians could lay their hands on them. Eagerly the T-Team men purloined a sample of the hidden factory's wares, a supposedly ingenious electronic device for which the Germans were famous, called *'Luftwaffenzielgerat EZ 42'*. But the soldier-scientists were in for a disappointment. It turned out to be the Norden bomb-sight.

However, there is one aspect of the saga of the Norden bomb-sight and its reputed ability to drop a bomb 'in a pickle barrel', which only came to light in 1999. It is to be found in concrete form in the sagebrush desert that belongs to the US Army's 'Dugway Proving Ground', some sixty miles south-west of the state capital of Utah, Salt Lake City. After fifty-seven years the abandoned buildings, which once occupied the attention not only of the US bombing strategists but of no less a person than President Roosevelt himself, still bear the strange name of 'the German Village'.*

The German Village is the surviving part of what during the Second World War was a larger complex, built by the technicians of the Standard Oil Company, whose pre-war bosses had made those secret deals with the Nazis and were probably still receiving dividends from their German partners via Switzerland. Standard Oil had been given the task by the US Corps of Chemical Warfare, located at the Dugway Testing Ground. Here all types of probably illegal warfare, including the use of anthrax, were being tried out in secrecy.

Now the US Army and Standard Oil contracted an emigre German-Jewish architect to come out to this remote place to take part in another experiment which, connected with the Norden sight as it was, has remained secret long after those devices have been forgotten.

The architect's name was Erich Mendelsohn and, before he had been forced to flee, had been one of Germany's leading architects. He had been particularly prominent in Berlin, building a model in the capital's suburb of Charlottenburg of the Einsteinturm Observatory in Potsdam.

His new assignment was much more humble. Out in the desert, under strict guard, he was to create a typical working-class Berlin apartment block (six different types in the end). They had to be exact replicas of ones already standing in Berlin, down to the very last detail.

Mendelsohn went to work with his customary thorough-ness, though he knew he wasn't going to win any award for this little Berlin in the middle of nowhere. The timber for the roof frames was imported especially from Murmansk; a highly dangerous undertaking in itself. In that year, 1943, five thousand British merchant seamen lost their lives on convoys between Hull and Murmansk. The timber had then to be

* Professor E. Davis, 'The German Village' *Grandstreet Magazine*, New York, 1998.

constantly sprayed with water to simulate the rainfall of Berlin.

Mendelsohn went further. Jewish he might be, but he worked with typical German thoroughness. He contracted RKO Studios in Hollywood to supply a team of decorators, the same people who had been praised for the high quality of their work on Orson Welles' *Citizen Kane*. Now, aided by craftsmen who had been trained in Germany, they created typical low-class interiors. Solid, heavy, cheap furniture of the kind pre-war working class Berliners had bought at *Karstadt*, at *Kaufhof* and the like was hand-made at prohibitive cost by these Hollywood design specialists and their German-trained carpenters and painters. Mendelsohn even managed to find a supply of German textiles from which seamstresses (also German-trained) made carpets, covers, drapes and the like.

By June of 1943 the six apartment blocks which made up the German Village were finished and ready for use. But the American military authorities waited before they went into action. They wanted to see how the British under 'Bomber' Harris got on. For that summer Harris, who did not have much time for pinpoint bombing – he favoured Professor Lindemann's 'de-housing policy' – was going to try out one of his pet theories – the destruction of an enemy city by massive bomb-induced blazes. Hamburg was to be his first target for what became known later as 'fire-storms'.

Harris's four-engined bombers went in first with incendiaries. When these had been dropped and were well alight, especially around the inner docks area of the city, where the buildings dated back to medieval times and were partly made of wood and wattle, there came a second wave, which dropped high explosive. The bursts from these fanned the flames which grew higher and higher, creating a great vacuum in which a wall of fire jumped from street to street with terrible effect. At the height of the raid Hamburg's fire brigade recorded temperatures of 1,000° Celsius. That terrible week of fire storms caused the death of some 30,000 citizens, reduced whole areas of the city to 'death zones', areas sealed off by police and troops. Hundreds of thousands fled the city, jamming the country roads out to Reinbek, Glinde, Berge-dorf and other smaller towns in the area. Hamburg had been well and truly 'fire-stormed' and nearly a million of its inhabitants 'de-housed'.

The US Eighth Air Force, stationed in Britain and bombing the same targets, couldn't possibly emulate the 'Limeys'. Their generals believed in the 'democratic value' of precision bombing. But unfortunately for the Americans they were not achieving a 'kill rate' to justify their high losses. The Norden sight was 'just too accurate'. Something had to be done.

Roosevelt shared the feelings of his 'hawks'. In 1944 he told his virulently anti-German Treasury Minister, the Jewish Henry Morgenthau, 'We've got to be hard on the Germans and I mean Germans not Nazis. Either we castrate them or deal with them in such manner that they can't produce another generation to carry on the way they have been doing in the past.' Roosevelt ordered that Berlin should one day suffer the same 'fire-storming' as Hamburg. He demanded a single attack by 2,000 US bombers which would cause 220,000 casualties. The British agreed. A spokesman for Harris (and probably Churchill) stated: 'The complete destruction of an inner city such as the centre of Berlin would convince our Russian allies, and the neutrals too, of the power of the Anglo-American air forces.'

It was for this reason that the German Village had been constructed. The armchair warriors had had enough of the Norden sight and precision bombing. They wanted mass destruction. Here in the desert they practised that mass destruction, without the aid of the Norden sight.

In the event the great American raid of Berlin on 3 February, 1945, didn't turn out to be a second Hamburg, though it did, incidentally, knock out the *Abwehr* HQ. It failed to create another, American-manufactured, fire-storm; nevertheless 3,000 Berliners died that day. Dresden followed. There the 'Anglo-American terror fliers', as the Germans called them, created a second fire-storm and an estimated 35/40,000 Germans were killed. The raid on Dresden has been a matter of controversy ever since.

Mendelsohn's Observatory and the workers' flats in Berlin-Wilmersdorf still survive, occupied by young Berliners who have no idea who built them and the fate their architect had intended for them. It has become part of the secret history of the war in the shadows.

It is the same with that pride of pre-war US technology, for which men of half a dozen nationalities wheeled and dealed, betrayed and were betrayed, the Norden bomb-sight. Today it is merely an object of scientific curiosity, openly displayed in a handful of poorly visited museums. All that effort, for what?

WIR MARSCHIEREN GEGEN ENGELAND (1940)

'The British Secret Service has a great tradition.
Germany possesses nothing comparable to it. . . .
The cunning and perfidy of the British Secret
Service is known to the world, but it will avail
them little unless Germans themselves are ready
to betray Germany.'

Adolf Hitler to SS General Schellenberg

On the evening of 26 June 1940 a gathering of some of the US's most distinguished and richest men descended on the Waldorf-Astoria, which itself had been built by the scion of a German-American family, the Astors, to dine at this, New York's most upper-crust hotel.

Officially they had come at the invitation of a certain Dr Westrick, one day to be a prominent figure in postwar Germany. In 1940 he was accredited as the Commercial Attaché at the German Legation in Washington and was in the States on a secret mission 'to build up goodwill for Germany among American businessmen and financiers'.

They had come to celebrate the surrender of France the day before. Not that the French defeat particularly interested these 'prominent businessmen [who] did not want to be further identified in any circumstance at this time', as Westrick put it in his report to Berlin. But the German victory did. It meant their investments in Hitler's Germany would prosper and with Germany now dominating Western Europe, save for Britain, which didn't matter anyway, the room for US expansion there was boundless.

They were a powerful bunch who assembled that night to toast Germany's victory, in French champagne of course. They included Colonel Behn, chief executive of International Telephone and Telegraph, James Mooney, chief of General Motors' overseas operations, Henry Ford's son Edsel, representatives of Eastman Kodak and many others.

The guest of honour, in reality the behind-the-scenes organizer of the party, was Norwegian-American 'Cap'n' Torkild Rieber of the Texas Oil Company, who financed Westrick and ensured that he met the right people in the States. He had worked personally with Hermann Goering, who, among his many offices, was head of the Nazi Four-Year Economic Plan. Rieber, who proclaimed to anyone prepared to listen, 'Some of my best friends are kikes like Bernie Gimbel and Sol Guggenheim,' was, in fact, the only one present who was open about the fact that German victory would mean enormously enlarged business potentials. As the head of the firm which would become Texaco, the Cap'n wanted a large slice of the cake for himself and his investors. The Germans knew that and behind his back they nicknamed him *'Leichengaenger'*, a man who would walk over dead bodies to achieve his aims.

It was Rieber who paid Westrick's rent for the house he had leased in fashionable Scarsdale, New York, bought him a new Buick for a couple of thousand dollars and this night was paying for the party at the Waldorf.

These American businessmen were doing nothing illegal. Indeed the US Ambassador to the Court of St James in London, Joseph Kennedy, another big businessman himself and the father of President Kennedy, represented the same point of view. They wanted America out of the war for they believed, as Kennedy did, that Britain would not win. A neutral USA could then get on with the task of making money in a booming Germany and her new empire in Europe.

The day after the Waldorf dinner Westrick reported to Berlin that an influential group of the diners, under Mooney of GM, had agreed to put pressure on President Roosevelt to improve relations with Germany by 'immediately sending an American ambassador to Berlin' and by 'suspending shipments of armaments to Great Britain'.

44

It was a view with which Rieber concurred, for he was the representative not only of US big business but the German *Abwehr* as well, and one which was whole-heartedly supported by the Führer, who at this moment did not want any trouble on the other side of the Atlantic.

That hot June night in New York, however, something occurred which brought matters to a head as far as *Abwehr* activity in the United States was concerned.* For another espionage service had been watching the activities of the *Abwehr*, and more importantly pro-Nazi US businessmen, with growing alarm ever since Dr Westrick had arrived in the United States.

The covert British operation, which helped to bring to an end the first phase of German Intelligence operations in America, had its offices on the 38th floor of New York City's Rockefeller Center and was led by an undersized, boastful, former pilot and ex-amateur boxer, William Stephenson, a Canadian millionaire. Ian Fleming, then a member of Naval Intelligence and later famous as the creator of James Bond said of him that he 'became . . . the scourge of the enemy throughout the Americas'.

Stephenson, whose main task was to counter German influence in the United States, stopped at nothing. 'Intrepid', as he was code-named after his New York cable address, was prepared to use threats, blackmail and, in one case perhaps even murder to stop the Germans and their American big business friends in the USA.

In the black summer of defeat in Europe, while Hitler was prepared to go to any length to keep America *out* of the war, Stephenson used all the means at his disposal to help President Roosevelt take the country *into* the war.

That summer one of his prime targets was those US big businessmen who, in his eyes, put profit before patriotism. They and their Swiss banker associates in New York, who laundered their money as well as the Nazi gold needed for military purchases in the US and elsewhere abroad, had, in Stephenson's opinion, to

* The *Abwehr* had two major spy rings operating in the US at that time, with agents apparently employed at all major industrial plants, plus the many amateur spies watching shipping transporting arms to Britain, sailing from New York and other Eastern seaboard ports.

45

be shown up for what they were to John Doe and the Great American Public – capitalist bigots who were anti-labour, anti-Jewish and prepared to contravene American laws about trading with the Germans in the interests of their own greed.

The dinner at the Waldorf was the kind of opportunity Stephenson needed to show the average American what kind of skunks they had in their midst. Enlisting the support of Arthur Hays Sulzburger, the democrat, pro-Jewish owner of the *New York Times*, read throughout the States and naturally in the world's largest Jewish city, New York, he revealed the full details of that grand, invitation-only dinner.

Stephenson did an excellent hatchet job and Sulzburger loved it. In it he detailed the whole Rieber-Westrick alliance, and the involvement of Texas Oil was revealed. Stephenson's agents even found out that Westrick had contravened the law by applying for a licence to drive the Texaco Buick without mentioning that he had a wooden leg! A list of prominent US businessmen who had visited the German 'diplomat' at Scarsdale was also published, much to their and their firms' embarrassment.

The scandal that ensued swiftly brought about the end of the Westrick-Rieber alliance, and their US business associates dived for cover. Westrick was declared *persona non grata* by the Washington State Department and Rieber was asked by his Board to resign at the time that Westrick was sailing back to the Reich and an uncertain future. (He need not have worried. Postwar German governments would look after him.*)

But one thing reported in the *New York Times* set the alarm bells ringing in Admiral Canaris' HQ. It was that 'a number of comparatively obscure young Americans of German descent' had visited Westrick's Scarsdale home, New York. Strangely enough, they were 'employed in strategic factories'.

If the Great American Public didn't tumble to what their function was, Admiral Canaris very quickly did. They were more of those amateur *Abwehr* German-American agents prepared to

---

* Rieber also had a soft landing. A year later he became president of the Barber Asphalt Company, ironically enough a subsidiary of the Guggenheims. 30-odd years later he died, aged 86, in his Fifth Avenue apartment.

betray their host country in an effort to aid the *Heimat*. Canaris had no time for amateurs and *'ihre verdammte Scheisse'* (their damned shit), as he habitually called their reports. He knew, too, that the Führer was now concentrating all his efforts on Europe, in particular Britain, and that this was no time for more scandals in the United States. The fact that some German-American amateur spy might produce an important snippet of information about some US weapon paled against the game that the Swiss bankers and their friends the American businessmen were playing on Germany's behalf. Canaris ordered *Abwehr* operations in neutral America to be kept to a minimum. Under no circumstances could the combination of the *Abwehr* and the German Foreign Service be shown to be working against the best interests of the United States, a viewpoint supported whole-heartedly by the Führer.

Roosevelt, he knew, welcomed any opportunity to turn the basically isolationist attitude of the American public into a pro-war stance in favour of Britain. As Hitler saw it, Roosevelt lusted for war against Germany. It was no different with the powerful Jews who supported Henry Morgenthau, the rabid anti-German and personal friend of the President. Although the Jewish movie moguls of Hollywood still valued the German market and wouldn't allow anti-German propaganda to be smuggled into that most popular medium of all, the rest of the media Jews, like Sulzburger, yearned to find material which would malign the New Germany. Already they and their agents in the Treasury and the FBI were closing in on those vital Swiss banks which Hitler needed to keep the German war economy going.

So for the next two years all *Abwehr* operations against the United States were restricted to a low level, and Captain (soon Major) Ritter, who had initiated them was now ordered to concentrate on Britain. The time had come for Ritter to begin *'Operation Lena'*.

Back in 1937 when Ritter had first taken up his appointment as a trainee spymaster in Hamburg, he had, as we have seen, been a spymaster without a single spy. His big safe in the *Abwehr* HQ had been empty not only of codebooks and the usual tools of spymasters but also of one single hint on paper that somewhere in the world that there was an agent being paid to work for him.

Fortunately for him, a colleague, Dierks, in charge of naval intelligence, took pity on him and gave him his first agent, 'a Welshman who offered his services in Brussels when he was there on a business trip'.

Ritter had become acquainted with his first spy, a double-dealing traitor who thus earned his place in the secret history of espionage in the Second World War. He was a disreputable Welsh electrical engineer named Arthur Owens, who had an eye for the women and on whom he spent all his money, both honestly and dishonestly earned.

Naturally he wasn't what he seemed, though Ritter never seemed to grasp the fact. Owens, code-named 'Johnny' by the Germans, was 'Snow' to British Intelligence, for whom he also worked. Money was his main motive, though he told the Germans and his 'sub-agents' in Britain (all Welsh) that he was a fervent Welsh nationalist who desired an immediate end to 'English rule and tyranny'. According to Owens, by the time war had started he had thirty-eight Welsh agents located in strategic spots from Catterick to Chatham. *

Whatever the value of 'Johnny' was, he did unwittingly start Ritter off in search of his own spies, some of them passed on to him by Owens on the orders of his SIS masters in London's Queen Anne's gate.

Thus by the time Hitler had knocked France out of the war and had personally gazed at the white cliffs of Dover, Ritter had assembled a team of a dozen agents. They were a strange bunch, prepared to go on what the *Abwehr* staff at Hamburg's *Fleischhauerstrasse* called *Himmelfahrtkommando* or Ascension Day operation, ie, a one-way ticket to heaven. The more astute of the *Abwehr* personnel realized that most of Ritter's agents hadn't a chance in hell once they landed in Britain; half of them didn't even speak English!

* There is ample evidence, however, that a small bunch of Welsh nationalists, probably financed by the *Abwehr*, did carry out sabotage and other covert ops in North Wales after war broke out. One notorious incident involved the lighting of huge arrows on the hills of North Wales pointing in the general direction of Mersyside during the heavy bombing of Liverpool in 1940 as a guide for German bombers. The incident, naturally, was hushed up.

There was Theodore Druegge, smart and middle class, who had been born in Hamburg but bummed around Europe drinking and chasing women, earning the money by acting as an *Abwehr* 'researcher'. He was one of the key men in 'Operation Lena'. Others were Jose Waldberg, who spoke fluent French and German, but no English; a thick-witted ex-chauffeur from Switzerland, Werner Walti; a Dutch Indonesian, Caarlie van den Boom; Sjord Pons, his friend from their time in the Dutch Army and both members of the Dutch Fascist Organization led by Mussert, an arch-traitor; two Norwegian traitors, whom British Intelligence later nick-named 'Mutt and Jeff' for obvious reasons – the usual fools and rogues who drift into the world of espionage through greed, patriotism, a spirit of adventure, or an amalgam of all three. But the outstanding member of the 'Lena' team was a woman!

Ritter code-named her 'Viola', but he might as well have called her Mata Hari, for she became the outstanding German female agent of the Second World War, still sought after by historians of Intelligence after her mysterious disappearance once she arrived in England, one whose history has remained a tantalizing enigma to this day.*

'Viola' certainly fascinated all the men with whom she worked in Hamburg. Ritter said later, 'There was not a man who worked with her who was not attracted to her.' Indeed, with the dour Victorian morality that he had inherited from his Rhenish father, Ritter never allowed himself to meet her alone and ordered his subordinate officers to do the same. But of course they didn't. Her charms were too great.

She has entered the annals of espionage as 'Vera de Witte', 'Vera von Schalenburg', 'Vera von Schalburg' and in the British Intelligence dossier on her released in the spring of 1999 as 'Vera Starizky' and, in a surviving signature as 'Vera Chalburg'.

The present author has come to the conclusion that she was born Vera Chalburg because of her race and where she was born,

---

* Even in 1999, the author has been unable to find out her true identity or whether she is still alive sixty years after her disappearance, for, although MI5 have released some of her details in recent years, the authorities still censor her most important details.

probably illegitimately – Kiev in 1914. She is described in MI5's release as 'in her mid-twenties, dark and attractive with blue eyes, who had suffered a miscarriage not long after being arrested'. In a report submitted by a graphologist, who examined her handwriting at the time, which is surprising, as, unlike the Continentals, the British were not accustomed to using hand-writing experts in the diagnosis of character, she was described as a 'cold and calculating person, who took too much interest in other people's affairs'. In addition, according to the graphologist, she had 'suffered a great erotic disappointment'.

In essence the salient points of MI5's assessment of their suspect were true. She was attractive. She was nosey. She was cool and calculating. All excellent qualities in a spy, who used her sexual charms to entrap men and worm information out of them. As for the fact that she once had 'suffered a great erotic dis-appointment', one might think that was an understatement. For throughout her career as a spy, she must have suffered many 'great erotic disappointments' with the older gentlemen with whom she was obliged to go to bed. Ritter once confided to the author in his house in Blankenese on the River Elbe, after his secretary-girl-friend and later wife had left the room, *'Man sagte sie war scharf wie ein Rasiermesser'* (he said she was as sharp as a cut-throat razor).

One thing is certain about her origins, however: she was Jewish, born in Russia, and her father had been wealthy enough to smuggle her and her brother out of Kiev after the Bolshevik Revolution, when, with new foster parents, they began life again in Copenhagen. Some researchers maintain that she and her brother were supported by their hard-working mother in a one-room flat in a suburb of Brussels, but this seems hardly likely since her brother, described as handsome and Aryan-looking, became an officer of the Danish Palace Guard. He also became a secret member of the Danish Nazi Party, which must have helped Vera to be accepted in Germany, but did the brother little good. Volunteering for the SS, he was killed in action fighting in Russia. *

---

* There are several misconceptions about the fate of Jews in wartime Germany. Not all German Jews disappeared into concentration camps, as is generally

Vera Chalburg, as we shall call her, using the name she and her brother were known by in Copenhagen, and, in his case, later in the *Waffen SS*, apparently had no anti-communist prejudices. After training in Paris, she became a night club dancer. Here, among other lovers, and there were plenty of them, Vera took up with a White Russian 'general'. In those days the French capital was filled with Russian ex-officers of the Garde du Corps and the like and naturally they were all generals. This one was twice her age, down on his luck and a secret agent for Beria, the Russian spymaster and head of the feared GPU. By the time Vera reached her majority she was already a spy for her first espionage outfit. It wouldn't be the last.

As the Dane Joergen Boerresen, another *Abwehr* agent, has recorded: 'Before the war Vera worked in France for the GPU and it was there she was recruited by British Intelligence in order to penetrate the *Abwehr*. It is more than likely that Commander Dunderdale, station head for MI6 and an old Russia hand (he spoke Russian fluently, had lived in pre-communist Russia and, after the failed White Russian counter-revolutions, had kept in contact with their foreign organizations) used Vera to spy on her lover-controller. But after her lover stabbed her in a fit of jealousy, she lost her value in that area and we can assume that she was switched to a completely new field of activity, the *Abwehr*.

For a while there is a gap in our knowledge of her activities in Paris, if that was where she really was. The MI5 record speaks vaguely of 'her time in Gloucestershire'. Had Admiral Sinclair, head of the MI6 at that time, removed her for some kind of

---

supposed. In Berlin alone in 1943 there were still 15–20,000 Jews (mostly regarded as '*Halbjuden*', half-Jews, by their persecutors; some of these were recruited by the Gestapo as agents). A good number went 'underground' by joining the German Army; there were others who went into the German administration. Up to quite recently two well-known media figures, both awarded Nazi decorations for war services, Herr Lowenthal and Herr Max Rosenthal, were, for instance, popular on German TV. Hermann Goering, head of the *Luftwaffe*, summed up one Nazi attitude when he proclaimed, after being told that one of his generals was Jewish, '*Hier bestimme ich wer Jude ist*' (Here I decide who is Jewish).

training to one of those remote country houses that the upper-class chiefs of British Intelligence preferred for the instruction of their novice agents? We don't know. What we do know is that Vera turns up again in Hamburg as the mistress of Hilmar Dierks, the naval intelligence expert of the Hamburg *Abwehr*, an area of expertise that was always of interest to Britain. Dierks, much older than she, enjoyed her strong sex drive and, despite her dubious background (the *Abwehr* probably knew she was Jewish), convinced his superiors that Vera could be very valuable due to her knowledge of languages and her contacts. If Dierks had only known just who those contacts were he would have tried to get rid of Vera earlier than he did.

By the outbreak of war Dierks had tired of Vera. He seemed never to stay with one woman long enough to establish a permanent relationship. He asked Captain Wichmann, the head of the *Abwehr* station in Hamburg, for a posting to get away from her and was promised one in newly occupied Poland.

Vera went crazy. She took an overdose of tablets at the *Pension Klopstock*, the hotel which housed the *Abwehr*'s agents, where Dierks found her just in time. Her first cry when the doctors brought her round was supposedly for her treacherous lover.

But Dierks had had enough. He tried to convince Vera to become an agent and, surprisingly enough, she agreed. Naturally none of the *Abwehr* spymasters in Hamburg who felt *they* were doing the manipulating realized that, in fact, it was they who were being manipulated. Ritter tried to dissuade her. In the end, however, he gave in and by way of a start introduced her to one of his English agents, probably directed to him through 'Johnny', whom he called 'the Duchess of Château-Thierry', after his first battle during the First World War in France. Ritter and all the other agents of 'Operation Lena' were slowly but inevitably being drawn into the deadly spiderweb spun for them by the gentlemen at Queen Anne's Gate.

Ritter had first met the 'Duchess' the year before when she had been introduced to him by 'Lady May', a young German-born widow in her mid-forties, who had been married to an older Swedish officer and who, when he died, had gone to housekeep for a British naval officer in the Lincolnshire fishing port of Grimsby. Anyone but Ritter would have immediately suspected a background like that. You could have run a train through its loopholes. But not Ritter. 'May', or Mrs Erikson as she was really called, was of German birth, so she could be trusted implicitly.

In due course 'Lady May' introduced Ritter to the Countess Montabelli di Condo, whom the former, with his love of titles, immediately elevated to the status of 'Duchess'. The 'Duchess of Château-Thierry' was a lively old bird in her sixties, with a taste for expensive hotels and equally expensive malt whisky, but without the wherewithal to pay for either. Straight off she told Ritter that she was short of cash and, 'If you help me, I'll help you.'

Ritter bought it hook, line and sinker. But what use could he put the old bird to and justify the money he was spending on her and on 'Lady May'? Then he hit upon the idea of letting her open a kind of modified 'Green House' in the smart part of Mayfair.

Over half a century before, Bismarck's despicable chief of police, Wilhelm Stieber, had run a brothel called the Green House. It had catered for all tastes among its special clients, who were usually from the higher rungs of the Prussian social ladder. Once these clients had been hooked by the specialized services offered by Stieber's boys and girls they were wide open to blackmail. Homosexuality was rife at the court of the Kaiser Wilhelm II whom Bismarck disliked, and later probably hated after the former had dismissed him from his post as Chancellor.

By 1939 Canaris' former cadet and now secret rival, Reinhard Heydrich, head of the SS's own secret service, was running a similar establishment in Berlin. Known as 'Madame Kitty's' after its blowsy, ex-prostitute owner, it too catered for upper-crust Germans and foreigners passing through the nation's capital, including Count Ciano, the Italian Foreign Minister and Mussolini's son-in-law. Madame Kitty's girls, however, were different from ordinary whores. They spoke several languages, were trained intelligence agents and their bedrooms were wired to a listening post in the cellar. The reports of these listeners were passed on to young Walter Schellenberg, Heydrich's assistant, of whom we shall hear more, known affectionately to Kitty as *Bubi* or Laddie. Some laddie!

Ritter was no Stieber or even Schellenberg. He was too straight-laced. All the same he liked the idea of a salon in which high-ranking British officers and officials could relax in pleasant female company and naturally spill the beans to his attentive and charming agents.

In 1939 he expounded the idea to the penniless 'Duchess' and naturally she jumped at it. 'That's a wonderful idea,' she exclaimed, according to Ritter. 'But we need a beautiful woman.' Of course that beautiful woman was going to be Vera.

Ritter arranged for the two to meet at the smart Alsterpavillon, a stone's throw from the swank *Vier Jahreszeiten* Hotel in which he normally housed those agents he wished to impress. There, over coffee, looking out over the port's beautiful internal lake, the Alster, they planned for the future.

Vera would be given the cover name 'Vera Erikson' and pose as the Norwegian niece of May Erikson. The Duchess, given sufficient funds, would do the rest. She'd open a salon in Mayfair where handsome members of the upper classes would confess all to Vera, who, in case of necessity, would oblige them in bed. Anything to obtain the information that the Führer needed for his invasion of England.

Naturally the poor, innocent Ritter hadn't the faintest idea that afternoon that he was being set up. His good times as a spymaster were about to end.

'Operation Lobster', as this section of the 'Lena' mission was named, misfired from the very start. The group led by Druegge, who secretly loved Vera, but who had passed her dutifully on to his superior, Dierks, was due to leave Hamburg on the first leg of its dangerous mission to Britain on 3 September 1940. As was customary with Germans and *Abwehr* agents, *'Feste werden gefeiert wie sie fallen'* (feasts are celebrated as they occur) and the group went out to dine and get drunk at Jacob, a well-known restaurant on Hamburg's *Elbchaussee*.

One bottle led to another. 'It was an exciting evening,' Ritter noted later. They ate and they drank well. Dierks, in particular, drank more than normal. Perhaps he was celebrating the fact that he was finally getting rid of the volatile Vera. Outside in the blackout he insisted drunkenly that he should drive the car back to their quarters. But Druegge, the frustrated lover, overruled him. He'd take the wheel, though he didn't know the route too well, particularly in the blackout. So they set off.

A thin mist was creeping in from the water. To their right the Inner Alster was camouflaged against enemy bombers with huge nets. The cobbled Chaussee was empty and Druegge drove fast. Suddenly another car raced towards them. In spite of the blackout regulations which stipulated that cars should have dimmed headlights, this car had its headlights full on. Druegge hit the brakes and the car skidded on the wet cobbles. Druegge was not sober enough to react correctly. The car spun round out of control, hit one of the great oaks lining the Chaussee and came to an abrupt halt.

Dierks, in the back, was flung forward, hitting the window with a bang. His head went through, blood splattering everywhere. According to Ritter, he was killed instantly.

Captain Boeckel, Ritter's assistant, found the group white-faced and trembling in a hospital just off Hamburg's *Dammtor*. Vera was sobbing. 'Where's Dierks?' he asked. 'Is he badly hurt?' Vera didn't answer. Walti, another member of the 'Lobster' team, answered for her. He shook his head. Boeckel understood. Dierks was dead. The operation had got off to a very bad start. It was going to get worse.

For a while the spymasters hesitated. The death of Dierks seemed a bad omen. But in the end it was decided to continue with the operation. The German High Command was crying out for information; after all Operation Sea-Lion, the planned invasion of Britain, was running at full speed. Already one of Ritter's teams from 'Lena' had set off for England, but nothing more had been heard from them. On 21 September the 'Lobster' team were ordered to fly to Stavanger in Norway where a seaplane that would take them across the North Sea would be waiting for them.

They arrived at the newly captured Norwegian port with their hands and faces still covered with sticking plaster. Here they were taught how to launch the rubber dinghy which would convey them and their ancient British Raleigh cycles, found in the cellar of the British consulate in Bergen, to the Scottish shore. For it had been decided that, to make things easier for them, on account of their poor English, they'd cycle the six hundred miles from Scotland to London! Here Vera would contact the 'Duchess', while the others would go to ground and carry out their various missions: Druegge as a Belgian refugee, Walti as a neutral Swiss. Vera was to be a Dane, residing, according to her poorly forged identity card, at 18 Sussex Place, London, W2.

Still they were dogged by misfortune. On 26 September their Heinkel HE 115 was forced to turn back due to bad weather. Finally at two thirty on the morning of 30 September 1940 they were on their way.

England that autumn was undergoing the strangest period of the whole war. Instead of the men in khaki fighting their battles in some far-off country, the war was being fought in the skies above the civilians' heads. Britain was on its own and the Continent might have been twenty thousand miles away instead of a mere twenty. As Churchill complained that month to his intelligence chiefs, 'I can read the time on the clock at Calais with my binoculars, but that's about all I know of what is going on.'

The country was going through a period of invasion fever, though the Prime Minister knew that the Germans were beginning to call off their Sea Lion plans since the *Luftwaffe* was apparently failing to conquer the skies over the British Isles, a prerequisite for a successful invasion.

Every large open space, especially near rivers and estuaries, was covered with tall poles with wires strung between them. These were supposed to stop German gliders landing. Other poles, already there, became the object of a major MI5 investigation after it was discovered that they had strange markings on them. Were these a guide for German paratroopers? In the event the markings turned out to be the work of pre-war Boy Scouts and Girl Guides.

Pigeons, naturally, became a major object of suspicion. The Germans had banned the Belgians from keeping pigeons in the First World War in case they were used by spies. A hard-pressed Britain had better do the same. Teams of falcons were trained to combat the supposed menace. Then, under interrogation, captured 'German pigeon personnel' (as the MI5 report put it, presumably meaning captured German Army signallers) revealed that Himmler was a pigeon fancier and was going to use pigeons as a vital component of the coming invasion. And they say the Germans have no sense of humour!

The pigeon scare continued for a long while, as did the early harvesting by farmers, who might be signalling to the enemy by this means. Two pigeons of foreign origin were discovered and held by MI5 as 'prisoners-of war'. As an unknown intelligence officer reported, perhaps tongue in cheek, 'Both birds are now prisoners-of-war, working hard at breeding English pigeons.' There was even a new Army Pigeon Service Special Section, composed of birds of prey, used to set up 'an airborne net' over the Scilly Isles, following the sightings of 'pigeons disappearing towards France'. *

But the scare was not altogether imaginary. By 1940 the UK was swamped with refugees from Europe of all creeds and political persuasions, each of whom needed a detailed security check, which was exceedingly difficult in view of the fact that most of their homelands were now occupied by the Germans.

There was good reason for caution, good enough for Churchill to snarl, 'Collar the lot'. He meant the mass internment of 'enemy aliens', whatever their reasons for fleeing to Britain. The head of Naval Intelligence was suspected by MI6 of having an Austrian-Jewish mistress who might well be an enemy agent. Even Vic Oliver, Churchill's son-in-law and a well-known comedian of Austrian-Jewish origin, was suspect for a time. Perhaps Churchill would have liked to have seen Oliver behind barbed wire in the Isle of Man, whence most 'collared' enemy aliens were eventually sent.

However, one thing came of the spy scare of 1940: for the first time in British history everyone was issued with an official identity card. A curfew was instituted for 'aliens' still not interned and the nation as a whole, including the almost one-million-strong Local Defence Volunteers, the forerunner of the Home Guard, was now committed to *not* 'minding their own business' in the traditional British fashion. Suddenly the nation was on its guard. It was a factor that was to prove the downfall for so many of Ritter's ill-trained and ill-prepared spies.

The seaplane carrying the three spies landed on the sea off the

* MI5 recorded at the time: 'Himmler, who has been a pigeon fancier and enthusiast all his life, is the head or president of the German National Pigeon Society'. Highly doubtful, even for that ex-chicken farmer. In 1940 the head of the SS had other matters on his mind.

small Scottish town of Buckie, but again luck was against them. Their bicycles were lost in the choppy waves as they were being transferred from the Heinkel to the rubber dinghy. A few minutes later they reached the deserted shore safely and buried their boat. Without the Raleigh bikes that might have taken them the six hundred miles to London, they had to change their plans. Or, as it now looks, Vera changed their plans for them, for by this time she was definitely in charge of the two male agents, despite the fact that, unknown to them, she was pregnant.

Vera decided that they would split up. She and Druegge would go south, while Walti would head east. It was obvious that the couple's first destination was London, presumably there to meet the 'Duchess'. Walti's was more uncertain and is not mentioned in the recently released MI5 papers. Probably they were protecting their agent 'Snow', known to the Germans, as we have seen, as 'Johnny'. It might well have been that Walti had been told he could contact one of the little Welsh traitor's nationalists on the other side of the country. But it didn't really matter. None of them were going to get very far.

At seven thirty that Monday morning Vera and Druegge found themselves at the little country station of Portgordon. They were carrying a large suitcase and two smaller bags, which surprised the stationmaster, John Donald, and the lone porter, John Geddes. Where were the strangers going at this time of the morning and how had they got here with such heavy luggage? The two were even more surprised when the travellers asked where they were, having tried to find out from the fading railway map on the wall. Even in this remote area the spy scare had taken root and the stationmaster's suspicions were further aroused when he noted two more strange things: firstly, the man's wallet, when he opened it to pay for two third-class tickets, was crammed with banknotes, and, secondly, the man's trouser bottoms and the woman's shoes and stockings were both soaking wet. Telling the porter to keep a watchful eye on the strange pair, Donald called the local bobby, John Grieve, who arrived promptly on his bike and examined the pair's identity cards.

Immediately he noticed something wrong. Both said they were 'continentals', but there were no immigration stamps on the cards and both were filled in in a funny un-British script. He called his Inspector, John Simpson. They were on to something big.

'On the morning of 30 September 1940 I went to Portgordon Police Station,' the Inspector reported later in typical officialese. 'There I saw a man and a woman. I asked the man who he was and the woman said, "He cannot speak English". I was suspicious of them and ran my hands over the man for firearms and found a box containing nineteen rounds of revolver ammunition. The woman gave her name as Vera Erikson. She told me she was twenty-seven years of age, that she was a widow and had no occupation. She also said she was a Danish subject born in Siberia. I asked her to produce her identity papers and she produced National Registration Card CNFX/141/2. Constable Grieve and I had the man and woman conveyed to Buckie Police Station where a thorough check was made of their possessions and inquiries set going regarding them, as by this time we were satisfied they were enemy agents.'

The ball now started gathering momentum. Vera was questioned again (she was the only one who spoke English). She told the Inspector that they had come down from Bergen in a small boat named the *Norstar*, the name of the captain being Andersen. She said they had spent the previous night at a hotel in Banff and had hired a taxi to within a mile of Portgordon and walked to the railway station. The Inspector reported that 'The man had the following in his possession: an electric torch with a blue bulb and the word "Hawe" and "made in Bohemia" on the bottom; a watch with a monogram H.W.D. engraved on the back; a pocket knife, safety razor blades, propelling pencil . . . and £327 in Bank of England notes and 10s 3d in coins.' The Inspector's eyes must have popped out of his head. That kind of money was a fortune, a year's wages in 1940.

In effect the game was up. Though British Intelligence had not planned it like that, there the story of Vera ended. All that there is to trace her passing is her signature at Buckie Police Station. It reads 'Vera de Cottani Chalbur', yet another name used by the war's most enigmatic female spy.

That scrap of paper Vera gave Inspector Simpson is still in the possession of the family. But that is about all we know of her fate. Druegge was subsequently executed and Vera gave evidence against him *in camera*. Thereafter she disappeared. Some 'experts' maintain she married a Royal Navy officer in Intelligence and remained in this country. But as late as 1999, when Intelligence finally released the supposedly full details of 'Lena', no mention is made of Vera after 1940, save that she survived the war. Today she remains as much of an enigma as she was to her *Abwehr* spymasters sixty years ago.

But what of her fellow spy, the thick-witted Swiss chauffeur, Walti? He survived a little longer than Vera and Druegge. Perhaps because he knew he had to get away from the coast as quickly as possible, and away from Vera, he managed to get as far as Edinburgh's Waverley Station. Here he deposited his suitcase at four-thirty that Monday afternoon. He asked an attendant named Cameron when the next train for London left and then walked to Prince's Street where he had a meal and a shave, having told Cameron that he'd return to pick up his case before the ten o'clock when his train for King's Cross was due. By now the police, on orders from Special Branch, were already looking for him and the deposited case was found at Waverley Station by officers under the command of Chief Constable Merrilees. They noticed that it had a 'whitish irregular mark from which they were able to deduce that the case had been standing in salt water,' Merriless wrote afterwards. Porters then told them about the man who had deposited the case.

Merrilees then set a trap in which he took the leading role. He borrowed a porter's uniform and waited. In the meantime, as he wrote later, 'I fear I misdirected numerous travellers to the wrong platforms.'

In his three-hour wait he spotted many foreigners, mainly Poles in uniform and refugee civilians, but no one answering to the description of the suspect. Finally at about nine 'a man in foreign-type clothing' made his appearance. He seemed hesitant, walking past the left-luggage office several times before handing in his ticket, saying in a foreign accent, 'Now please'.

'The porter took the ticket and went to get the luggage. The suspect retreated, with his back towards the paling and kiosk with his left hand hidden in his pocket, arm apparently rigid.' The Chief Constable guessed there was going to be trouble. As he sauntered towards the agent Walti spotted him and his face changed. Merrilees pulled an old trick and gestured behind him with his hand.

'When he turned to see who was there, I sprang forward and gripped his wrist. I can assure you it was no light grip. I wrenched and his hand was jerked out of his pocket, grasping a Mauser automatic pistol fully loaded. I hung on to him till my assistants arrived and we bundled him into the left luggage office and bolted the door.'

The third agent had been captured. He had ten months left to live.

A similar fate met most of Ritter's 'Lena' agents, save those few who became double agents working for British Intelligence. Most were caught almost immediately after landing and surrendered tamely. After all, the British knew as much about them as Ritter did. 'Johnny-Snow', the arch-traitor saved his neck by being particularly helpful. A few managed to escape the net for a while, but in the end they were caught.

One such was Karl Richter, who had come to bring funds for another German agent, who had run out of money. Naturally Richter had been set up. The burly 6'2" ex-SS man managed to dodge his pursuers for a little while, but inevitably in the end he was caught and sentenced to death, betrayed by his fellow countryman. Albert Pierrepoint, the celebrated hangman, was scheduled to do the job at Wandsworth Prison, but Richter wasn't the usual tame victim that Pierrepoint was accustomed to.

Kicking aside the Catholic priest who had come to give him final absolution, Richter fought his two prison guards. 'Get your straps on him, Albert, for God's sake,' someone shouted. Pierrepoint managed to do so and appeased the prisoner, 'Follow me lad. It will be all right.' But it wouldn't.

A moment later someone else cried, 'Albert, come back!'

Pierrepoint swung round. As he recorded it later, 'I turned and saw that Richter's arms were free and it was a free-for-all again. I went back and got into the fray. Richter fought me, fought everyone.' And he continued to fight to the very end as the drop opened and Pierrepoint saw 'with horror that the noose was slipping'. But at the final moment it held.

One by one Ritter's agents were either 'turned' or hanged. Only one escaped, Jan Willem Ter Braak. Although he had been set up by British double agents so that British Intelligence knew he was coming he managed to dodge the 'reception committee' when he landed safely at Amersham, Buckinghamshire. From there he travelled to Cambridge where he took lodgings in the old university town. Here he lived without hindrance for several months, posing as a fossil researcher of Dutch origin. But he showed much more interest in Mr Churchill's movements than he ever did in fossils. He even followed the Prime Minister on his wartime visits to factories all over the United Kingdom. Later it was discovered from his notes that his task was to assassinate wartime leaders if and when the opportunity arose. It never did. On 1 April, 1941, Mrs Alice Stutely, Air Raid Shelter Marshal for the area, was walking her dog in a park in the centre of Cambridge, known as 'Christ's Pieces', when a small boy approached her and told her that there was a dead body in the nearby air-raid shelter. She found the body of a man dressed in a black overcoat and wearing horn-rimmed glasses. It was the body of Ter Braak. He had committed suicide. No one at the time could reason why. Now we can guess he did so out of despair.

In Hamburg Ritter also despaired in a milder sort of a way. He was among friends and associates, able to speak as freely as the Gestapo would allow and converse in his native language. He was not fighting the lone, nerve-racking battle of the agent in a foreign land. Naturally he was worried what had happened to the 'Lena' team, for after two weeks they had still not reported in to the *Abwehr* listening station just outside Hamburg at Wohltorf.

Another week passed and then an obscure item in a Swiss paper seemed to clear up a little of the mystery of what had happened to the team. It stated that a Swiss citizen had been arrested, accused of being a spy for the Germans. Immediately Ritter asked the *Abwehr*'s legal department to take up the case of the 'innocent neutral'.

Using Swiss lawyers as cover, the *Abwehr* researchers found out that Walti had managed to reach Edinburgh. There he had been apprehended by the police after a brave struggle. Druegge's fate had been little different. According to Ritter's garbled and incorrect version, he had managed to get to Birmingham (sic) by varied and devious routes. Just as he was about to board the train for London, the police attempted to arrest him. Loyal to his original statement that he would not be taken alive, he drew his pistol and shot one of the policemen. Then he turned the pistol on himself. But fate was against his suicide. Just as previously, Boeckel had knocked the pistol out of his hands at the hospital (back in Hamburg), the policeman did the same. He was taken off to jail.'

As Ritter commented after the war: 'We don't know how the police got to know of his presence. We supposed that the Swiss had betrayed him after his arrest.'

Naturally Ritter was wrong. Druegge had already been captured with Vera on the coast before Walti was taken at Waverley station. The 'Lena Operation' had been betrayed even before it had left Hamburg, thanks to 'Johnny'. All sixteen would-be spies who couldn't be 'turned' ended on the gallows. Those who could be used by MI5 continued to betray Canaris' *Abwehr* right till the end of the war. *

In the end Ritter dismissed the whole nasty business. In the cold-blooded manner of spymasters all over the world, he remarked: 'Apparently there was a court case. Druegge was shot and Walti hanged.' Besides, the global espionage war was heating up. Canaris had new tasks for him.

Hitler and his Chief of Military Intelligence in the west, General Ulrich Liss, felt that Canaris had failed them over Operation Sea Lion. As the General wrote, 'I came to the conclusion during *Case Yellow* [the Attack on the West] that his [Canaris'] offensive intelligence operations against the French, Norway, Belgium and the Low Countries were all models of efficiency. But the same could not be said for his Sea Lion operations. I thought then that, while he appeared to be trying to be efficient, he was not doing his job against England with conviction. We never quite got the intelligence from England that we needed to make correct estimates of England's strengths and dispositions on the ground.'

Canaris knew he had to do better. His main rival was forging

---

* One of them, code-named 'Tate', for instance (real name Jensen) was actually awarded the Iron Cross for his bravery 'in the face of the enemy', though as we have seen he was instrumental in having that ill-fated SS Richter parachuted into Britain with funds for him. He continued to live in the UK, with a British wife, until his death, engaged in civic work, at one time being presented to the Queen Mother.

ahead in the intelligence field and in his own career. The former naval cadet whom Hitler called the 'man with the iron heart', Reinhard Heydrich, was going places, while he was just marking time. As for Ritter, Canaris had other tasks awaiting him. He was going on his travels once more.

MAJOR RITTER GETS HIS KNEES BROWN

'In these new weeks I need an absolutely reliable unit in Egypt. It is absolutely essential for the success of my planned offensive.'

Field Marshal Erwin Rommel to Admiral Canaris,
1942.

In 1941 Canaris realized that Goering had been correct when the latter had told him in a moment of confidence that the invasion of England was off and he should turn his attention to more global matters.

Canaris had failed in Britain and America was still neutral and out of bounds, but he felt he was now in a position to strike a blow at the British Empire. His organization had expanded tremendously since the outbreak of war. Funds were plentiful, Intelligence was urgently needed from every quarter and his 3,000 full-time officers were spread all over the world. He was now in a position to organize missions on a global scale, some realistic, some decidedly crackpot.

By 1941 he had agents and agitators trying to raise the native population in India, on the North-West Frontier, in Iraq and in Iran. Closer to home he had agents dropped to help a Welsh Nationalist Organization, though it didn't really exist. His agent landed by parachute at the feet of the supposed liberation movement's head. He turned out to be a disguised Welsh police inspector.

Guns, money and agents were run into Southern Ireland to aid the IRA, but they turned out to be a bunch of ageing confidence men who used good German money to indulge themselves in the bars of Dublin. One of Canaris' agents, former Hamburg lawyer Hermann Goertz, found the IRA's 'Chief-of-Staff', Stephen Hayes, to be scared of offensive action, but with a liking for money and drink. As Goertz noted in his diary – he wasn't a very professional spy – Hayes looked 'like a superannuated football player, his dignity sadly impaired by alcohol and anxiety'. Later he was arrested by the authorities and interned until the end of the war. Bitterly, Goetz wrote, 'The IRA is rotten to the very core.'

But failure in Ireland and Wales and only semi-success in the Moslem countries didn't deter the Admiral. Captured Indian Army soldiers who went over to the Germans (in the end there was a 3,000-strong 'Indian Legion', composed of turncoat former Indian POWs) were given crash-courses in sabotage and spying and parachuted back into their home countries. Most of them were never heard of again.

But Canaris kept at it. He even introduced *Abwehr* agents into British-occupied Palestine. There they worked with the Jewish underground against the British and the Arabs, who, they thought, the British favoured. Strange bedfellows indeed! But after all Heydrich, one of the fathers of the 'Final Solution', had worked with Jewish representatives of those same organizations in Berlin itself until the outbreak of war.

But one scheme in particular, suggested in 1941 and designed to hurt the British at a critical spot in their world-wide empire, became more important than all the others put together. It was a daring and imaginative scheme which was later given the name *Unternehmen Kondor* – Operation Condor.

When Ritter first suggested it to Canaris, he snapped '*Mensch, das ist doch eine verruckte Idee*' (Man that's a crazy idea). He looked at his subordinate, as Ritter said later, as if to say, 'My dear fellow, you can't be altogether right in the head.' Then he added, 'Forget it,' and dismissed the matter.

Four weeks later Canaris changed his mind. He called Ritter in Hamburg and told him that he was considering the idea. Ritter would be hearing from him again soon.

The next day Major Ritter was on the way to Budapest, capital of Germany's fascist ally, Hungary. There he met once again the man who had given him the idea to aid General Rommel, now leading his first drive against the British Eighth Army in North Africa. He was an Hungarian aristocrat and adventurer called Count Laszlo von Almaszy, a tall, skinny man with a fine-featured face and the careless but genteel gestures of a *Kavalier der alten Schule* (a cavalier of the old school) as Ritter was to call him to the author.

Almaszy had served as an officer in the fledgling air force of the Austro-Hungarian Empire in the First World War, but when he returned from the front in 1918 he found that the Hungarian revolution, led by the Communist Bela Kun, had deprived him of his family estates; all he had left was a derelict town house in Budapest. As a result he had to earn a living and trained as a surveyor. Some time later he was grateful to accept a position with the Anglo-Egyptian Survey Team mapping the Sahara Desert.

Almaszy fell in love with the country. He loved the carefree life of Cairo's rich international set with whom anything went, for his sexual tastes were not standard by any means. He even came to love the desert, though he confessed to his intimates, 'Once I'm out of it, I never want to go back into that burning hell, with no water and no whisky, but after a few weeks of Cairo, I'm always ready to go in once more to get away from people.' By the end of the thirties the desert had indeed become a kind of drug to him, an escape from the leisured society into which he had been born and with which he conducted a kind of love-hate relationship.

On the outbreak of war Almaszy had been forced to leave Egypt and by the time Ritter got to know him he was living off his memories, spending hours alone in his 18th century Budapest apartment, surrounded by ancient Arab weapons, stuffed gazelle heads and other dusty souvenirs. When Ritter expressed some interest in Egypt, Almaszy had dropped his customary bored cynicism and never stopped talking; he was delighted with the German's curiosity about the country he feared he would never see again.

He drew Ritter's attention to his friend the ex-chief-of-staff of the Egyptian Army, El Masri Pasha. He had been dismissed under pressure from the British when the latter discovered, during their first victorious campaign against the Italians, that the Egyptian General had betrayed their plans to the enemy.

The General now formed part of a group of dissident nationalist officers who were plotting to overthrow King Farouk, the gross and sensual King of Egypt, who reputedly had the largest collection of pornographic photographs in the world. Among these were young officers such as Gamal Abdel Nasser and Anwar El Sadat, both of whom would later become rulers of their native country. Now in 1941 they were regarded by the British as traitors who would throw in their lot with the enemy at the drop of a hat. But they needed a figurehead, a senior officer with authority. Almaszy suggested that Masri Pasha was that person.

'Do you really think that we could use this general to work with us against the British?' Ritter had asked.

'I'm convinced he would. I've often considered the possibility, but until I met you, I couldn't think of anyone to whom I could suggest the idea.'

Now as Rommel prepared to bail out the Italians, Germany's new allies, with his decisive attack on the British Eighth Army, the *Abwehr* went into action and tried to get Masri out of the Delta. The first two attempts failed and it was up to Ritter and Almaszy to ensure that the third succeeded.

So Ritter reported back to Canaris at his Berlin HQ on February 1941 with the details of what he intended to do. The Admiral had lost all his initial doubts, but during their discussions he said something Ritter found difficult to understand at the time: 'Watch out for the SD down there.' He meant Heydrich's own spy organization and added, 'In peacetime, my dear Ritter, one can overthrow a government when one is dissatisfied with it. But when one attempts to do so in wartime, then that is treachery to one's own people.' And with that enigmatic statement, the only one of a political nature that Ritter ever heard the Admiral utter, they parted. Ritter never saw him again.

At three in the afternoon on a burning June day the two Heinkel IIIs which were going to bring the Egyptian general back to the *Luftwaffe-Abwehr* base at Derna took off. They were to fly to the Red Djebel, an elevated plateau south-west of Cairo, not far from the road linking the Egyptian capital with one of the main desert oases. There the Pasha would be waiting for his German rescuers near a giant sign made of bedsheets spread out in the sand in the shape of a cross. While one of the twin-engined planes landed to pick the Egyptian up, the other would circle the area to ensure that no one interfered.

As the two planes disappeared behind the dangerous mountains south of the landing strip Ritter returned to his HQ to wait for news of the operation over the radio. The hours passed slowly. Time and again he got up for a drink in the half-wrecked house recently captured from the Australians by the Afrika Korps. At the radio the operator sweated, his half-naked body looking as if it had been greased. Then came a long crackle of static and a voice broke in. It was the pilot of the first Heinkel. He was flying over Tobruk. A little later the plane touched down. But the op had been a failure. Almaszy was alone. The 'Pasha' hadn't appeared. Later they heard that they had run out of petrol on the road from Cairo. It was typical of the Egyptians. Almaszy consoled Ritter that night. 'It's no use worrying,' he said. 'We'll have to wait for the next broadcast from our contacts in the morning.'

But the morning brought even worse news. Radio Cairo reported that the General had been arrested. The newscaster didn't say by whom, but Ritter guessed it was the English. At the height of the first great 'flap' in Cairo the British had suspended the rules of habeas corpus. They'd simply taken the Egyptian into custody indefinitely.

But Ritter had no time to reflect on the failure of his plan. Rommel wanted agents in place in Cairo immediately. At that time there were several German agents sending information on the British in that general area. The main agent there, however, didn't know he was working for Canaris, for he was a neutral, a soldier of a country which would soon be at war with Germany, but totally unaware, it seems, that his information was being passed on to his country's future enemies. He was, in fact, the US military attaché in Cairo, Colonel Bonner Frank Fellers.

The anglophobic West Pointer, who had once served on MacArthur's staff with Eisenhower, had been posted to Cairo in October 1940. As a potential ally, he was afforded every assistance by the British Army. Industriously, this middle-aged soldier toured the Western Desert from corps HQ to battalion front line and soon acquired an unrivalled knowledge of the British Army in action – of its weaknesses and its strengths. He then signalled his findings to Washington in long, detailed and frequent reports.

Little did he know, however, that the Germans in Africa had already broken the US 'Black Code' he used for his messages and that they were passed on immediately to the very top, to Rommel himself.

The unwitting American spy passed on details of withdrawals of British equipment from the Far East, the rundown of available British armour in the Middle East, the location of three new British infantry divisions, the details of a planned British commando raid behind German lines, its main aim apparently the kidnapping of Rommel himself, and so on and so on.

But Rommel suspected that the American wouldn't last much longer. When the British tumbled to him he would be deprived of one of his main sources of information. He needed new agents in place as soon as possible ready for his great march on Cairo, which might well end the war in the Middle East in Germany's favour.*

Ritter was given the task of infiltrating that new agent. In fact there were two of them, nicknamed Pat and Patichon, one fat, one long and miserable, who looked like the Danish comedy couple of that name, popular in Germany. But their mission was a failure. The pilot was scared to land due to the terrain and they turned back, with Ritter in the back of the plane planning the punishment he would gladly inflict on the cowardly pilot once they got back to base.

They were not fated to do so. As they started their approach to Derna a voice came in from the tower crying, 'Don't land here. We're being bombed. Use the alternative field at Benghazi.' Thereupon the radio went dead.

Benghazi was three hundred kilometres away and the plane was low on fuel, but before they had much time to consider what to do next, the rear gunner cried over the intercom, '*Feindliche*

---

* Fellers was finally blown when a team from Washington came to check him out as a possible source of leaks. They cleared him. But before the Americans could return him, the British captured one of Rommel's radio operators who had worked on the American's signals. Fellers was sent home, but not in disgrace. He was awarded the Distinguished Service Medal with a citation of supreme irony. It stated that Fellers' 'reports . . . were models of clarity and accuracy'. The Germans must have thought so too.

70

Flieger'. Enemy bombers were approaching. The pilot, coward though he was, reacted promptly and correctly. He threw the twin-engined plane into a tight curve. Tracer zipped by, but in the next instant they had reached the cover of the nearest clouds and vanished.

But they weren't out of the mess yet. A little later the Heinkel started to shake violently. Then the left engine cut out totally and the remaining engine threatened to do the same. They would have to land soon. But where? The pilot clicked on a searchlight and to their horror they saw that they were flying just above the surface of the Mediterranean. There was nothing but water as far as the beam would reach.

As Ritter said later, 'We now saw nothing but the deep blue of the African midnight sky. . . . All we could hear was the howl of the wind over the wings. The motors had stopped altogether. Suddenly there was a blow as hard as steel. That was the last thing my mind registered.'

Ritter's *Abwehr* career was over.*

Two months later Canaris himself appeared in Africa, which didn't particularly surprise anyone. In those days he travelled all the time with his two dogs and his black servant Mohammed, who might have been something else as well. The only surprise he achieved when he appeared at Rommel's African HQ at the Hotel Uaddan was his dress.

The Afrika Korps had by this time adopted the kind of dress customary among its opponents, the British 'African types', who 'up in the blue', as they called the Western Desert, were inclined to be decidedly casual – shorts, no shirt, desert boots and sunglasses. Even their new chief, General Montgomery, who had

---

* He survived the crash, however. After thirty-six hours floating in the sea he was picked up. His arm was badly mangled and the doctors wanted to remove it, but he refused. Later Canaris wanted to post him to Brazil. Here, under diplomatic cover, he would serve in a less strenuous position. But a spy scandal broke out in the States in which Ritter was named and Brazil wouldn't accept him. He ended the war as a colonel in charge of a flak regiment. After the war he was recruited into the German Gehlen Spy organization and, in due course, began working indirectly for the CIA.

not yet got his 'knees brown' wore civvie trousers and carried a green umbrella. The Germans were just as casual and, although Rommel wore regulation uniform, he did wear a scarf round his neck and a pair of captured British goggles on his peaked cap.

But Canaris outdid the lot. Just before Rommel made his usual rushed entrance Canaris shuffled into the briefing room. He wore a new and cheap jacket he had just bought in Madrid and a pair of shabby, unpressed grey flannel trousers. It was the start of a strange new phobia. From now on he seemed to abhor wearing uniform or decorations, unusual in a man who had been in the Armed Services for nearly four decades. Once, in Africa, he was photographed wearing his naval tunic and an Italian infantry officer's cap.

Rommel was wearing home service *Wehrmacht* uniform, the thick field grey of the regular Army, and was sweating accordingly. It did not seem to bother him, but the ugly desert sores around his thick lips did. However, he briefed the assembled company in his usual efficient manner concluding with, 'Before us we are faced with our major task, to drive to the Suez Canal and take Cairo. If we succeed – and we *must* succeed – then the British will lose the whole of the Near East.'

He then turned to the men of Canaris' own special commando battalion, the Brandenburgers. In particular he addressed the newest infiltration team of 'Sandy' and 'Buddy' who would be first to go. 'We need information about the enemy's intentions,' he told them. 'I need another network in Cairo.' He nodded to Canaris, who seemed bored. 'For that reason I have taken up your suggestion to run a new team before the old network folds up. In the next few weeks I need a totally reliable unit in Egypt. It is absolutely essential. I don't want a second failure like that business with the aeroplane.'

Canaris awoke from his reverie. 'I am afraid we can never give a hundred per cent assurance that things will work out well, but this time I am inclined to think that everything will be all right.' He nodded to 'Buddy', a small, thickset officer in the Brandenburgers who didn't look very German, but then many in the regiment weren't of German origin. 'Captain Eppler and I have selected the group personally. They've all spent years in the Orient, speak perfect English and in some cases Arabic. The doctors have checked them out and they are absolutely fit to face up to the rigours of the desert.'

Rommel nodded his approval. He turned to Captain Almaszy: 'It's a bold plan. I hope you don't die in the damned desert.'

Almaszy acknowledged the remark with a smile: 'If you knew how often I've been in that desert, *Herr Feldmarschall*,' he replied, 'then you'd believe that we can do it.'

Rommel gave him a hard smile. 'Oh, well, they say lunatics are usually lucky. Why shouldn't you be?' And with that he went, leaving Canaris to discuss the minor details of *Unternehmen Kondor* with his subordinates, in particular Captain Eppler, who Rommel thought looked the most unlikely German officer he'd ever seen.

Johannes Eppler had in fact been born not more than a couple of hundred miles from where they were now, in the Egyptian port of Alexandria, of German parents, or so it was said. When he was still a baby, his father had died and two years later his mother had married an Egyptian judge, a member of the powerful and rich Gafer family. Pasha Gafer had brought up his stepson as a Moslem so that by the time Johannes Eppler-Gafer was ready to go out into society he spoke Arabic and German, as well as English and French, the languages of the port's society set.

But Johannes didn't turn out to be the serious young Moslem his stepfather had wished for. In Cairo he neglected his studies, became a gambler and skirt-chaser with expensive tastes. As his high society friends punned, he 'loved slow horses and fast ladies'.

As the future President of Egypt, Anwar Sadat, was to write of him at that time in his *Secret Diary of the Egyptian Revolution*, 'The boy had not matched up to the hopes placed in him. Under the influence of doubtful companions he spent his nights in dubious establishments, much to the sorrow of his stepfather who finally gave up on him.' If Eppler ever read that passage he must have laughed up his sleeve at the naive straight-laced peasant who rose, thanks to him in a way, to become Father of his Country.

In 1939 Eppler felt he'd had enough. Perhaps he knew he'd be arrested by the British sooner or later. He went to Germany and joined the *Wehrmacht* as a tanker, but any enthusiasm he might have had when wore broke out soon vanished. However, his superiors saw that he was a young man of good education and recommended him for Intelligence. Later Eppler was to record: 'I shall never forget the name of the man who recruited me. He was called "Major Bean" [*Bohne*]. He put me through my paces and then accepted me into the organization [the *Abwehr*] from which I was freed years later with a broken nose and a crushed kidney.'

Thereafter Eppler trained for special missions in the Near East. That had been in late 1940. Now, with the crisis in Egypt reaching a head, he was finally being employed in an operation for which his whole life had been a kind of training.

With Almaszy as their guide through virtually unexplored desert, the two-truck team of Brandenburgers would leave the coastal road that ran the length of the whole area of the two-year-long desert campaign. Just beyond the last Italian positions at the Jalo Oasis they would plunge into the real sand waste. Driving south into the heart of the desert, they would make for the Kufra Oasis, where they would head east to cross the Libyan-Egyptian border. By this means, Canaris hoped, they'd be able to infiltrate Egypt without risking crossing the official frontier.

Almaszy would then lead the group through the Japsa Pass into the Glif Kebir, a pass which he had reconnoitred in 1937, 'one of nature's airfields', as he told Eppler. 'When I saw it then I was struck by that fact. I realized that one could land squadron after squadron of planes there behind British lines.'

There Almaszy would survey the whole area; it was still a blank on British Army maps. Thereafter he would lead the 'Condor' mission through the first British-held oasis at El Kharga. Once that obstacle had been overcome, Eppler and Sandberg ('Sandy's' real name) would go on alone by rail and slip into Cairo where they would adopt the names 'Gafar' and, in 'Sandy's' case, that of an American civilian, Peter Monkaster. In due course they would form a spy ring from Egyptian Army nationalists and from Eppler's friends, radioing back what they found out to Rommel's HQ.

It was a bold plan. The journey through the unexplored desert was fraught with danger. The ten-man team was young and fit, but had no idea of what they faced in the sand waste. Canaris was also worried about 'Sandy' and Eppler. What would the two young rogues do once they reached Cairo? They had £20,000 with them, a fortune in those days. With Eppler's reputation, it might well be that he and Sandy would forget their mission and waste the money in Cairo's fleshpots.

But now on this April day in 1942 when the war hadn't yet gone sour for the Nazis, the long preparations were over. They selected as the base of the code they would use when they reached Cairo Daphne du Maurier's best-selling novel *Rebecca*, unaware that in a year's time her husband, General 'Boy' Browning, would not be a million miles away planning the invasion of Europe from Africa ('Husky', the invasion of Sicily in July, 1943). Canaris saw them off. He shook the hand of each young man, saying to Eppler and the rest that same old phrase with which he had sped so many young men to their death, 'I'd like to wish you the best of luck. . . . best of luck . . . I'd like to . . .'

Then they were gone.

The weather was wonderful when they set off, a bright fine day, not too hot with perfect visibility. According to Almaszy, they were able to see objects fifty kilometres away. One hour after they started he spotted the turn-off and then they were on a rough, rutted track heading straight into the desert. The real journey had begun. A day later the going became more difficult. As Eppler wrote after the war, 'The desert is merciless. It destroys everyone who goes into it without training. Fanaticism and fatalism are the products of the desert.'

But they pressed on. On the third day they spotted a plane, a black dot in the far distance, but it disappeared without coming close to the little expedition. That same day Almaszy gathered the German drivers together and explained how to tackle the great sand dunes: 'Position your vehicle directly facing the top of the ridge,' he said, 'then let her have it! Drive at top speed for the crest. Once on top, brake hard momentarily, swing the wheel to left or right and go down the other side at an angle. If you don't, you'll go straight down, all twenty to thirty metres, and after that the bone-flicker here,' he indicated the red-face M.O. who seemed to be suffering most of all from the heat, 'won't be able to help you.'

They rolled on. Another day passed in back-breaking labour. Time and again one or other of the trucks stalled and became bogged down. Then they had to go through the murderous routine of unloading all their gear, digging trenches below the wheels and slipping metal strips underneath so they could obtain some traction in the sliding sand.

Then they began experiencing their first casualties. Their chief mechanic collapsed with a suspected heart attack, suspected because their M.O. had gone temporarily crazy and they had been forced to punch him into unconsciousness, tie him up for his own safety and fling him in the back of one of the trucks.

On the fifth day they gave up. Almaszy sighed wearily, 'Five days out and two casualties. It's no go.' In moody silence they turned and set off back for the Italian outpost at Jalo.

On 11 May, reinforced by three new volunteers from the Brandenburg Regiment, they set off once again. Once more the almost unbearable misery of the burning hot desert began. Temperatures reached 120 degrees, but Almaszy didn't appear to notice. 'Have you ever thought,' he snapped at anyone who began to complain, 'that at this very moment, other people don't just have to exist in this heat, they have to fight in it?'

On the fourth day out they spotted other vehicles, black against the sun's glare in that infinite sea of sand. 'Trucks to the north,' someone cried. Eppler's face paled under his tan. Almaszy had warned them that the British had their own long range desert patrols deep in the desert. There was also a young Guards officer out here somewhere with a new irregular formation called the SAS, whatever that meant.

While the Brandenburgers scattered, Almaszy and Eppler crept forward to observe the little group of ten vehicles drawn up in a wadi in a circle like US prairie schooners in some Hollywood epic. 'They look like the Lawrence patrol,' Almaszy concluded, lowering his glasses. 'It's led by Clayton.' He meant one of the British long-range penetration patrols started by Major Clayton, whom he had known before the war in Egypt. Clayton had named his group after Lawrence of Arabia. 'Clayton's obviously left the trucks behind as a base for one of his teams.'

He explained to Eppler that when Clayton's patrols went out they usually left behind at certain fixed points a depot of spare parts, petrol, watercans, even trucks, following the example of the desert Arabs who never ventured deep into the sand waste without two camels, in case one died. Now he said to Eppler, 'God has sent those trucks.'

Whether the deity had or not, the Germans helped themselves to the fortuitously stationed British supplies and pushed on ever deeper into the desert. But the men were starting to get jumpy and impatient. Using an old Arab trick to calm people in the desert, Almaszy would say, 'I know it's a long way off, but we'll get there.' Then, after a few more hours, he'd try to make it appear that they really were by adding, 'Yes, we're getting there now.' Some hours after that he would conclude for the day with 'Now we'll soon be there.' It seemed to work, for a while at least.

After six days out they were stretched to their limit. One young officer had gone mad and was tied up in a bundle at the back of a truck. More importantly, their water was running out again and it was proving very hard to impose water discipline.

It was about then that Almaszy stopped the little convoy and announced, pointing at the dark smudge of the Kebir Mountains on the burning horizon, 'Up there we'll find water.' He was like some ancient prophet making a biblical pronouncement as he looked at their sweating, hollow faces from which red-rimmed eyes looked back at him, 'We've only got to find the pass through the mountains. If we do, I'll give you water. I was here in 1937 when I buried a water depot up there.'

Eppler later remarked that he thought it was a 'slim chance', but there was no alternative. All the water they had left was the rust-tasting liquid in their radiators, and they daren't drink that. They just had to go on.

Five hours later they found the pass and then the precious water. Almaszy stopped the lead truck, grabbed a shovel and started digging. The blade of his shovel struck metal and, moments afterwards, a two-gallon British can was revealed. They had found the life-saving water. Turning to Eppler triumphantly, Almaszy wiped the sweat off his brow and exclaimed proudly, 'What did I tell you? That's genuinely filtered water from the Nile. Five years ago I put it here in English cans, just in case.' He bent and rubbed away the last of the sand. 'Look, they're still sealed.'

'Do you mean that people can still drink that stuff after *five* years?'

'*Drink* it, that's not the word for it!' Almaszy cried exuberantly.

'We shall savour it!' And he splashed some into Eppler's surprised face.

Greedily Eppler licked up the drops pouring down into his lips, while the others darted forward, all weariness gone, eyes bulging from emaciated faces like those of men demented. 'Now little man,' Almaszy said, finally helping himself to a can. 'What do you say to that?'

'I feel as if I've been reborn,' Eppler stuttered between gulps of water.

On 22 May 1942, eleven days after they had entered the desert proper, they saw their first lights on the horizon, glimmering through the velvet African evening. They were well within the Egyptian border area and had reached the first British Army outpost at El Kharga Oasis.

Almaszy ordered the convoy to stop and solemnly announced, 'We've reached our destination.'

Eppler followed the direction of his gaze and, as he wrote later, experienced 'a strange feeling. After days out in the desert, down there were people, eating, drinking, smoking – perhaps even making love.' Perhaps too, he realized for the first time that soon he and 'Sandy' would be on their own, minus the wise guidance of the older man, with every man's hand against them once they reached Cairo. If they slipped up now and were captured in civilian clothes it would be the firing squad for them.

Almaszy tapped Eppler on the shoulder and broke into his reverie. Perhaps he realized what was going through Eppler's mind. With a slight smile he said, 'Tomorrow you are on your own. I think that tonight Sandy and you should celebrate. I have a few cans of Australian food left, and a little bit of whisky.'

Ten hours later Sandy and Eppler were on their way, heading east into the unknown which lay ahead of them. Almaszy, for his part, duly set out on his return to the west with the Brandenburg saboteurs to become yet another footnote in Hitler's war in the shadows.*

---

* Fifty years later he made an astonishing return from the past as the 'English Patient' in the movie of the same name. He had made an astonishing transformation from the skinny, middle-aged homosexual he had been in 1942!

BOOK TWO

TAKE CARE, THE YANKS ARE COMING

'Come back to the firm. We'll clean up together.
An awful lot of things are opening up.'

John Foster Dulles to his brother
Allen Dulles, 1945.

AN AMERICAN GENTLEMAN
AT HERRENGASSE 23

'The fact that the Americans sent a sharp Wall
Street banking lawyer and not a soldier to run the
OSS in Berne is very significant. That tells us a
lot. They didn't send a military lawyer; they sent
a lawyer – a smart fast lawyer. He could look
behind things; he had a clear picture of how
finance and goods are the base for a war drive.
He played games, like all secret services do.'

Jacques Picard, Swiss Historian.

Eppler and Peter Monkaster, as the latter was now known,
arrived in Cairo at a turning-point in the Second World War. Nazi
Germany was still attacking in the Western Desert and was
preparing for yet another 'decisive' assault in Russia, while the
USA, at war with both Germany and Japan for the past five
months, was still confused and reeling from the Japs' 'surprise
attack' at Pearl Harbor. Despite President Roosevelt's secret
attempts to prepare America for the war which he knew *had* to
come (after all, he had been actively engaged in trying to take the
USA into it) the country was woefully unready. Her army was raw,
untrained and under-equipped. Even the two more professional
services, the Navy and the Air Force, were definitely not combat-
ready, sticking to outdated and old-fashioned procedures. *

---

* The US Merchant Marine lost more tonnage to German subs (400,000 tons)
sunk off the coast of New England in the first four months of war than did the
Navy at Pearl Harbor. The cause was the US Navy's stubborn refusal to adopt
the British convoy system.

Yet the seeds of Germany's defeat were already sown. She was now engaged in a two-front war – Britain, and now America, in the west and Russia in the east. Hitler had stupidly declared war on the world's greatest industrial power, a fact which Canaris deplored. He knew that the USA was still 'a sleeping giant', but he knew, too, from his US big business contacts in the States, and more importantly in Switzerland, of which we will hear more, that once American industrialists scented money there was no stopping their ingenuity. Hitler might well laugh at the prediction that America could be turning out up to 50,000 bombers within the next year, but Canaris didn't. He knew America's industrial capacity and he was beginning to realize that his prediction to the giant, half-blind Gestapo agent Hans Gisevius at the outbreak of war was starting to come true.

Back in September 1939 Canaris had bumped into Gisevius in his Tirpitzufer HQ and whispered to him, 'My God, if England comes into this, it will be the end of our poor Germany.' For, as he had gone on to explain, if England came into the war, America, with its huge industrial and military potential would follow, as it had done back in 1917.

Although Germany was still seemingly victorious everywhere, with Hitler ruling over 300 million people, events were now beginning to prove Canaris right. His agents were not getting the support they were accustomed to from their sub-agents, mostly foreign, nor from the neutral governments who until 1942 had banked on a German victory. All of them, from Sweden to Spain, were reluctant to supply Germany with the essential goods that the latter needed for its war machine. It was only the stolen gold and foreign currencies that Switzerland provided for Nazi Germany that now appeared to keep them in the German camp. Sweden, Switzerland, Turkey and others were making ever more anti-German noises and concessions to the Allies, now that the latter had started to win.

Everywhere in occupied Europe pro-German groups were getting cold feet. The days when young Dutchmen, Frenchmen, Belgians, even neutral Swiss and Swedes, streamed voluntarily into the *Waffen SS* recruitment offices were over; now, where they could not be encouraged to join Himmler's elite, they were forced. It was no different in countries under British rule,

82

1. "Reinhard Heydrich (right), the one-time naval cadet whom Canaris (left) had befriended in the '20s" (p.19).

2. Berchtesgaden: "up the steep road to the Führer's modest mountain chalet" (p.22).

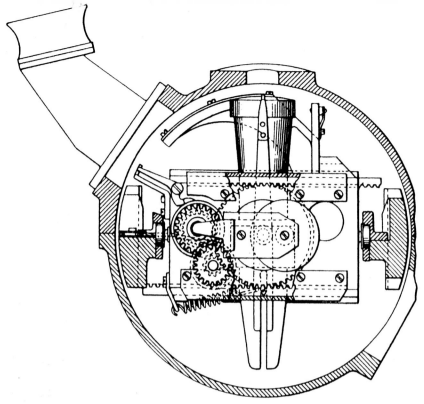

3. The Norden Bomb-sight: "this country's most jealously guarded air defense weapon" (p.32).

4. "After fifty-seven years the abandoned buildings...still bear the strange name of 'the German Village'" (p.39).

5. "The new agent used many names" (p.33). In reality he was Nikolaus Ritter, seen here in Hamburg after the war.

6. "Ian Fleming, then a member of Naval Intelligence and later famous as the creator of James Bond" (p.45).

7. "Henry Morgenthau, the rabid anti-German and personal friend of the President" (p.47).

8. Vera Chalburg: "the outstanding German female agent of the Second World War" (p.49).

9. "Thereafter Eppler trained for special missions in the Near East" (p.74).

where native resisters were losing confidence in a German victory.*

Egypt proved to be typical. Eppler's high hopes of help from the Egyptian Army's 'Young Turks' were soon dashed. Sadat, for instance, turned out to be a sore disappointment. He was suspicious of the 'spy' who was really a playboy. As Eppler wrote after the war, 'As soon as he entered our houseboat [he and 'Sandy' had hired one on the Nile as an ideal place to send their radio signals back to the *Afrika Korps*] and saw the somewhat pompous living room, I could see the look of rejection on his face.'

Indeed Sadat, who was Eppler's main contact with the anti-Farouk nationalist generals, became a serious problem. 'Sadat was too loud,' he told a newspaper correspondent twenty years later, 'too passionate. He could have betrayed us unwittingly at any moment. I was forced to drop him.'

Sandy had formed an association with a luscious belly-dancer at the Kit-Kat Club in Cairo, very popular with Eighth Army staff officers stationed there. Not only was she generous with her ample charms, she was also an Egyptian nationalist and started to work for the Germans as a spy. In time she found out about General Montgomery's plans for the Western Desert which might well have helped Rommel to victory in the Near East. Time and again Sandy tried to raise Rommel's HQ from their secret radio aboard the Nile houseboat, but in vain. His call-sign went unanswered.

It wasn't surprising. The frontline *Afrika Korps* listening and relaying station, which passed such messages on to Rommel, had been overrun by the British and no one had been found to replace the German operators.

And so, on 14 October 1942, the whole grandiose plan came to an end. The Germans had played for very high stakes, which, if they had won, might well have changed the whole course of the war. If Rommel had succeeded, it was planned that he would link up with the German advance through Southern Russia, thus

* The Indian leader, Subhas Chandra Bose, who helped to form the 'Indian Legion', although Hitler commented contemptuously, 'What good is a soldier who refuses to crush a beetle and will walk round it?', went over to Japan and there built up an 'army' of two divisions to fight the British in Burma.

cutting off both Britain and Russia from their vital oil supplies in the Near East.

Eppler and Sandy were on their houseboat, still trying to make radio contact with the German HQ, when they were startled by a thunderous knocking on their door. This was followed by the sound of heavy army boots running across the deck. They didn't need a crystal ball to know that they had been discovered.

'Okay,' Sandy said, playing it as cool as ever, 'look after yourself, old buddy.'

The knocking on the door gave way to the battering of rifle butts. The two agents started to destroy the radio, while at the same time setting fire to their secret papers. With the evidence destroyed, they hoped the enemy wouldn't have a good enough case against them in the trial that was bound to come.

The door flew open with a crash. Captain 'Sammy' Samson, dark-haired intelligence officer who had often played a round of golf with the two spies during the last couple of months, stood there, .38 revolver in his hand. Behind him stood a squad of British military policemen, weapons in their hands. Samson had been led to them by the indiscretions of the belly-dancer at the Kit-Kat club, Hekmat Fahmy.

Eppler, who was naked, faced up to the intelligence man bravely, surprised all the same to see Samson in a British Army captain's uniform. 'The black market currency king,' he said. For he had thought that his well-heeled golf partner had been a black marketeer.

'The playboy of the Eastern World,' Samson retorted warily. 'Take my tip and talk if you want to live.'

Both Eppler and Sandy had been ordered by Canaris to commit suicide if they were apprehended and Sandy did indeed try to do so afterwards, but was foiled in his attempt. Eppler was more realistic. He sang. Sadat was arrested, cashiered and imprisoned for the rest of the war. Eppler went on to make money out of his wartime experiences in books and in a German film made of the Cairo spying episode. Indeed he became a kind of friend with his former captor, Samson, when the two met again for the first time since the war in Cairo in 1960.

But in that October of 1942 it was the British who profited from the failure of Canaris' greatest operation in the Near East. Under

84

the command of General Montgomery, the Eighth Army surprised the *Afrika Korps* at El Alamein, a remote railway halt on the way to Cairo.* It was the start of the finish of German ambitions in Africa. It marked, too, the beginning of the German rollback in the West. After three years of war and defeat after defeat, there was light at the end of the tunnel for Britain and America at last. Less than nine months later, the Allies would be making their first landings in Occupied Europe.

Two weeks after the Battle of El Alamein began a middle-aged, pipe-smoking American civilian slipped over the border between Unoccupied France at Annemasse into neutral Switzerland. Just in time. That very day the Germans sealed off the border and took over control in Unoccupied France in response to the Anglo-American landings in North Africa.** Once across the border, the American continued his journey to Berne. Here he took up his residence at *Herrengasse 23*, not far from the River Aare in the old section of the city.

Berne in that winter of 1942 seemed very remote from the conflict raging all around. It had an air of solid, even smug, bourgeois contentment. After the Depression of the '30s, its citizens were prosperous once more. Switzerland was safely neutral.† War meant that the only important neutral country in Western Europe boomed; there was plenty of business while both the Allies and the Germans needed Swiss financial expertise. So the burghers of Berne could concentrate in 1942 on what they did best, making money!

In fact, behind the scenes in this neutral backwater the war also

---

* Rommel was in Germany on sick leave when Montgomery attacked at El Alamein.
** Codenamed 'Operation Torch', the Anglo-Americans landed, believing that the 'invasion' would be a walkover; after all they were coming to *liberate* the French. They were in for a surprise. 1,000 young Americans were killed or wounded by the grateful French.
† After the war Switzerland excused its tolerance of the Nazis to the bitter end by maintaining that the country feared a German invasion. But the only invasion that they should have feared was the secret one planned by the Western Allies in 1944, the details of which are still a close secret.

raged. It was not a shooting war, but a war in the shadows – one that was fought with perhaps more intensity than anywhere else in German-dominated Europe. For Berne was the nexus of global intrigue.

Half a dozen great and small powers waged their intelligence – and financial – battles (they were interlinked in virtually every case) here in those prim, 19th century offices and rustic inns, with their heavy solid meals, the like of which could be bought only on the black market in the rest of war-torn Europe.

It was a battle that was fought primarily over gold and what gold could buy, a secret battle, much of which remains secret to this day. For too many important people, and the institutions they once represented, are still involved. They don't want the murky past revealed, even in the year 2000. Now, in the person of this harmless-looking, middle-aged American who had just managed to slip over the Swiss border, the United States had entered what in the years to come would be called 'America's dirty wars'.

At first sight the American seemed an unlikely backstreet fighter. He was grey-haired, stooped slightly, wore a moustache and smoked a pipe. Indeed he looked like a graduate of an Ivy League college, who voted Democrat, subscribed to liberal causes and might be a lawyer or perhaps a clergyman of the Episcopalian kind.

Allen Welsh Dulles was all of that. That type of breeding had formed him. But his sense of ethics owed little to 'Stoker of Yale'. They were those of a big city corporation lawyer, out to earn an easy buck, used to wheeling and dealing in some panelled inner sanctum. His morals weren't of the highest either. He liked women and whenever he travelled he made a point of finding some bedworthy female.

Indeed in some ways the new arrival, who with his brother Foster would later do much to formulate America's foreign policies in the '50s, was akin to those German *Schreibtischtater** across the border. They too, apparently harmless bureaucrats, would give their orders from behind their imposing desks in some

---

* Literally 'writing desk criminals', the Nazi bureaucrats who made the Reich and its camps function so efficiently.

safe haven and then let others carry them out with ruthless brutality. Later, when the game was up, they would wring their hands and proclaim, 'It wasn't *me*! I had orders from above. I just signed the order.' Naturally they'd die in bed of old age, probably honoured by their fellow citizens on account of the good works they did later.

Officially the newcomer had arrived in Switzerland as the 'Special Legal Assistant' to the US Minister to the Swiss Government, Mr Leland Harrison. Naturally those in the know about such covers, and there were many, didn't believe the description. However, the Swiss Press described Dulles as the 'personal representative of President Roosevelt'.

In a way the Swiss journalists weren't far off the mark, not that Roosevelt liked Dulles one bit. It was said that he had approved his appointment just to get him out of Washington. Dulles, in fact, had come to Berne as the European head of a new and very powerful secret organization, the OSS, the country's first spy organization since the First World War. Although he was a lawyer by profession, Dulles had not been sent as an embassy legal adviser. Far from it. He had come as Canaris' main opponent. He, too, was a spymaster in Hitler's war in the shadows, which America had now joined.

At first sight Dulles seemed a very unlikely spymaster. He wasn't a military man like Canaris or Menzies, head of the British opposition, MI6. He hadn't had any connection with the intelligence world since 1929 and his contacts in Europe were definitely with the wrong people; most of them were Nazis!

All the same he had had job experience in Europe, which was rare in the ranks of America's new spy organization. Indeed, a quarter of a century before he had begun a career in intelligence in this same Berne. Then, as a young Foreign Service officer, he had collected information on wartime Imperial Germany and its ally, the dying Austro-Hungarian Double Monarchy.

In 1919 he had moved to France and worked with his older brother, sour-faced John Foster Dulles, the future US Secretary of State to Eisenhower and Kennedy, on the US team at the post-war peace conference at Versailles.

By the age of 29 Allen Dulles was the chief of the Near Eastern Division of the US Foreign Service. But the pay was poor and

America had already entered its isolationist phase. Nobody in the States was much interested in 'abroad'. So Dulles thought he needed a change of direction. He left the State Department and joined his brother's prestigious New York law firm, Sullivan and Cromwell. It was here that he started to make the real contacts with Germany which would stand him in good stead in what was to come.

In particular his contacts with the massive IG Farben Group, whose holdings in Switzerland and in the USA not even the experts were able to unravel, were very important in his later career. It put him in touch with the representatives of the German Rhine-Ruhr industrial barons, the creators of the Ruhr as Germany's workshop. For example, his chief wartime aide, German-American von Gævernitz, who was half-Jewish, was a scion of the great Ruhr industrialist Stinnes family, and it was through the bisexual von Gævernitz that Dulles was able to 'consort with the enemy', as one biographer of Dulles put it, in the form of German businessmen and right-wing officers who were now plotting against Hitler. In due course Dulles would, in 1944, start dealing with Himmler himself through one of his senior SS officers, General Wolff.

Naturally the *Abwehr*, which was involved, knew of Dulles's German contacts, and in due course the Gestapo would find them out as well. But although he and his somewhat naive bosses in Washington must have felt they were hoodwinking the enemy representatives in Berne, the Germans didn't mind, even those from the Party. If Dulles, as the US's man in Switzerland, could keep Washington off their backs, let the new spymaster fool himself as much as he pleased. Switzerland was vital for their conduct of the war. Without the Swiss bankers and their agents all over the world, including, probably, Anglo-American ones in London and New York, they would be unable to finance the war. As far back as 1937 Dr Schacht, the Nazi Minister of Economics, had warned Hitler that Germany would be bankrupt, meaning she would have no foreign currency left, by early 1940.* It was

* The Governor of the Bank of England, still the most powerful bank in the world, Montagu Norman, was decidedly pro-German. Schacht even named his son after him.

88

essential, therefore, that the Swiss conduit to foreign currency and the goods that currency would purchase should be kept open. Both Nazis *and* German anti-Nazis knew that. The alternative was a total collapse of the German economy and its war machine, with consequent chaos that could then lead to a communist Russian take-over. That was something that neither the Germans, whatever their political views, nor Dulles and his American business associates wanted.

It is an aspect of the latter half of the Second World War that has remained obscure, even to this day. In the face of the new threat that Soviet Russia now presented, total collapse had to be prevented at all costs. If Germany went, the rest of Western Europe, save perhaps Britain, would go communist. In 1942/43 those in power in the West were no longer just fighting for democracy, human rights and all those fancy phrases that the politicians utter so glibly. The West was fighting to defeat Germany admittedly, but at the same time to preserve her in a governable form for the future of Europe. There was only one fly in the ointment – the Jews.

By the time Allen Dulles arrived in Berne war was big business in Germany. The capitalists were making money hand over fist. Naturally they were expected to pay their tribute to the Nazi state, whether they were Nazis or not (and most were), in the form of assets which could be turned into foreign currency. All the same they were making huge profits and buying up great estates as a security for the future. Even Canaris' *Abwehr* was involved. His agents and their spymasters were making personal fortunes by smuggling goods out of Germany under cover of their nefarious activities or by selling passes to those who had need to get out of Hitler's Reich.

Naturally the ones who made the most profit were the Nazis themselves, in particular *Reichsführer* SS Heinrich Himmler, whose technically illegal activities* were foolproof due to the fact that he was the boss of the investigating service, the Gestapo.

* The export of foreign currencies and assets to be used for the purchase of the same was an offence which could be punished by seven years' imprisonment or in some cases by death.

By 1942 Himmler not only ran the half-a-million-strong *Waffen SS* and Germany's gigantic police *apparat*, but he was also in charge of a huge 'cottage industry', supplying labour and services to Germany's business giants. IG Farben built chemical plants; Himmler supplied the labour from the nearest concentration camps. Volkswagen turned over its production full-time to the *Wehrmacht*'s version of the 'people's car' *à la* Henry Ford's Model-T. Himmler and Speer, Minister of Munitions, provided a quarter to half of the slave labour to keep the little cars coming off the production line. (It should be noted here that Ford (Germany) and Opel (read GM), which supplied the *Wehrmacht*'s trucks and halftracks also used slave labour.) Indirectly Germany's major banks profited from the slave-based production boom too. The Deutsche Bank, the Commerz, the Dresdner (founded by a Jew), for example, all provided the funds for the industrial giants to build the plants, while insurance companies such as *Allianz* insured them, even down to personal insurance to the concentration camp guards in case they were 'injured' by their charges.

Being no economist himself, Himmler turned to German bankers to assist him in the proper use of the enormous gains being made by the SS prison-industrial complex. For, mass murderer that he was, Himmler seems to have been an honest man in the best German civil service tradition. For instance, when he wished to provide a home for his new mistress and her child, he asked the Party treasury for a proper mortgage and paid up monthly.

The German bankers, already greatly enriched by their role in the 'Aryanization' of Jewish property* before the war, were only too eager to help. They had the contacts, Himmler had the 'goodies'. They'd bring the two together, do their patriotic duty in helping the Fatherland and naturally make a tidy profit for themselves.

The whole scheme, which became known after the war as the 'Melmer Shipments', had begun in the summer of 1942 when an

---

* Forced sales of Jewish property at a nominal sum to the bank, which would then sell it to an honest Aryan German at a profit.

SS man (no one ever found out what his rank was) had had the audacity to call Emil Puhl, a Nazi and vice-president of the Berlin Reichsbank. He was also a senior member of the Swiss-based Bank of International Settlements, of which we shall hear more. Surprisingly enough, Puhl had a long talk with the SS man before switching him to *Direktor* Albert Thoms, Chief of the Reichsbank's Precious Metal Department. The latter was told by the SS man to expect to receive 'deliveries from the East', starting in the near future. These deliveries would be carried out by an SS Captain named Melmer. The deliveries would normally be in the form of precious metal and Thoms was told to assess their value and credit the amount in marks to a 'Max Heiliger' account. Later it would be realized that someone in the SS was having a bizarre joke on the uninitiated. For *Heiliger* means 'saint' in German and, whether the owners of these deliveries were saints or not, they were now presumably in heaven!

Thoms revealed, during his post-war interrogation by the Americans, that Melmer shipments arrived in truckloads of suitcases, boxes and packages, each of which was unmarked, save a couple stamped *Konzentrationslager*. Obviously the senior Reichsbank official knew something of the origin of these shipments from the East. He definitely knew what happened next. If the shipments contained precious metals, and they usually did, they were sent to the firm of Degussa, then, as now, Germany's premier firm dealing with precious metals. Here the metals were melted down. In the case of gold objects they were re-cast into standard-sized bullion bars, bearing the stamp of the Reichsbank. These bars had now lost all trace of their origin and could be accepted on the international gold market. It is said that there are 25 million dollars worth of such bars in a New York bank's vaults to this day and the Bank of England possesses just short of two million pounds' worth of 'Melmer shipment' bullion.

Twelve days after Dulles arrived in Berne on 20 November 1942 twenty Melmer bars were assayed by Degussa. They were melted and refined until they had a purity of 999.9. In the despatch book of Degussa there is a note for 7 December, 1942, that it had returned twelve bars of total weight of 143.2 kilos to the Reichsbank. The accompanying certificate includes the notation of 'Ref Melmer Shipment IX'.

From the Reichsbank the major part of this shipment went to the capital of Germany's ally, Bulgaria. There its receipt was registered in Sofia on 23 February 1943. The rest was sent to a Swiss bank in Zurich on the 22nd of the same month. Thereafter the source and the final resting place of that particular entry in the 'Max Heiliger' account has vanished, presumably for ever.

This single example shows how the system worked and, according to the documents seized by the Americans at the end of the war, there were many 'Melmer Shipments'.* In essence, therefore, the Nazi state, fronted here by Himmler, was using stolen gold and other valuables, plus the stolen labour of hundreds of thousands of people from a dozen different countries (including Britain and the USA, it will surprise some to learn**) to finance the war. In effect, the victims paid for their torturers to be able to continue torturing them.

But how was it kept secret, right up to our own time? The bullion was exported to half a dozen foreign countries. The currency gained from its sale was used to buy essential war goods in Sweden, Switzerland, Spain, Portugal, Turkey and elsewhere. Surely others apart from the officials of the Reichsbank and the staff at Himmler's Economic Office must have known the source of this sudden wealth in a nation that had supposedly been bankrupt in 1940? After all, German tourists going abroad on their 'Strength Through Joy' cruises did so in German ships, eating German food and buying German souvenirs in order to save foreign currency. Housewives were forced to use rhubarb instead of currency-expensive lemons in their cooking and Goering ordered 'Guns before Butter'. By 1940 Germany was dependent upon something akin to a barter economy as far as overseas trade was concerned. Naturally there were those at the top who were

* The Americans returned the documents in the early fifties. Promptly the German authorities 'lost' them. They were refound, but were 'lost' once more when Jewish and other organizations started to look into the shipments.
** In the early '90s the author lived in Wittlich, Germany, next to the graves of two Channel Islanders. Both had died working as slave labourers for this SS economy. In the summer of 1999 US Jewish GIs captured by the Germans and forced into concentration camps received a multi-dollar compensation from the Germans, which has gone totally unpublicized – for obvious reasons.

92

in the know, not only in Switzerland but also in German-occupied countries and, of course, in Allied ones.

Thomas McKittrick, the American banker who was President of the Bank of International Settlements in Switzerland, must, for example, have known. He had dined with Pohl until America entered the war. Senior British bankers, including the Germano-phile Montagu Norman, must also have been aware of what was going on. And there must have been a whole host of senior Swiss bankers and ministers who were privy to the secret. They, after all, were the ones who were carrying and sanctioning the German bullion for foreign currency dealings.

Naturally Canaris was well aware of what was going on. It was part of the *Abwehr*'s task not only to obtain enemy secrets, but also to protect Germany's secrets. The ex-Gestapo man Gisevius had been sent to Switzerland under the customary diplomatic cover to do many things. Most importantly he was to spy for Canaris, but at the same time he was to make contact with the Allies (the British turned him down as 'unreliable', so it had to be Dulles and the Americans). Here it was his mission to discover how the Americans stood on the matter of German resistance to Hitler. At least, that is what Dulles later wanted Washington to believe.

But was that all? Canaris may have come to hate the Hitler regime, but his whole career as a right-wing professional officer had shown that he was also a deeply patriotic German. He would not betray his fatherland without ensuring there was something in it for a Germany after Hitler. Germany would have to have a bargaining counter once Hitler had been removed by the anti-Nazi plotters, to which he appeared to belong. And that had to be the ability to fight on if the Allied terms weren't satisfactory, and to do that Germany needed the foreign currency provided by the Melmer shipments and the like. That major source of purchasing power for weapons of war had to be preserved at all costs. No one in America could be allowed to be in a position to point the finger of accusation at the 'neutral' Swiss and force them to break their ties with Germany.

In Switzerland Gisevius would be able to report on any change in Dulles's attitude; after all he was also the representative of US big business with great investments in Germany. His reports to Washington had to be controlled, ensuring that nothing of

Switzerland's underhand currency deals was revealed in them to those in the nation's capital who wanted to destroy Germany.

In Washington itself Canaris also needed a top-level source to keep him informed of what those anti-German groups might find out about what has since come to be called the Swiss Gold. He found it virtually at the top, in no less a person than the Vice-President of the United States, Henry Wallace! *

By 1940 Canaris had succeeded in planting two *Abwehr* agents, one code-named 'Habakuk' in the Swiss Foreign Ministry and another code-named 'Jakob' in the Swiss Secret Service, small but powerful and out to protect Swiss interests, whatever the cost. At first the two were relatively minor sources of information for Berlin. Then 'Habakuk' struck lucky. In 1941 he managed to obtain a long report on the Roosevelt–Churchill meeting at Placentia Bay where the Atlantic Charter was laid down. But how had the unimportant Swiss Minister in Washington, Dr Charles Bruggmann, managed to obtain such high-level information, which 'Habakuk' was able to pass on to Canaris?

Washington had now become a spy centre too, though America was still not at war. Russia and Germany vied with each other (and Britain too, in a minor sort of way) to obtain information on America's (read Roosevelt's) intentions. But Dr Bruggmann was no spy. So how had he obtained such highly classified information, which seemed to come right from Roosevelt's own cabinet meetings?

The answer was simple. One of Roosevelt's cabinet was leaking details. In both reports from Bruggmann, which 'Habakuk' managed to obtain in 1941, there was only one member of the Roosevelt cabinet present at both. He was the Vice-President, the radical New Dealer Henry Wallace, who would make an attempt at the presidency himself in 1948; and Wallace was the brother-in-law of Dr Bruggmann!

* There had been another source of top-level information, located in London. He was a clerk at the US Embassy while Joseph Kennedy, anglophobe and unscrupulous member of that same big business set, who believed in a German victory, was Minister. The clerk, Tyler Kent, who had an outsized chip on his shoulder, was in a position to read top-level despatches between Churchill and Roosevelt. He got eight years in a British jail.

The 52-year-old Swiss diplomat had married Henry Wallace's sister Mary in 1924. Thereafter a close relationship developed between the two men. When Bruggmann was appointed Swiss Minister to the States in 1932, Wallace was in the habit of calling on him personally and phoning him whenever he could. At these meetings Wallace let slip privileged information. Naturally the Vice-President, foolish as he was in some ways, never thought that this information would finally land on Canaris' desk in Berlin.

Bruggmann, for his part, was probably interested mainly in what Wallace might reveal of the activities of his cabinet colleague, the Secretary of the Treasury, Henry Morgenthau, who was attempting to take stringent measures against those Swiss banks in the States which represented the Nazis. At all events, as a good minister-ambassador should, Bruggmann passed on comprehensive accounts of top-level US thinking and intentions to the Swiss Foreign Office, from where 'Habakuk' and 'Jakob' forwarded it to the *Abwehr* and Ribbentrop's Foreign Ministry.

The coup was doomed by a 1943 Bruggmann report to Canaris and Ribbentrop on Wallace's thoughts on the new Russo–American relationship. Wallace, who was suspected of left-wing populist tendencies, was pessimistic about the new alliance born of the war. According to Bruggmann, his brother-in-law had said the alliance had deteriorated to the level where America and Britain would have to win the war 'alone' and *'possibly even against the Russians'*. Naturally this information, which also had Wallace stating that 'The American Government may be compelled eventually to make momentous decisions,' was manna from heaven to the Nazis. With the war turning against them, they prayed now that the strange alliance between communism and capitalism would fall apart and allow the Führer to sue for a fairer peace than Roosevelt's uncompromising 'unconditional surrender'.

It might well be that Dulles, who was actively attempting to cut out all left-wing American influences on how Germany should be treated during the war and afterwards, felt the same as Ribbentrop, but for different reasons. This damning leak, which he obtained with surprising ease from his own spy in the German

Foreign Ministry*, could be used to eradicate Wallace from such influence as he had as Vice-President in Roosevelt's government.

At all events Dulles forwarded the information he had on Wallace to his boss, General 'Bill' Donovan, in Washington. The head of the OSS decided to bypass the Vice-President and sent Dulles's alarming signal, plus a copy of the German intercept of the Bruggmann despatch, to Admiral William D. Leahy, Roosevelt's Chief-of-Staff, confidant in matters of security and general 'minder'.

At his daily briefing on 11 January, 1944, Admiral Leahy presented his case on Wallace to Roosevelt. FDR was not impressed or alarmed. He shrugged it off. As Leahy put it later, 'The OSS report did not seem to surprise Roosevelt. . . . I do not recall that he commented on it at all except to say that it was quite interesting.'

There, it seemed, the matter ended. The vital Swiss-German-American contact presumably continued a little longer. Whether Wallace's de-selection as Roosevelt's running mate that year in the coming election was due to his foolish leaks is not known. What is known is that he was replaced by a chirpy little ex-haberdasher Harry S. Truman, who had no Swiss brother-in-law and would become the biggest anti-communist of them all. Dulles's schemes had seemingly worked yet again and the Swiss gold secret had been preserved for a while longer.

But now the American spymaster and naturally the German one in Berlin, who was feeding off the American's pro-German, anti-Soviet intentions, was to be faced by another member of Roosevelt's cabinet and he was not going to be got rid of so easily.

In the same winter that Allen Dulles took up his spymaster post in Berne a seedy ex-journalist in Washington decided he needed some sort of security for what might soon come. In retrospect some

---

* This was Fritz Kolbe, a humble clerk code-named 'George Wood'. He supplied Dulles with 1,800 documents taken from his ministry. How he got away with it when the Germans had long been reading Dulles's coded messages to Washington is anybody's guess. When the present author tried to find out about Kolbe with the active support of a German cabinet minister, he was met by a blank wall at the present day German Foreign Ministry. Perhaps Dulles's 'ace of agents' was really a plant.

might consider the ex-journalist to have been a little paranoid. After all a great war was raging. What did his fate matter against the background of a global conflict? Besides, he had already confessed to the authorities about his 'crimes' back in 1939. In May 1942, when he had tried to re-establish contact with the former spymasters he had betrayed, they seemed reluctant to have any dealings with him. That was understandable enough. What, however, was puzzling was that they didn't even seem to know him.

The ex-journalist was named David Whittaker Chambers. One day he'd go down in the history of espionage and betrayal during the Cold War. Now he was a total unknown, a man one wouldn't give a second look if one passed him in the street. But his unkempt appearance hid a foxy intelligence, a crazy sense of mission and a desire for self-preservation.

Despite his cunning though, Chambers had been a failure for most of his life. Two decades earlier he had dropped out of Columbia Law School and become a communist journalist. It was not the most promising of career choices in isolationist America in the '20s. He went even further. In 1925 he joined the US Communist Party, the bugbear of big business and the FBI. From the CP he drifted into the fringes of espionage. He became a courier and then a manager of a Communist network in Washington, which had links with the GRU, the Soviet Intelligence Agency of that time.

Perhaps he made the choice because of his job; he was the editor of *The New Masses*. Perhaps he was carried away by those early US revolutionaries who went to Moscow in the early '20s, full of left-wing fervour, expecting the 'New Dawn' to appear the very next day. All that changed when Stalin began his great purges in 1937. As Chambers confessed later, 'Those show trials and purges aroused in me a profound upheaval of spirit.' In 1938 he broke with the Party.

What was he to do? Perhaps it was his journalist's sense that he had a great story to sell that compelled him to do what he did next. Indeed there would be a ready market for what he was about to sell; there were plenty in business and in the media who were convinced that Roosevelt and his 'New Dealers' on Capitol Hill were preparing the way for a 'red' takeover. But Chambers was smart enough to know that to tell his story he first needed

97

freedom from prosecution. The only way to do that was to 'name names' and do a deal with the authorities.

However, Chambers didn't head off to the nearest police station. Instead he went almost to the top in Washington, approached the US Assistant Secretary of State, Adolf Berle, in mid-1939 and gave him a list of Communist contacts that he had had inside Roosevelt's administration.

Chambers' list was a bombshell and Berle knew it. But the bomb wasn't going to explode yet. Indeed it was going to take nearly a decade before it really went off. For Berle's memo to the President on the 'Underground Espionage Agent', with Chambers' list of covert communists among the 'New Dealers', couldn't have arrived on Roosevelt's desk at a worse time. The President was going to have a crack at an unprecedented third term in office. If it were revealed that some of his best men were 'commies', the Republicans and their big business supporters who hated him would have a field day. He'd never make it.

So the Berle memo was quietly shelved and didn't appear again till Hoover, the head of the FBI, got hold of it. Chambers was summoned by the FBI for cross-examination, but the agents were foxed by him. By turn he was revealing and then reluctant. He wasn't the best of witnesses. He categorically refused to elaborate on his original disclosures to Berle in 1939 and he wanted cover names for himself and anyone else he might betray to the FBI chief.

Hoover wouldn't buy that. He wasn't so kosher himself. He was said to keep a male live-in lover and at times wear drag. He knew a funny guy when he saw one. If he were going to take Chambers seriously, he demanded names – *now*. Still Chambers refused. And there apparently the matter rested. (Perhaps pressure was put on Hoover, and in his case it could come only from the very top.) It was not until 1948 that Chambers started to reveal what he knew and helped to start that period of witch-hunting that has become known as the 'age of McCarthyism'.

All the same Chambers knew he was in trouble. He could be arrested at any time. If the worst came to the worst he could be sentenced to twenty years' imprisonment under the 'Espionage Act' if convicted. He decided to take some sort of precaution, a kind of blackmailer's insurance.

98

So the lethal war in the shadows was extended to, of all places, Brooklyn. There two of the key documents in his possession were hidden in the shaft of the dumb waiter at his wife's sister's home. Another was concealed inside a hollowed-out pumpkin that he kept on his farm in Maryland. One of these contained filmed copies of State Department documents that would be used years later in an attempt to incriminate Alger Hiss, the Harvard-educated American patrician in the State Department hounded by Senator McCarthy. Another contained a hand-written memo from a certain Harry Dexter White, who would end his career as Assistant Secretary to the head of the US Treasury, Henry Morgenthau. It was the latter's name which would be branded onto German folk consciousness as Germany's most vindictive persecutor for the rest of the 20th century.

In 1943 Morgenthau, then aged 52, had been Roosevelt's Secretary of the Treasury for nine years. Although a farmer by profession, the balding, bespectacled friend and neighbour of the newly elected FDR had been selected by Roosevelt to lead the Treasury and ensure the USA's recovery from the Great Depression. Morgenthau had not been successful, but he had built up massive gold reserves, primarily by squeezing the rich, so that when the war began for America in December 1941 he had been able to finance the great rearmament programme and thus bring the Depression to an end. He had also been instrumental in devising the Lend-Lease agreements which had indirectly brought the USA into the war on Britain's side.

In the years since 1941 Morgenthau, who was Jewish, had been formulating his ideas on the future of Nazi Germany once that country was beaten. They were of a totally punitive nature and would result in the famous (or infamous, according to your point of view) 'Morgenthau Plan'. This envisaged the destruction of a beaten Germany's industrial potential. Morgenthau thought that German imperialism, which had resulted in two world wars, had been caused in the first place by her economic aspirations. In his opinion the one way to prevent a third 'German war' was to put an end to those aspirations by transforming industrial Germany into an agricultural state, as she had once been back in the 18th century. His ideas were shared by Roosevelt, who, like Morgenthau, disliked, even hated, the Germans intensely.

Master planner behind the Morgenthau Plans as he was in shaping the International Monetary Fund and the World Bank, both of which function to this day, was Dr Harry Dexter White. He was also a Soviet spy, code-name 'Jurist'. White, a former Harvard lecturer, who as a young man had considered going to Moscow University to study, had been a member of the Communist Party and an 'agent of influence' probably since the mid-thirties. Chambers said of him, 'He enjoyed being a member of the Communist Party, but he didn't like the discipline'. But now he was disciplined and influential enough to follow Stalin's line in regard to Germany. A beaten Germany was to be rendered impotent and ripe for a communist takeover.

From 1942 Morgenthau and Dexter White worked in relative secrecy, as far as anything could be secret in Washington that year, ironing out the complicated details of the Morgenthau Plan. What did you do with German industry, for example? Did you shut down *all* German factories? If you did, what did you do with the hundreds of thousands of unemployed industrial workers? Could you employ these city folk on the land in this new agricultural Germany?

In due course Morgenthau gained FDR's approval for the still secret plan named after him. But Germany had not yet been beaten. Morgenthau knew that her war economy was booming. Germany was still trading covertly with the rest of the world, even as far afield as Latin American countries like the Argentine. How were the Anglo-Americans going to stop this secret trading, which was financed by Nazi gold shipments to Switzerland and by the Swiss bankers using it to buy strategic goods on the world market?*

In due course the US Treasury and the State Department developed a plan that would pinpoint those areas of finance and trade in which neutral countries would be punished by sanctions and seizures if they used them to aid Nazi Germany. At the same

---

* Churchill, for obvious geopolitical reasons, didn't like Morgenthau's plans for a post-war Germany. He wanted to keep post-war Germany 'impotent but fat'. Otherwise he was afraid that Germany might go communist. But he was, in essence, blackmailed by Morgenthau into accepting the plan by the threat of America cutting off her essential loans in dollars to a virtually bankrupt Britain.

time the planners around Morgenthau set about preventing the build-up of German assets abroad for post-war use. This time, unlike what happened after Germany's defeat in the First World War, the beaten Germans would not be allowed to hide financial assets in other countries to be used in due course to set up yet another aggressive Germany.

The American programme, code-named 'Safehaven', would ensure that the Nazis didn't smuggle gold, currency or diamonds through Switzerland to South America. The neutrals were warned of what was to come. They didn't like it, in particular Switzerland, and mostly determined to keep up their trading with the Germans to the bitter end, despite aggressive American threats.

The Swiss fought their corner cleverly and with iron determination. They invented the standard ploy, which became their major excuse then and into our own time for their continued co-operation with the proscribed Germans. It was that they *had* to work with the Germans if they didn't want the latter to invade their country. Besides, without German iron ore, coal and oil, the Swiss economy would grind to a halt.

Morgenthau put on the pressure. He sent a mission, headed by one Lauchlin Currie, called thereafter the 'Currie Mission', to obtain yet further concessions under pressure from the Swiss Government in Berne. The Swiss gave way a little, but they said that there could not be an immediate termination to exports, military or otherwise. By now Switzerland was exporting sixty per cent of her industrial production to Germany, all paid for by the 'Melmer Shipments'.

Morgenthau relaxed the pressure a little. He was quite pleased, it seemed, with the 'Currie Mission'. He wrote to the team leader, 'Dear Lauchlin, I want to congratulate you on the fine job you have just done in Switzerland. . . . I feel that you have not only thwarted the Nazis' plan for using Switzerland as a financial hideout, but also have laid the basis for the Allied Military Government in Germany to take control of German assets in Switzerland.'

Morgenthau, who, in essence, was attempting to ruin Germany for decades to come by turning the clock back, was not alone in being pleased at the supposed success of the Currie Mission.

Moscow was too. For anything that would disrupt the affairs of post-war Germany, especially her financial ruin, brought joy to the Russian spymasters and their political bosses in the Kremlin. Their plan had worked. For, just like Morgenthau's closest associate, Harry Dexter White, Lauchlin Currie was also not what he seemed. He was a Soviet spy!*

In May 1943, when the Morgenthau Plan was still in the planning stage and as secret as anything could be in gossip-plagued Washington, a Swedish economist of international standing asked three prominent German bankers to meet him on the neutral ground of Switzerland. He wanted to have an informal chat with the Germans in the discreet surroundings of Zurich's Hotel Baur en Ville.

The Swede, Per Jacobssen, was the chief economic adviser to the American-led Bank of International Settlements in Basle. He was also a friend of Dulles and had, more than likely, connections

---

* In later years, when the thirty-odd Americans accused by Chambers and Elizabeth Bentley, another undercover communist, including Hiss, White and Currie, were tried, the charges against them were regarded by US liberals as a Republican backlash. Harry Dexter White died of a heart attack just after his first official interrogation in 1948 and was popularly regarded as a 'martyr'. Hiss was another.

However, although Truman, then President, was *not* informed of it, US codebreakers had already cracked the spies' code, used by their Russian case officers in Washington to send the details of their agents' reports to Moscow. The 'Venona Decodes', as they are now called, were given the top classification and although the first were cracked as far back as 1943, they were still classified long after the Ultra decodes were made available to the general public. Even today some are not available. Without the code-names the Russians gave to their US agents (as we have seen, White was code-named 'Jurist') it is still very difficult to make sense of those which have been released since the early '80s to the public.

In the light of the fuss the American authorities made of the British spies, 'the Cambridge Five', Philby and the like, it is clear that they were not too keen to inform the Great American Public that America, too, had spies working for the Russians at virtually cabinet level. It is clear, too, that the McCarthy era has now, in view of the real treachery of the supposedly innocent Hiss, to be re-appraised.

What is *not* clear is who in the USA in the mid-forties started the ball rolling, knowing that there was hard evidence (in the form of the Venona decodes) available to back up these accusations of high-level treachery. Could it have been Dulles himself?

with at least three intelligence services. Now his main duty was to advise Thomas McKittrick, the US head of the Swiss-based bank, which had been set up by the major world powers after the First World War primarily to regulate defeated Germany's monetary obligations. As we have seen, the Bank still functioned, with its board composed of both enemy and allied nationals, ensuring, among other things, that dividends gained in Nazi Germany were paid out to Allied shareholders. That was just a minor aspect of this strange bank, set in neutral Switzerland, in the midst of war-torn Europe.[*]

Just as strange was this meeting between the Swede, who worked for both an American boss and his German deputy, and his three German guests. They were all determined to ensure the flow of Melmer shipments to Switzerland. There was Emil Puhl of the Reichsbank, Carl Goetz of the Dresdner and German banking's mystery man, 42-year-old Hermann Abs, head of Foreign Assets for the Deutsche Bank, a man who would dominate German finance long after the war. He died in 1994.

Jacobssen told them of a disquieting American plan which would affect not only the Bank of International Settlements, with which all three had connections, but the whole future of post-war German economy if America won the war.

That afternoon Jacobssen revealed that not only were the Americans intending to regulate post-war currencies, but that Morgenthau was proposing that Germany should be turned into an 18th century agricultural economy.

If Abs, the banker who would become *the* major player in the post-war German economy, although imprisoned for three months and accused of being a war criminal, recorded his thoughts that day we are not privy to them. His private papers are locked up until the year 2015. But Jacobssen's revelations must have come as a shock, as they did later to the average German. Some maintain that when the ordinary German Army *landser* learned of the Morgenthau Plan, it kept him fighting much longer than necessary. Fighting was better than surrendering, it seemed.

---

[*] The bank still exists, despite the fact that the US authorities had decided they'd close it as soon as victory was achieved.

But Abs, a pragmatist who was not only concerned about Germany's future but also his own, must have been shocked by the Swede's disclosures. As a good banker should, he had left his options open. He knew that there was a clique among the aristocratic professional caste who wanted to get rid of the Führer, by force if necessary. He knew that Germany, now faced with the might of Russia *and* America, and in the process of being kicked out of Russia and North Africa, with the prospect of an Allied invasion of *Festung Europa* soon to come, would, in the end, be defeated by the Allied powers.

However, the longer Germany kept going the better her chances were of negotiating a peace that would not include 'unconditional surrender' that would be the necessary base for the forced introduction of the Morgenthau Plan. Germany simply needed time to plan her own post-war future after defeat and at the same time somehow or other kill the Morgenthau Plan which would be the ruination of Germany for decades to come. It was therefore essential that the Swiss connection be kept going for as long as possible.

Abs and his fellow bankers, along with the right-wing plotters against Hitler, attempted that summer to make approaches to Allied governments in order to stave off the disaster looming on the horizon while Hitler and his war could still be used as a bargaining counter. Naturally they used their contacts with the Bank of International Settlements. But that cut little ice with the American patriots in Washington. As an officer of the New York Federal Reserve Bank noted at the time, the BIS was a club, 'where representatives of Allied high finance gather round a table with their opposite numbers from Germany in order to participate in fat dividend distributions while our boys are dying at the front'. The Bank of International Settlements' reputation was so stained that it could never be accepted in Washington as a mediator, especially as the 1944 presidential elections were now looming up.

The British were tried. The Germans told themselves the British were Europeans. Their businessmen and bankers also had large stakes in Germany. They might help the plotters to put off the evil day, and the Morgenthau Plan. The Germans were right. The City and the Bank of England were definitely anxious to keep

Germany's economy going after that country's defeat. But the plotters hadn't reckoned with Churchill. Britain's previous war-time dealings, secret as they had been, with Germany had turned out a disaster. There had been plenty of high-ranking politicians, bankers, secret service chiefs, even the King's own brother, the Duke of Windsor, who had tried to come to some sort of agreement with the German anti-Nazi plotters. All had fallen flat and scandal had only been avoided through wartime censorship. Churchill was not going to have any repetition of that, especially now he was relying virtually one hundred per cent on Roosevelt to win the war for him and help reshape post-war Europe according to the plans he had formulated for the continent.

If Britain was out, that left only the USA for the right-wing plotters. But naturally it could not be the America represented by Morgenthau and his left-wing advisers who were secretly working for Russian communist interests.* It had to be those Americans who were business-minded, had German financial interests, were anti-communist *and* knew the importance of the Swiss connection, not only for the Germans but for those of a like mind as the erstwhile enemy. It didn't take the Germans long to discover who their American contact should be, one they could approach without difficulty and who was himself something of a loner, cut off from the mainstream of US activity. Naturally it was Allen Dulles in Berne.

Now Dulles was contacted by a whole stream of Germans from the 'resistance'. There was of course Gisevius, who started to make his first contacts through Dulles's mistress Mary Bancroft. Often Dulles used to pop in to her bedroom on their twice-weekly 'engagements' so that he could 'clear my head'. There was the notorious Prince Max von Hohenlohe, who was the happy

* In recent years research has shown that there were a large number of Americans at the top who weren't so politically naive as the British thought. In some cases, they were more anti-British than anti-German. They wanted the break-up of the British Empire. Their motives were either economic or anti-colonial. Steering them were ideologues of a communist persuasion. Even Vice-President Wallace came into this category in his woolly and confused manner. These people definitely influenced US military strategy in the last twelve months of the war.

possessor of a rich wife and a Liechtenstein passport. Later the Prince, who seemed to have been everyone's agent, including Himmler's, hurt Dulles's reputation greatly. In his reports, which were published in the States after the war, he maintained that during their first meeting Dulles had said that he was 'sick of listening to bankrupt politicians, emigrés and prejudiced Jews'.

In addition there were German industrialists. Eduard Schulte, for instance, was managing director of the giant Giesche mining complex in Upper Silesia. After the First World War the firm had been sold to a US consortium led by the US financier Averell Harriman. Now Schulte, who is reputed to have been the first German to reveal the details of Himmler's holocaust to the West, wanted to work with Dulles. Whether Harriman, currently Roosevelt's fact-finder in London and lover of Pamela Churchill,* estranged wife of Churchill's son Randolph, had a hand in Schulte's decision to approach Dulles is not known, but it would add another enigmatic dimension to this strange business if he had. For right-wing Germans seemed to be dropping out of the very woodwork in Berne, all of them dying to meet and work with the US spymaster. Yet not one of them appeared to be worried by the fact that they were guilty of high treason by consorting with this influential enemy of the Reich, if that was what Dulles really was.

Why were they so eager? The answer is not hard to find. Admiral Canaris, via von Gævernitz's protégé Gisevius, a paid-up member of the *Abwehr*, was steering them Dulles's way to help Germany keep the vital Melmer-Swiss banking operation going and as secret as possible. If anyone could stop Morgenthau and the stringent application of his Safehaven operation, which was soon due to arrive in England under the control of a certain Colonel Bernstein** it would be Dulles with his important banking and Republican connections in the States.

* Harriman, who was at least 30 years older than Mrs Churchill, later married her and left her his huge fortune. The family are still trying to get some of it back.
** In 1944 Bernstein was feared by almost everyone in the Allied camp, including Eisenhower. He was overbearing, arrogant and what one would today call 'a control freak'. But when FDR died in April, 1945 Morgenthau and Bernstein both fell from grace.

In the end Canaris succeeded. The Morgenthau Plan was never put into operation and the Safehaven operation failed. People are arguing about the missing Melmer gold to this day, with the current German and US Governments publicly at loggerheads over what happened to the stolen assets and which German firms should pay compensation to whom.

The bamboozlement of Allen Dulles and those he represented in this question of the Melmer gold and the role the Swiss played in the affair can be regarded as Canaris' major achievement against the Allies in the Second World War. The British, in particular, have always been rightly proud of their achievements in the field of wartime deception. But the greatest of their triumphs, the mass turning of the *Abwehr* agents in Britain under the accurately named 'Double Cross Committee' and the way MI6 and MI5 fooled the Germans about where the 1944 Invasion would take place, were of limited value. Once these coups had been pulled off, that was that. The matter was over.

Canaris' achievement in Switzerland was of a totally different nature. As hopelessly corrupt as the *Abwehr* was by this time, not even trusted by its political and military masters, it was still able to carry out a feat of deception which has lasted into our own time. Not only that, but their efforts were to ensure that post-war Germany was not reduced to the level of an 18th century agricultural state as Morgenthau had envisaged, and that, when the time was ripe, Germany could emerge as a great economic power, the home of the vaunted *Wirtschaftswunder*, the 'Economic Miracle'.

British Intelligence, as I have said, made the invasion and liberation of Europe possible in 1945, but in the long run the effort ruined the British Empire and eventually reduced Britain to a third or fourth-class power. German intelligence, although it lost the war and in all other fields was hopelessly outclassed by the gifted amateurs and professionals of its opposing service, helped make the Germany we know today Europe's most powerful nation, economically and politically.*

* Naturally British Intelligence knew a great deal of what was going on in Switzerland at that time, but it was hampered by powerful people in the British establishment from doing much about it. Recently released SOE papers

But there was a price to be paid for their success in this secret war in Switzerland. It wasn't obvious at the time, indeed it was just a minor incident in a whole series of failures that Canaris experienced in 1942. As far as is known, Canaris never learned of the incident which would finally lead to his slow death by the SS in one of his own country's concentration camps.

By the autumn of 1942 when the Melmer operation was getting into its stride, Admiral Canaris had been hopelessly compromised in the eyes of his enemies in the Reich. General Muller, head of the Gestapo, had already prepared a long dossier on him. His associate General Walter Schellenberg, head of the SS's own secret service, the *SD*, which he had taken over from the murdered Reinhardt Heydrich, wanted to take over the *Abwehr* as well. To do this, he needed to get Canaris out of the way. He too had prepared a dossier on his daily riding companion and supposed 'elderly friend and adviser'.

As the Austrian SD secret agent Wilhelm Hoettl wrote later: 'The papers on Canaris in the Gestapo archives ran to several volumes, for everything unsatisfactory in the *Abwehr* organization was debited to the personal account of the Admiral.'

Surprisingly enough, at first Himmler, who was both Muller's and Schellenberg's chief, did nothing about it. According to Hoettl, Ernst Kaltenbrunner, evil head of the *Polizeiapparat*, once took the Gestapo file to the *Reichsführer SS*, expecting action, but Himmler sent him away, surprising him by 'declaring that he was well aware of the contents of the file [as Hoettl wrote] but he had for good reasons nevertheless refrained from taking any action against Canaris and that any future action by Kaltenbrunner on his own initiative was undesirable'.

All the same Muller continued to collect details of Canaris' downright anti-Nazi stance and in the autumn of 1942 was able to add another little snippet to the growing *'Canaris-Akte'*. It was the arrest of a supposed Munich businessman named

---

(October, 1999) reveal that a special section of that organization was formed to infiltrate into the bands smuggling Nazi assets into Switzerland, Spain, Turkey and other countries and that SOE was empowered to carry out specific assassinations if required. This activity apparently continued after the war was ended.

Schmidthuber who was picked up between Switzerland and Bavaria for smuggling foreign currency. That was a serious offence under Nazi law. The Gestapo 'squeezed' him a little. As the older Gestapo officials always boasted, they could 'make even a mummy talk'.

Schmidthuber began to sing. He turned out to be not just another Bavarian businessman trying to rescue what he could from the sinking ship of Nazi Germany. In fact he was an *Abwehr* agent who was smuggling foreign currency out of the country for a group of German-Jewish refugees in Switzerland.

It was a surprising admission and Muller was very gratified. Now he sat back in his office in Berlin and waited to see what the *Abwehr* would do. They did nothing and he got angry.

Back in Munich Schmidthuber started to get the wind up and began to talk and talk. He had been an *Abwehr* agent for several years and he knew a lot about the organization's activities. He had also memorized much of the agents' gossip. What he didn't know he made up, in the manner of so many who attempt to please their interrogators by telling them what they want to know.

He told Muller's cops that in 1940 Canaris had attempted to make contact with the British through the Pope, but the pro-German Pius XII had refused to help. Schmidthuber also told his interrogators that Canaris had sent an anti-Hitler protestant clergyman, Dr Dietrich Bonhoeffer, later executed by the Nazis, to meet Dr Bell, the Bishop of Chichester, in Stockholm. Dr Bell, who appeared sympathetic to the aspirations of the German anti-Nazis, had also attempted to seek peace. Again nothing came of it.

Schmidthuber also confessed that the *Abwehr* had not only smuggled money but also Jews! They might have worked for Canaris as agents (the Admiral was not averse to using Jewish agents, including a very prominent German-Jewish banker, who survived the war*) but more than likely Canaris's men smuggled

* In the USA one of Canaris' long-term agents, for instance, was a Miss Stein, hairdresser and so-called 'artist's model', although she weighed a good two hundred pounds. Despite all she must have known about the Nazis' persecution of the Jews (she was herself a German Jewess) she continued to work for the *Abwehr* until the FBI apprehended her.

them into Switzerland on account of the foreign currency with which they could pay for their rescue.

All that winter of 1942/43 the captive *Abwehr* agent continued to blab to his interrogators. In the end he gave away one of the *Abwehr*'s greatest secrets. Two of Canaris' key staff, General Oster, his chief-of-staff, and Hans von Dohnanyi, a senior *Abwehr* political adviser, had both betrayed Hitler's military secrets, including the invasion of Belgium and Holland, to the representatives of those countries in 1940. More importantly, they were implicated in plans to assassinate the Führer.

In due course they were arrested and interrogations were begun which would end in the execution of both for high treason. But, strangely enough, Canaris remained a free man. No one has ever been able to explain why in the years that have passed since Schmidthuber's arrest started the ball rolling which finally came to rest in Flossenburg Concentration Camp. Canaris has remained an enigma.

Wilhelm Hoettl of the SD wrote of him: 'Abroad he was widely regarded as the sinister *deus ex machina* behind all the crimes of the National Socialist regime: his friends profess to see in him the spiritual leader of all the opposition movements against Hitler and a martyr in the cause of the fight against National Socialism. A section of the German people, on the other hand, agree with neither of these verdicts, but condemn him as a traitor to his country and the man largely responsible for Germany's defeat.*

So we shall probably never know how it was that Canaris could do seemingly impossible things, even commit known crimes against the state for which most Germans would have been despatched to the state executioner and get away with it. Was it luck? Was it that he had some really high-ranking protector who shielded him until his 'crimes' became such that it was no longer

---

* When the author asked Colonel Ritter and his wife, experts in the vagaries of human nature (Mrs Ritter had also worked for the *Abwehr*), how they would characterize Canaris, both were at a loss for words. Ritter recalled, 'He always tried to maintain his distance. When he came to visit our branch in Hamburg, he would invite us to dinner after his inspection. But unlike most Germans who tell you their life story within five minutes of meeting them, the Admiral was always close. We never got anything out of him.'

possible to prevent the wrath of the Gestapo descending upon him? Again we simply don't know.

But one thing *is* clear. In 1942/43, at the turning point of the war, his fate was balanced on a knife-edge. Twice in 1942 he had incurred the Führer's public wrath. Hitler had taken him to task for his inability to provide him with information on the strength of the Red Army. In 1941 he had felt the attack on Russia would be a walkover. Although the Russians had suffered enormous losses, the Red Army had been able to fight on, even make the *Wehrmacht* retreat on the Moscow Front. Then, seemingly out of nowhere, the Russians had sprung a tremendous and shocking surprise on the Germans. They had sent the T-34 tank into battle in large numbers, as if they had been producing the tank, which could outgun and outfight every German tank at that time, for some years.

The second occasion on which the Führer vented his rage on Canaris had been in November, 1942, when the German High Command had been completely surprised by 'Operation Torch', the Anglo-American landings in North Africa. Why hadn't Canaris seen the operation coming? He had always boasted that he had excellent sources of information in Spain and Italy. At that time he was conducting a homosexual affair with the chauffeur of General Amé, the head of the Italian Secret Service. Why hadn't he learned from him that a large enemy fleet was sailing through the Straits of Gibraltar to land in the French North African ports, faced not by the German Army, but by the worthless French one?

Canaris managed to find some sort of explanation to appease the Führer, but he knew he wouldn't get away with it a second time. The operations he now planned against the Anglo-Americans for 1942/43 had to succeed, or else.

THE *ABWEHR* STRIKES BACK

'It is undoubtedly one of the most remarkable
feats in the history of espionage.'

Admiral Canaris, 1943.

At one o'clock on the morning of Wednesday 10 March, 1943, a
four-engined RAF Halifax bomber was slowly approaching the
Dutch provincial town of Apeldoorn. On board there were, in
addition to the crew, three Dutchmen. All were spies, volunteers,
exiles from their homeland for nearly three years. Now they were
going back to fight the Germans. Only one of them, a 25-year-old
former Dutch naval petty officer, Pieter Dourlein, would survive
the battle to come.

The pilot spotted what he had been looking for for the last ten
minutes – a fleck of winking red light. It was the signal beacon lit
by the Dutch underground. They had almost reached the DZ. The
three Dutch SOE, recruited a few months before in the UK by
a British Major Anthony Blunt, who looked at the world with a
haughty stare as if he had just discovered an unpleasant smell
underneath his long nose, tensed at the door.

Now the green light inside the door started to wink on and off.
It was time to go. They went out one after another like clockwork,
as they had been taught to do. Their instructors had told them the
reception party didn't want to spend half the night looking for
them. The 'stick' had to be very tight. For a novice Dourlein didn't
make a bad landing – in the branches of a tree. He dropped to the
ground and in a flash had his pistol out.

The drone of the Halifax's engines died away as the bomber
turned and headed westwards back to its base and an early

morning breakfast of eggs and bacon. Now there was total silence. Dourlein must have felt he was the last man left alive in the world. He grasped his pistol more tightly as he heard heavy boots swishing through the damp grass. There was someone coming. If it was the *Moppen*, the Germans, he swore they wouldn't take him alive. A figure came into view. Someone called his cover name softly. 'Paul? Paul, is it you?' It was the reception committee after all.

He stepped out of the trees to find two men waiting for him, followed a moment later by a third. As Dourlein recorded after the war, 'Their welcome was hearty and their manner jovial. We shook hands and they told me they were taking me straight to the leader of the reception committee.'

A little while later they found the other two agents. Dourlein spotted plenty of lamp signals in the distance, presumably from the Dutch underground. He thought, 'These people are being very lavish with their lights,' then dismissed what he regarded as his new friends' carelessness.

After half an hour they had a break and were each given an English cigarette, apparently a great luxury in Holland. They also had a nip from the new arrivals' whisky flasks. It was now four in the morning and they were given the signal to move on.

By now Dourlein was very tired and let his head hang with weariness. It was an unfortunate move. Suddenly the two men behind him twisted his arms and clicked a pair of handcuffs around his wrists. 'Come on,' he said. 'Don't start playing around now.' But they weren't joking. A pistol was jammed into his side. A whistle shrilled. A cynical voice said in Dutch, 'Well, well, so you thought you'd be clever and jump from an English plane, did you? You've been caught by German counter-espionage. You've been betrayed and we've got all of your organization in our hands.'

As Dourlein recalled afterwards, 'I was too taken aback to speak. The whole structure of my plans and hopes had collapsed.' At last he found words and gasped, 'In our hands, *our* hands? What do you mean, you dirty Judas. Think you're a German do you? Come on, then. Shoot, you coward.'

The response from his unknown captor was accompanied by a cynical laugh. 'No,' he replied. 'That's just what we're not going to do. First you're going to tell us all you know. The war's over for you. You've had it. If you do what we tell you, you'll stay alive and well.'

But Dourlein was not prepared to do that. In his boot he had a razor-sharp fighting knife. As they walked on he worked his handcuffs free. It would be an exquisite pleasure to send these traitors to kingdom come and escape in their car. But that wasn't to be. Just as he had finished working the knife free one of the men reacted and slammed his revolver into Dourlein's neck. A moment later the others joined in. He had failed, his only reward the sight of his captors suddenly 'white with fear'.

Yet another spy had walked into the German trap. Major Giskes of the *Abwehr* would add another whisky flask to the collection on his mantelpiece, one of forty-odd, each signifying a dead or turned enemy agent.*

Indeed in the end Giskes would become the *Abwehr*'s greatest spy-catcher of the Second World War, perhaps with even more agents taken prisoner to his credit than those celebrated Britons who made up Britain's famed 'Double Cross' committee.** As long as Giskes kept up his work in Holland, Canaris, who had given him his first appointment, could prove to the Führer that his organization was producing results.

Major Hermann Giskes had joined the *Abwehr* before the war. An ex-First World War artillery officer, he had been told by an old comrade that if he accepted the post offered him in the anti-tank artillery, he'd probably be 'shot to pieces'. He'd better look for a rear-echelon job. So he went into the *Abwehr*, just as Ritter had done.

Almost immediately this former travelling salesman from the Rhineland was engaged in counter-espionage operations against the British in his own native area, where the SIS operated in strength from nearby Holland. During that period he helped to break up the celebrated British 'Z-Ring', commanded by an old

---

* When the author visited him in his retirement home in Bavaria those same flasks, which still decorated his swanky little apartment, had been taken down for the day.
** The London-based Intelligence committee that dealt with turning captured German agents in the UK.

114

10. "At first sight Dulles seemed a very unlikely spymaster" (p.87). Seen here being decorated by President Kennedy.

11. "The *Abwehr* secret prison, the converted seminary for students of theology at Haaren" (p.116).

12. "Thomas McKittrick... President of
the Bank of International Settlements
in Switzerland... must have known"
about the Melmer Shipments (p.93).

13. "General Walter Schellenberg, head of the
SS's own secret service, the SD" (p.108).

14. "Major Giskes of the *Abwehr* would
add another whisky flask to the
collection on his mantlepiece" (p.114).

15. "Gregg Riddenhof, a small-time crook
and black marketeer" (p.115).

16. Eddie Chapman: "By profession he was what was known as a gellyman" (p.127).

17. "George Dasch, the ex-waiter who betrayed the whole operation" (p.132).

18. Concentration camp labour working on V2 missiles.

hand at espionage, Colonel Dansey. This was the major SIS operation in Europe, directed against the Nazis, employing German agents ranging from bicycle racers to Catholic nuns.

There followed spy-catching ops in the Low Countries and France until Giskes, now a major, was transferred in November, 1941, to Occupied Holland. In two years he had passed from an apprentice who knew nothing about the clandestine world of intelligence to a pro with all the dirty tricks of the trade at his fingertips. For the next two years he was to be Germany's greatest counter-intelligence expert.

In the same month that Giskes took up his new post a fat, lame Dutchman named Gregg Ridderhof, a small-time crook and black marketeer, who spoke an odd mixture of English and Spanish when he was drunk, which was most of the time, offered to work for him. Giskes hesitated. He didn't think much of the would-be Dutch traitor, but in the end he took Ridderhof on the payroll.

Shortly thereafter Ridderhof sent in a written report in which he wrote that British Intelligence had recently parachuted two Dutch SOE agents into the country. They were Hubertus Lauwers and Thijs Taconis. It was their task to set up an agent network in Holland for their British spymasters.

Giskes read the report, didn't believe one word of it and in a fit of pique scribbled in the margin, *'Gehen Sie zum Nordpol mit Ihren Geschichten'*, 'Go to the North Pole with your tales'. Giskes knew his petty Dutch traitors. They were all cheap crooks. They'd tell any kind of crazy tale for money.

But Ridderhof had a kind of thieves' honour and Giskes' comment made him angry. Perhaps he thought that Giskes didn't trust him, and he would have been right. Over the next two months he set to work to prove to Giskes that Radio Orange, the Free Dutch radio station, broadcasting from London, was being used, as all 'free' radio stations were, to send details of agents' landings to the Dutch Underground.

Giskes was convinced when, on 1 March 1942, as Ridderhof had predicted, an RAF bomber dropped weapons to a Dutch resistance group led by a tall man whose real name was Taconis. The latter worked for the Dutch branch of the SOE, which was commanded by a British Major Blunt and a Captain Bingham.

Giskes' first impulse was to arrest the Dutch resistance people.

115

It would look good on his record. Then he changed his mind. It was a stroke of genius. He decided that instead of arresting the whole bunch and handing them over to the Gestapo for subsequent execution, he would take them prisoner and make them work for him. Thus 'Operation North Pole', a reference to that first angry rebuff to Ridderhof, was born.

By the summer of 1942 the captured Dutch agents, who were now double agents under Major Giskes' command, had thirty DZs in operation. They were the supposed drop zones for British supplies, arms and agents to the grateful Dutch underground. Giskes, careful and thorough as he was, even had *Luftwaffe* spotter planes fly over the remoter areas of that flat, over-populated country looking for suitable 'secret' sites. And here agent after agent fell out of the sky and parachuted straight into the hands of the waiting *Abwehr*.

At first Giskes would turn out in the middle of the night to receive them personally. He'd allow the newly captured spy a drink out of his own little whisky bottle, before having the 'new boy' whisked off to the *Abwehr* secret prison, the converted seminary for students of theology at Haaren. Here the 'new boys' would 'get religion' quickly – or else! Later, however, there were so many of them that he got bored with meeting them. As he said afterwards, he was 'getting too old for those long night waits'. So he left the business of welcoming the new boys to his subordinates. But he did insist on having each new agent's whisky flask handed over to him as a souvenir.

Operation North Pole was an unqualified success. Nearly fifty Dutch agents from SOE went into the bag. The booty dropped by the RAF was also an eye-opener. For the first time the Germans were able to obtain British secret weapons, almost straight from the factory. And what weapons they were: coal filled with plastic explosive, Chianti bottles with explosives in the base, folding motorbikes, armoured canoes for attacking shipping, even dead rats filled with plastic explosive and rusty bolts which were, in reality, limpet mines for destroying railway bridges.

Berlin was impressed. Even the SS couldn't conceal their admiration. Although Schellenberg hated Canaris and secretly coveted the command of the *Abwehr* as well as his own SD, he sent the head of the new SA 'Hunting Commando' (the equivalent of the British SAS), Otto Skorzeny, to study Giskes' methods. The scarfaced giant who would rescue Mussolini from Italian imprisonment later that year, recorded that he 'followed the operation with the greatest of interest'.*

To test Giskes' operation, Skorzeny 'ordered' a new one-shot, silenced British revolver to be sent out with the next shipment. In due course it was delivered from London, courtesy of a four-engined bomber of the RAF. Skorzeny tried it out there and then. Opening the window of Giskes' office, he took aim at one of the ducks sailing along the canal outside. He pulled the trigger. A soft plop. The duck keeled over. Not a single Dutch civilian walking by the canal took a bit of notice.

Skorzeny was suitably impressed and returned to Berlin to report very favourably to Schellenberg on the Giskes operation. But Giskes was not taken by Skorzeny. 'Big, bold and brave,' was how he described him to the author, 'but not too bright'.

So the deception operation continued. Agents were dropped month after month. If they agreed to co-operate, they went to the seminary. If they didn't, they disappeared into another closed society from which there was rarely any return – the German concentration camps! Time and again the double agents tried to warn their British spymasters in London with specially built-in warning signals in their transmitters. But it was to no avail. London seemed to overlook them. Some thought later that the British appeared almost *not* to want to be warned, as if there was another secret intelligence 'scam' going on of which they were not aware.

As we shall see, that possibility was taken very seriously as a means of deflecting German interest away from the real, deep-cover intelligence network, an all-British affair, being run by the SIS. Others thought that the whole sad and, for too many Dutch agents, fatal business was another British deception operation, part of the great overall plan for D-Day. For in order to draw off the 80-odd German divisions which *could* have faced the Anglo-Americans when they landed in Normandy in 1944 instead of the

---

* The author, who interviewed Skorzeny in the years before his death, can testify that he was not given to praise of others.

117

six which met them on the beaches on 6 June, 1944, deception ops were launched which resulted in some 300,000 German soldiers being kept in Norway, for instance, with perhaps another 150,000 in Holland.

In other words the German deception plan carried within it, unknown to the Germans, yet another. Like those painted wooden dolls from Russia which contain a smaller version of the outer one and then yet another even smaller one, and so on, the plan bore one, perhaps even two or three, English-designed, secret deception games that fooled the Germans into concentrating their attentions on Holland.

But whatever lay behind this operation, which lasted for almost two years, those involved thought it very strange indeed. Dourlein, who had now been interrogated for six weeks, certainly did. As he wrote later, 'When I finally decided to give information, it was clear that it was not new to the Germans. It was also clear that the interrogator, who called himself Herr May, knew considerably more that I did. In replying to a question about the appearance of a certain officer, I described him as a clean-shaven man. "If that is so," May commented, "he must have changed his appearance. A fortnight ago he still wore a handlebar moustache."'

When Dourlein commented on the moderate treatment he was being given, though sometimes he was interrogated for forty hours without a break, May said, 'You didn't expect such fair treatment from the Gestapo did you? There are many things the British have not told you.' And, as Dourlein said to himself, 'I was inclined to admit this was true, but did not answer.'

Despite his relatively mild treatment and the promise that, if he collaborated, he would be saved, Dourlein had slowly retreated into a hard-shelled case of inner resistance which his interrogators couldn't penetrate. He remembered his hard-working peasant parents, how they had done so much for him, and his fellow citizens who, in a maddening peasant way, refused to be pushed around by their superiors. A new kind of pride and patriotism started to take him over, one that was increased by his growing isolation in his lonely cell.

He no longer despaired. His instructors back in England had told him that, if he was caught, his captors would attempt to break down his resistance with beatings, exhaustion and starvation. But, apart from the exhausting interrogations, none of these had taken place. Admittedly, the shock of realizing that he had been betrayed had been hard to take. But they hadn't beaten him and the food had not been too bad. His resilience had not been impaired and now he began studying the possibilities of escape. If he could only break out of the Seminary and somehow get back to England he'd tell them what was going on. Whatever the risk, he *had* to escape.

By the evening of Sunday, 29 August 1943 Pieter Dourlein had been a prisoner in the Haaren Seminary for six months. That Sunday morning he had woken his two cellmates to tell them that he was going. They pleaded with him not to do. 'For God's sake,' van der Boor had implored him, 'don't go. If you do, they'll shoot us.'

But their pleas only strengthened his resolve. That evening, after the guard had thrust the evening pail of watery soup into the cell, he stripped and tapped out the signal on the wall to his fellow escaper, Johann Ubbink. They were going.

'I sprang onto the bed,' Dourlein wrote later, 'pulled down the nail that held up the window and looked down the corridor. Everything clear! A bit further ahead I saw a blond head looking out too. A few moments later my future companion, whom I'd never even met, and I were both in the corridor. Our pals reached us our clothes and the rope. Together we ran into an empty cell that we knew was never locked. We looked at each other for the first time and we slapped each other on the back.'

But there was no time to waste. Anxiously they waited for the heavy tread of the sentry to pass. They had timed his beat accurately over the last few days. In stockinged feet, they crept cautiously to the latrine. This was the second stage of their escape.

They slipped inside and locked the door. Here they planned to wait until the prison had finally settled down for the night. After that they'd continue their escape. Twice guards rattled the door. Each time one of them cried in feigned anger, *'Um himmel-swillen. Besetzt Mensch'*. (Occupied, man.)

At last it was time to go on. They forced the window and

119

squeezed through the bars. At regular intervals the icy finger of the prison searchlight swept the façade of the Seminary, but it didn't worry them. They had already timed the sweep of the beam. They started to play out the rope they had stolen to the ground some twelve metres below. Pieter would have jumped, but he didn't want to risk a broken leg. Johann followed just as the beam swept by and momentarily blinded them.

They were outside, but there were still many obstacles to be overcome. 'Now,' Pieter recalled, 'we had to get over the barbed wire fences about fifty-five metres away. We approached them carefully. Suddenly we heard steps, the sound of heavily nailed boots. A guard. But the man didn't notice us and we continued.'

They crawled closer to the last big obstacle – Johann just cleared the fence. Now it was Pieter's turn. He ran forward, and moments later he was rolling on the damp ground on the other side. They had made it that far. But now they were alone in the world, with every man's hand seemingly against them. They had to be on the look-out not only for the Germans but also for fellow Dutchmen who were working with the Germans for ideological reasons or for dirty money.* They faced a journey into the unknown until they reached England. Here they would tell their tale of treachery and deceit and finally bring Operation North Pole to an end.

A month later, on 11 November, 1943, the 25th anniversary of Germany's defeat in the First World War, they left their hiding place in Tilburg and set off on the next stage of their journey. They were heading for Paris. But even there they didn't feel safe. As Dourlein wrote: 'We had been warned against French collaborators, dangerous people, and as there was no possibility of us passing ourselves off as natives. . . . We followed a method that we thought terrifying but which was, in actual fact, almost foolproof.' It was to declare themselves openly as Dutch workers who had volunteered to work on a *Luftwaffe* field under construction in the Marseilles area. When they travelled by train they sought out compartments filled with Germans. It had the added advan-

---

* It was estimated that in 1945 one-fifth of the *Wehrmacht* defenders of that country were Dutchmen.

tage that the French police checking papers, naturally in the service of the Germans, never came into such compartments. As Dourlein concluded, '[There] we were almost certain to be left alone, as we were so obviously friends of the German military.'

Of course, they never intended to go to Marseilles. They had another plan – to cross into Unoccupied France (though Vichy France had been occupied by the Germans a week before), as close to the border with Switzerland as possible and then cross the outlying Jura mountains into that country. By this means they thought they'd avoid the long and dangerous journey through Southern France into fascist Spain where they could be arrested and returned to the Germans at any time if they hadn't enough money to bribe the corrupt Spanish police.

So they set off on what they hoped would be the last leg of their journey. They took a bus. Then they walked. A chance contact told them there was a Dutch family in a nearby hamlet who might help them.

The travellers were 'received with open arms'. They were fed and told by the son of the household, 'Tomorrow I shall arrange for your trip across. Now you must sleep, for you are in for a strenuous time.'

They asked what their chances were of succeeding. 'Excellent,' he said, 'and if the Germans do become troublesome we'll shoot our way through. We have never failed yet. They are scared to death of the French Maquis.'

That cheered Dourlein and Ubbink no end. It was the first real fighting talk they had heard since their escape.

Next day they set out. The sun was shining. The air was clear. It was an ideal day for an escape. They climbed for hour after hour. Their rucksacks seemed now to weigh a ton. They dodged an armoured car filled with Germans. They waded an icy-cold stream with their bare feet tingling in the swift-running water. They crossed the line which divided Switzerland from France. But still their guides wouldn't let them rest. As Dourlein recalled, 'Though we were now on Swiss territory, we were by no means safe, for the Swiss customs men, if they caught us, would take us back to the frontier.' So much for Switzerland's supposedly neutral stance.

They pressed on. What seemed hours later they came 'to a

121

compound of simple barracks made of tarred tree-trunks and encircled by plain fencing'. It was an internment camp. They had finally reached safety. Now they could tell the British what was going on in Holland.

But it wasn't to be that easy. They were welcomed by the Dutch and British secret service representatives in Berne, not far from Dulles's HQ at the Herrengasse. Here Dourlein told his tale of treachery and betrayal, falling asleep on that first night of 'freedom' with the thought, 'I wish my friends at Haaren knew where we were. It would certainly put their minds at rest.' But it would be a long time before they could tell their tale in its entirety to the spymasters in London. Before that they'd have another long journey until on 1 December, 1943, they crossed from France into Spain. Two months later on 1 February, 1944, they were placed under arrest by the British authorities and secretly transferred to Brixton Prison. Operation North Pole wasn't over yet.

Dourlein's revelations to MI6's representative in Berne struck home like a bombshell at Queen Anne's Gate in London, the HQ of the British secret service. 'C', the head of that service, otherwise General Stewart Menzies, a long-term intelligence officer, was shocked beyond measure, it was reported. Both his own MI6 and what amounted to a rival service, brought into existence by Churchill in 1940, the SOE, were now totally geared up to preparing for D-Day. Both services had agents and contacts with the underground everywhere in Occupied Holland. But now it seemed that a great network had been turned – one that had contacts with other resistance and spy circuits in France and Belgium, which were also in danger. How was all this going to affect the plans for D-Day?

Up to now Menzies, who had the ear of the Court as well as Churchill, had thought that the British had a monopoly in turning enemy agents and using them in the service of Britain. Now it seemed that the Germans had done even better. They had managed to get a major SOE network to work for them in Holland.

Immediately 'C' instigated an investigation. Its premise was the frightening one that the Germans had, by means of the information they had gained through North Pole, penetrated the entire SOE system for the whole of Europe. At the very least, the thesis went, the Germans had infiltrated the key espionage system and had been controlling part of it since 1942.

Unknown to the public and of course to the agents of a dozen different nationalities involved, 'C' and the Joint Intelligence Committee started a top-level inquiry. Its seriousness was evidenced by the fact that those involved didn't even stop to celebrate Christmas and New Year, 1943. On the eve of that hoped for year of victory, 1944, it might well be that the whole success of Overlord had been compromised.

What really transpired at those high-level meetings is hard to piece together over five decades later. The papers relating to them were regarded as so important at the time that they were closed to the public till 1994. Most of the key participants are long dead and have taken their memories with them.

The matter was considered so important that it went up to the Joint Chiefs of Staff, probably even to Churchill himself, who was always interested in intelligence affairs. In the course of the investigation it is clear that the intelligence men discovered some unpleasant truths about the SOE and allied intelligence services, in particular those of Poland and France. But in the end the Joint Chiefs of Staff contented themselves with being highly critical of the Dutch operation, including, after Dourlein's disclosures, the despatch of two RAF 'supply' aircraft to test the extent of the German penetration. Both were shot down, adding to the forty-four aircraft which had already been lost and the scores of RAF crew members who had been killed or taken prisoner.

By the time the Joint Intelligence Committee's inquiries had come to an end Giskes knew the game was up. Operation North Pole was over.* Later he wrote, 'It was clear to me that the bottom had been knocked out of the whole *Englandspiel*.' Still his sardonic humour didn't desert him. Before he sent his remaining Dutch operators off to prison and perhaps to death in the camps, he despatched one final message to the SOE HQ at 22 Baker Street, London. It read:

'To Messrs Blunt, Bingham and Successors Ltd stop. You are

---

* Dourlein was finally released from Brixton Jail just after D-Day. He trained for the Dutch Air Force as a gunner and in late 1944 started on ops. He was awarded a decoration for his bravery, grudgingly it seems. Like surgeons, Intelligence chiefs bury their mistakes.

trying to do business in the Netherlands without our assistance stop. We think this is rather unfair in view of our long and successful co-operation as your sole agent stop. But never mind, whenever you pay a visit to the Continent, you may rest assured that you will be received with the same care as all those you sent us before stop. So long!'

We do not know General Gubbins' reaction to Giskes' message, but the SOE Chief's temper was volatile, so we can guess. His rival kept his moods to himself and Menzies' reaction also remains unrecorded, but we know that from now on the head of SIS went out of his way to discredit his opposite number in Berlin. *

Naturally 'C' knew a great deal about Canaris. One SIS executive thought he knew more about him than anyone else in the Allied camp and some historians believe that the two did actually meet in 1943. Of course 'C' had learned that Canaris was a homosexual and probably had something on Canaris' boyfriends in, say, Spain. But it would not have been the British spy chief's style to malign his opposite number in that manner. He'd let Canaris' own agents blacken their chief's character for him. They were mainly hopelessly corrupt. Many of them, at this turning-point of the war, were out to save their own skins and were in an excellent position to sell their service's secrets for the price of a new foreign passport and perhaps a new life in South America. These were the people 'C' would work on.

But what of the first addressee mentioned in Giskes' signal? Certainly Blunt was later the most famous (or infamous, according to your inclination) of the team. What was his reaction to the cheeky message? Neither then or later, when both intelligence and the newspapers examined his career from Marlborough College to his days as Keeper of the Queen's Pictures with a fine tooth comb, is there any mention of his reaction to *Englandspiel*. By the time Giskes' message was received he had already been promoted and transferred to a cosy niche in SHAEF Head-

---

* Fred Winterbotham told the author that Menzies' intended meeting with Canaris in Spain in 1943 was vetoed by Anthony Eden, the Foreign Minister, so he didn't go. But of course Menzies had ways of meeting Canaris without Eden's knowledge.

124

quarters. For the now Lieutenant-Colonel Blunt was regarded as an expert in 'double-cross operations' and was working for General Eisenhower. One wonders for whom else he was working.

Still, for one who had been working for the Russians as well as his own country since the outbreak of war, the disastrous Operation North Pole must have been good on-the-job training for what was to come. As for Petty Officer Dourlein, now a corporal-gunner in the Dutch Air Force, flying over his ruined country in a bomber, it had meant 'forty-eight of my companions in Haaren had been murdered by the Germans at Mauthausen Concentration Camp. I was lucky'. 'C' would see that Canaris, who had tricked him into the greatest fiasco of the war in the shadows, was not that lucky. Within the year he'd be dead at the hands of his own people, not a hundred miles from where those poor betrayed Dutch agents had died.

But Operation North Pole had pleased the Führer. Hitler had always thought that the British Intelligence Service was far superior to the German, indeed to every other Intelligence Service in the world. Now Giskes had proved that the British could make grave mistakes just like his own people. Canaris was in favour once more, but only for a short period. Soon he would blot his copybook once again.

EDDIE WITH THE GELLY

'The game of espionage is too dirty for anyone
but a gentleman.'

British Intelligence Officer

On the evening of Friday, 28 June, 1940 in the British Channel
Island of Guernsey long lines of ancient trucks, horse-drawn carts
and vans were lined up waiting to offload their cargoes of locally
grown tomatoes into the holds of mainland freighters alongside
the White Rock Quay.

It was a fine summer evening. Although the news from Europe
was bad, the farmers enjoyed the sunshine and chatted happily
about the wartime prices in their French patois. They were rising
and the growers were pleased. The war was far away and so far
all it had meant was increased profit.

At five minutes to seven that evening the war reached
Guernsey. Six planes flashed into sight. Three of them roared at
tree-top height across the island, whiplashing the grass with their
wash, and vanished in the direction of France. The other three
pilots had different ideas. They lost height rapidly. At three hundred miles an hour they screeched down towards the surprised
farmers. Flame crackled along the length of their black-painted
wings. Bullets splattered the area. In an instant all was chaos.
Horses reared up in terror. Carts overturned. Men cursed, women
screamed. Everywhere people threw themselves to the ground.
Some scrambled beneath the trucks. Others dropped to the wet
shingle.

In a moment the planes were gone. Twisting and turning, they
soared high into the sky, diminishing rapidly to black dots on the

horizon until they had vanished altogether. Behind them they left a mass of dead and dying civilians amid the red pulp of their ruined tomatoes.

A few hours later the first twin-engine reconnaissance plane of the German 122nd Squadron touched down at Guernsey Field. The cocky young *Oberleutnant* who piloted the plane reported later, 'Everything looked as if it were dead. Had everyone abandoned the place? Brown and white cows grazed in the fields. They looked at us peacefully. Where were the inhabitants?' Grabbing his machine pistol and putting on a helmet, the young pilot trotted across to the control tower, followed by the rest of his crew. All they found were two scared and elderly employees.* The Germans had arrived.

It was the same all over the islands. Churchill had evacuated all British troops, who had taken with them every able-bodied man willing to serve in the British forces. Remaining were the women, children, old men and those who were glad to see the back of British law and order for various reasons, political or otherwise. So the Channel Islands, the only part of Britain to be occupied by the German enemy in the Second World War, began its five years of occupation.

One person glad to see that British law and order had departed so hastily was discovered in a local Jersey jail that June day. He was undersized and clever-looking, with shifty if humorous, eyes, somewhere in his mid-thirties. His name was Eddie Chapman, a Londoner by birth. By profession he was what was known in his circles as a 'gellyman' or 'gelignite artiste' (Note the final 'e'). In other words Eddie was a well-known safe-cracker, wanted several times over by Scotland Yard, who had decided that he had deserved a little 'rest cure' in the moderate climate of the Channel Islands. The 'rest cure' had not taken place. One of the local constables had recognized him and he was imprisoned till Scotland Yard could come and fetch him back to the mainland. But the Met didn't arrive in time; the *Luftwaffe* beat them to it. So Eddie Chapman was not yet to return to the land of his birth.

* The author is indebted to that young pilot, now an old man, Lieutenant Schlichting, for these details.

When he did, he would do so at the end of a German parachute.

Slowly the Channel Islands returned to their normal sleepy existence. The Germans garrisoned the islands, but they were reserved and well-behaved. Here and there they built fortifications, but the great influx of slave workers required for such works had not arrived. The Germans instead concentrated on buying up what goodies they found in the local shops and in the manner of young soldiers the world over chasing nubile young ladies, 'Jerry Bags', as they became known, or 'Veronika Dankeschons' (Veronica, thankyou), VD for short, when an epidemic of that particular disease began to rage in the islands. Meanwhile Eddie Chapman, safe-cracker in waiting, did exactly that – he waited.

Around Christmas that year First Lieutenant Schlichting of the Luftwaffe's 122nd Reconnaissance Squadron was called to his squadron commander's office at Buc just outside Versailles. Inside Colonel Kopper, the CO, seemed lost in thought. He was staring out of the window at Louis Bleriot's old plane. From here in 1909 the French air pioneer had set off on his historic crossing of the English Channel. Finally he snapped out of his reverie, swung round and barked, 'Have you and Charlie', Schlichting's observer, 'got civilian clothes?'

The young officer answered in the negative.

'All right,' the CO said, 'buy some at the Luftwaffe's expense. You're both off to Paris.'

Schlichting spluttered a question, but he could get nothing out of Kopper save that he'd be told the why and wherefore when he reported to the Paris office of the Abwehr at the Hotel Lutetia.

A day later a nervous Schlichting met 'Fritz' (or Fritzchen as his case officers were in the habit of calling the cheeky little spy) for the first time. 'He was,' as the pilot recalled years later, 'sehr sympathisch' – very friendly. It was an opinion apparently shared by the Abwehr officers who looked after him, for one of them told Schlichting, 'He's very fond of animals, especially dogs.' No wonder, for the man they called Fritz was of course Eddie Chapman. A safe-breaker needs to get on well with dogs.

For a while the Abwehr officer, the two Luftwaffe men and the man who liked dogs chatted in a desultory fashion in the hotel room while Schlichting wondered what this had to do with a pilot in a reconnaissance squadron. Finally the *Abwehr* officer told him.

Apparently the Führer was annoyed by the success of a new British fighter-bomber-reconnaissance plane called the Mosquito. Unarmed and made of wood, the new plane had begun appearing over the Reich. Flashing in at four hundred miles an hour, it had seemed able to penetrate to the heart of the Reich with impunity.

Neither the *Luftwaffe* nor the German flak had been capable of shooting down a single Mosquito. Enraged, Hitler and Goering, head of the *Luftwaffe*, had demanded of Canaris that he take other measures for ridding the skies above the Reich of the British plane. Hadn't Goering solemnly sworn publically that if one single British bomber penetrated German air space the people could call him 'Meier', a supposedly Jewish name? Then it had been a joke. Now it was more than that.

It was the kind of order which fitted into Canaris' new strategy to please his political masters and to show them just how well in control of the German side of the war in the shadows he was. Already he was planning a new campaign in America. This time it was not going to be espionage only. Now he was going over to the attack. He was going to sabotage American industry.

It was to be the same with the Mosquito. Hitler's order had been to sabotage the de Havilland factory at Hatfield, north of London, where the Mosquito was made. But Canaris had discovered a snag to that plan. German agents had learnt that the British plane was so easy to construct that its assembly had been farmed out to subcontractors, some employing only half a dozen workers, all over southern England. De Havilland had established what amounted to a cottage industry.

That had stopped any further preparations for the sabotage attack on the Hatfield Plant. A little later, however, the same agents had had a breakthrough. They had discovered that the special laminated wood used in the plane's construction was stored on the premises of De Havilland's factory airfield. Now Eddie Chapman, after a year's training at an *Abwehr* secret sabotage school near the French port of Nantes, was going to carry out the Führer's order. In a plane to be manned by Schlichting and his observer, Charlie Ischenger, he was to be taken to England and dropped over Hatfield. Thereafter the safe-cracker-saboteur would be on his own.

The date of Chapman's mission, which if it failed and he was captured would mean an appointment with a firing squad at the miniature rifle range at the Tower of London, was 18 December, 1942.*

Six months before, on the evening of 12 June, 1942, *Kapitan-leutnant* Lindner of the German *U-202* noted in his log that he was twenty miles off the coast of Long Island. He was very pleased by his assessment of his position. He was right on course, due south of East Hampton and a hundred miles east of New York. He was actually opposite Amagansett, a summer resort on the coast three miles to the east.

850 miles to the south of Lindner's *U-202* another U-boat commander, *Kapitanleutnant* Deeke of the *U-584* was equally pleased with himself. He was heading for Florida's Atlantic coast and, just like Lindner, he had on board four civilians, dressed as submariners for the time being. Neither U-boat commander had encountered a single American warship. The *Amis* were un-believably slack. On shore the lights were still burning, although the United States had been at war for six months. Lindner and Deeke were pleased by the *Amis'* slackness. For they had strict orders from Admiral Doenitz, Head of the U-Boat Arm, not to become involved in offensive operations before they had landed their cargo of strange civilians.

That evening Lindner surfaced. It was eleven o'clock. Followed by a thin-faced civilian, a spy-saboteur named Dasch, Lindner went up top and opened the hatch. 'What do you think of the night, Dasch?' he asked softly.

'Christ, this is perfect,' the German-American replied.

For their purposes it was. They were fifty metres from the shore and still they couldn't see it. The night fog was that thick.

Lindner didn't waste time. The civilians' gear was brought up. Mainly it consisted of four big boxes and the rubber boat that

---

* The site is still there between the Tower's inner wall and the Constable and Martin Towers. Here in two wars twelve German spies were executed by firing squad.

would take them to the shore. Lindner's sailors got the dinghy inflated and carefully deposited the four big wooden crates in it. By midnight they were ready to go. Lindner had a last drink of cognac with the civilians, wished them good luck and then they were off, gently paddling into the mist.

Off Florida Deeke would repeat the same procedure four days later. Operation Pastorius had begun.

It was the first of Canaris' new approach to offensive operations. Just as the American Air Force was beginning their different type of bombing campaign over the Reich, what they called 'strategic bombing' – if they knocked out all Germany's ball-bearing plants not a German vehicle, military or otherwise, would be able to move – Canaris had dreamed up his 'strategic sabotage'. This entailed the sabotage of enemy plants which would have a far-ranging impact. Not only would an individual factory be knocked out, but the destruction of its product might well affect a whole industry.

The new US operation was such an undercover attack. Named after Daniel Pastorius, a German pioneer and one of the first to try his luck in 18th-century America, its mission was to cripple American aircraft production. Its agents were to blow up a cryolite factory in Philadelphia, which manufactured the essential materials for the production of aluminium, as well as Aluminum Company plants at Massena, New York, East St Louis, Illinois, Alcoa, Tennessee, and other sites. Again the Führer had specifically ordered the operation himself. For by now he had accepted Canaris' figure for the aircraft industry's output in the USA and, before that figure could be reached, he wanted to put a spoke in the wheel. Hence Operation Pastorius.

But there was one thing wrong with the plan, for which a number of German-Americans had been selected and trained by the *Abwehr* in their remote training ground near a lake some miles from Berlin. All were fluent speakers of what Germans call 'the Yankee dialect' and familiar with American ways. A couple of them had either served in the US Army or taken out naturalization papers. The problem was human greed!

None of the saboteurs had given any indication that they had any great love for the country which had given them a job and a roof over their heads during the twenties and thirties, though

131

most of them had emotional and family ties with America. For one it was a wife, for another a mistress, a third had both his parents living in Chicago. But the men who were to carry out Pastorius had returned to the *Heimat*, never expecting to see the USA again, fully convinced that their only loyalty was to the Fatherland.

But there was one of the saboteurs, the one who seemed to the *Abwehr* spymasters to be the most promising – he knew the States like the back of his hand, he was the best linguist, he had served in the German Army and had been threatened with a French prison sentence back in 1920 on account of his nationalist activities against the French occupation of his native region – who had apparently been prepared to betray the Operation as soon as he had learned of it. With the exception of the fact that he had been a German national, he seemed, like so many of Canaris' agents, ready to be bought at the drop of a hat.

In the case of George Dasch, the ex-waiter who betrayed the whole operation, it was the sum of 160,000 dollars which he held for the group as their 'slush fund' which caused his treachery, plus the fact that all his life he had felt he had held a subaltern position. As he told his interrogators, 'I was never satisfied.' Everything he had ever attempted, from studying for the priesthood to training as a pilot, had turned sour on him. Even working as a waiter had been too much for him. He had hated the fact that most of his income was dependent on the whim of a customer. 'I hated the tipping system and felt it was degrading.' As the saboteurs' training at various sites other than by the lake, including Aachen and Bitterfelde, progressed, Dasch's conviction grew that now at last he was in a position to better himself. All he had to do was to betray his comrades and at the same time ensure that that fortune in dollars should remain firmly in his own sticky hands.

At first everything went roughly according to plan. A total of eight saboteurs were landed in Florida and those under the command of Dasch in New England.

They had indeed bumped into a seemingly friendly (in reality scared stiff) Coastguard near Amagansett. But Dasch dealt with him smartly. He asked the unarmed 21-year-old Coastguard, 'Do you have a mother and father?' The man said he had and Dasch replied darkly, 'Well, I don't want to have to kill them.' Shortly after, he changed his tune. A man always motivated by money, he thought he had taken the measure of the frightened young American who was still hanging around the beach. 'Forget about this,' he whispered so the others couldn't hear, 'and I'll give you some money.'

The Coastguard at first refused, but Dasch was persistent. He held out two fifty dollar bills. Still the young man wouldn't be persuaded. Dasch added more money until there was three hundred dollars. 'Here,' he urged, 'take this.'

Now the young man gave in. But before he could go Dasch grabbed him by the arm. 'Wait a minute,' he ordered. 'Take a good look at me. Look into my eyes.'

The man did so, flashing his torch into Dasch's face. 'You'll be meeting me in East Hampton,' Dasch said slowly. 'Do you know me?'

'No sir, I never saw you before in my life.'

'My name is George John Davis. What's yours?'

'Frank Collins,' the young man said. Then he turned and ran off into the fog.

Then they broke up, going their various ways to safehouses, hotels and the like, until they would meet Dasch and another man in Cincinnati on 4 July, American Independence Day.

Naturally Collins had reported the incident to his superior who thought it might be the start of some sort of Nazi invasion. The search began, intensified when Dasch in New York phoned the FBI on Sunday 14 June, using the name John Davis.

But nothing happened. So on Friday 19 June he tried again, this time being put in touch with an FBI agent, Duane Traynor. Traynor thought that Dasch's story was the ramblings of yet another crackpot. Still he made some notes and a little later the FBI agents picked Dasch up at Washington's Mayflower Hotel. Naturally, as Dasch assured the agents, he'd only speak to Mr Edgar Hoover himself.

Dasch never did see the head of the FBI, but what he did encounter was FBI toughness, covered with a thin veneer of trained politeness. They had no time for Dasch's pretensions. All the 'G-men' wanted from the German turncoat were clues and more clues. Dasch was set to work. He was to reveal every stage of the operation, finally covering 255 typewritten pages. By the time he'd finished five of his erstwhile comrades had been arrested and the FBI was hot on the trail of a further two.

So it all ended in tragedy. There was a secret trial, though Hoover, being Hoover, always keen to achieve personal publicity whatever the cost, announced some of the details on 27 June, 1942. The announcement certainly grabbed the headlines in a nation starved of good news. Roosevelt himself was informed and was delighted. One wonders what the President would have made of it if he'd been also told that he personally was surrounded by spies of various hues, including British. *

Adolf Hitler was less than pleased when he heard the news. Fully occupied with the war in Russia as he was, and no great friend of espionage operations, he had, all the same, followed Canaris' various operations during 1942. There had been Operation Hawthorn, a plan to start a revolt of the Boers in South Africa; Operation Tiger, a similar plan to help the Afghans and Indians to rise against the British in the Sub-Continent; Operation Schamil, another revolt in the Caucasus against Russia, and so on. They had all been failures.

Operation Pastorius had been yet another failure. Canaris, it must have seemed to the Führer, simply couldn't get anything right. As Colonel-General Jodl, Hitler's main military adviser, would rage later that year after the Allied invasion of North Africa, 'Again Canaris has let us down with his foolishness and instability.'

Canaris knew he was making a vital contribution to the German war effort through the gold of the Melmer Shipments, but he also knew that he must not fail in the next op against Britain. So at the turn of 1942/43 his fate depended upon the efforts of an ex-London jailbird.

Eight days after the FBI handed over the *Abwehr* slush fund to Morgenthau's Treasury Department, 'Little Fritz' appeared at Buc Air Field. Here he met Schlichting and Charlie and they had a drink together before their departure.

---

* Dasch received a jail sentence for his treachery. Six of the others were sentenced to death. As for the money Dasch had coveted, it was turned over to the US Treasury.

Many years later Schlichting remembered, 'On the whole he was pretty calm. Naturally he was a bit worried about jumping with a parachute. But his main concern was that we should drop him near a certain railway station in southern England so that he could catch the morning train into London. He was so sure of himself.'

Soon after they were airborne the men's troubles started. At first they followed the radio beams up to the Dutch coast and across the North Sea. Here they picked the beams up again at the British port of Harwich. But the British picked them up, although they were flying at 20,000 feet, and blocked their receiving set. Schlichting was now virtually lost.

He came down in an attempt to orientate himself and after a few moments he spotted far to the south a vague white light reflected on the cloud bank. He knew it was a concentration of searchlights and guessed that the only place in that immediate area where there would be a concentration of that nature had to be London. He was on course, some forty miles north of the capital. He flew on.

But his troubles were not over. He had just corrected his course when Charlie's voice came crackling over the intercom. There was no mistaking the fear in his voice *'Achtung! Achtung! Nachtjager!'* He had spotted an enemy night-fighter.

Schlichting pushed the plane into the nearest bank of clouds. It was the correct procedure. But by now he had had enough of this mission. 'Charlie,' he ordered, pressing his throat mike, 'Eddie's got to go.'

Charlie prepared Eddie for the drop. Meanwhile the pilot brought the plane down to a safe height to make the drop. Somewhere down there was East Anglia, but in this blacked-out winter of 1942 he couldn't see a single light. He'd have to drop his passenger without guidance from the ground. 'Friend Eddie,' he told himself, 'will have to make out the best he can,' and gave the signal for Charlie to despatch Eddie into the black unknown.

Charlie was only too eager to carry out the order, but there was a hitch. The good living of the last months had had their effect. Eddie was too fat to go through the hatch. Stuck there with his legs dangling in midair, he yelled above the roar of the engines in his broken German, 'I can't get out!'

Charlie's reaction is not recorded, but Schlichting remembered that he turned around at the controls and cried, 'For God's sake Charlie – *push him out!*'

Charlie shouted for Franz, the radio operator, to come and help him. Together they exerted all their strength and the next moment Eddie disappeared into the darkness. The operation was underway.

The next night Schlichting and Charlie were waiting at *Abwehr*'s listening station in the Paris hotel when the receiving set burst into life. It was Eddie. He had come through right on the agreed time. Now, apparently in remarkably good spirits, he was sending his first piece of intelligence: as requested it was a weather forecast.

The *Abwehr* conducting officer looked over at the two *Luftwaffe* men in triumph. His spy had come up trumps. Schlichting winked at Charlie. Little did the *Abwehr* man know that immediately Fritz had departed the two of them had hastily inspected their Junkers 88 to check whether Fritz had left a grenade behind to blow them and their aircraft to kingdom come. That would have been an ideal way to cover his tracks.

One month later, at six on a foggy winter's evening, the de Havilland factory at Hatfield was blown up. The fire spread across the factory airfield to the huge piles of laminated timber waiting for the sub-contractors.

Two days later Schlichting was ordered to fly across the Channel to take photos of the Hatfield site. He spotted the traces of a blaze immediately, something confirmed not only by the photos he took but also by small items detailing a 'mysterious explosion and fire' carried in a local paper.

Later the papers carried reports of suspected sabotage, followed by the arrest of a 'suspect' carrying gelignite who had 'acted in a suspicious manner'.

Dr Graumann, Fritz's conducting officer from the *Abwehr*, was delighted. 'Gelly' was Eddie Chapman's trademark. He'd done the job all right. Canaris and the Führer would be happy. They wouldn't be seeing too many Mosquitoes over the Reich in the next few months.

A few days later Dr Graumann had further confirmation of the success of Fritz's mission. More recent aerial photos showed a huge area of blackened building at Hatfield with what appeared to be pieces of a transformer scattered all over the place. The British were so shocked, it seemed, that the German reconnaissance plane had been able to penetrate British air space over East Anglia without having a single shot fired at it. More than that, another local newspaper collected for the *Abwehr* by their friends in neutral Spanish and Portuguese embassies, reported that someone had successfully burgled a quarry at Sevenoaks. Graumann knew that could mean only one thing: Fritz had stolen 'gelly' from the place in order to carry out his sabotage. Where else would someone be able to obtain high explosive in wartime? It all fitted together nicely.

A few weeks later Eddie turned up in Lisbon. From there he travelled to Nantes and his first request after de-briefing was to have a night out with Schlichting and Charlie. This was duly allowed and the two were again ordered into civilian clothes and to report to the *Abwehr* HQ in Paris.

'Eddie was happy. He unpacked a couple of parcels he had brought with him from Lisbon or Madrid – I forget which,' Schlichting recalled. 'They contained chocolate and coffee – real bean coffee, a rarity in those days. Charlie and I were both moved. Then we asked him where he had come down.'

This was the question that Eddie had been waiting for them to ask. He knew his words would be reported back to Dr Graumann eventually.

'I was scared,' he told them. 'My head was stuck in the slip-stream and I could see the clouds rushing by. I thought, God I'm over the sea. They're gonna drop me in the drink. I dived through the clouds, but then found myself coming down over a house. I missed it and hid the parachute in some woods. But I thought they had seen me. I rushed back there [to the house].'

'I stared at him fascinated,' Schlichting explained to the author decades afterwards, 'well aware of what he would say next, and Eddie did. "If they had seen me I would have killed the lot of them."'

'But where did you come down?' Charlie persisted.

Eddie didn't hesitate. 'Right on the nose – at the spot where I'd planned to.'

He went on to explain that when he reached London he'd met

old friends from the underworld who had helped him to carry out the sabotage at Hatfield. That done, he'd headed straight for Liverpool. There he'd shipped out as a steward on the *City of Lancaster* bound for Lisbon.

'It was a terrible trip. Half the ships in the convoy were sunk.' Then, just before he deserted the ship, he prepared to sink it by dropping coal containing explosives into the ship's coaling bunkers. One hour later he was reporting to the German Embassy in Lisbon, his odyssey over.

As a proud Dr Graumann exclaimed the next morning, 'Isn't he just a great little fellow?' Little did the conducting officer know that the 'great little fellow' was the newest addition to the British Double Cross Committee's collection of double agents. Eddie Chapman was now playing for the highest stakes in his long criminal career. Double agents have always been a time-honoured method of deception and counter-espionage, but no country in the world can match Britain's performance in this field in the Second World War.

Between 1940 and 1945 British counter-intelligence experts not only subverted Germans spying in the UK by the score, they also 'turned them' and *ran* them and the whole German espionage *apparat* in Britain. In Berlin Admiral Canaris might have believed that he had some 130 agents working for him in Britain in the years leading up to D-Day, sending him vital information on the Anglo-American preparations for the landing. But, with perhaps the exception of two or three shadowy agents, the Twenty Committee, also called the Double Cross Committee from its XX abbreviation, controlled his whole network in Britain.

The double cross game had been started by a Scottish SIS agent, Major Thomas Robertson. He had seen the advantage of having captured German agents work for the British rather than shooting them. Not only would the presence of active *Abwehr* agents working in the UK prevent Canaris from sending more, they would also be useful in feeding their German controllers carefully faked information on British resources and intentions.

By the time Eddie Chapman had set off for England on behalf of the *Abwehr*, the Double Cross Committee had a hundred or more agents working for them, mainly in the south of England. It was to this force that Chapman was recruited under the code-name of 'Zigzag'.

'We knew a great deal about Zigzag before his arrival in the UK,' Major John Masterman, the ex-Oxford professor in charge of the Double Cross Operation, wrote later, 'and elaborate preparations had been made with regional and police authorities to secure him quickly and without advertisement as soon as he arrived.'

British SOE and SIS agents spying on the Nantes *Abwehr* training school had already informed London about 'Fritz's' presence there and that he could be easily identified because he had false teeth. As Masterman said, 'We knew indeed a great deal about him; we knew that he would be in possession of two identity cards; we knew the details of his equipment and we knew that an act of sabotage would be his primary assignment. What we did *not* know was whether he really was on our side or on that of the Germans.'

Masterman need not have worried. As soon as he landed Chapman reported to the local police. They took him to the Double Cross cage in a former mental home, where he told his story, as Masterman wrote, 'with apparent candour and completeness.'

Thus it was that Eddie was allowed to send his weather report so soon after landing and, a few days later, the details of US troop movements in the UK. But now the real problems began. Masterman's XX Committee would be forced to blow up the de Havilland plant if they weren't going to blow Eddie's cover.

Masterman was clever, despite his fuddy-duddy appearance. He knew that agents had a certain method of operation, what police today call their 'MO'. So he let Chapman proceed as he would have done under ordinary circumstances. The cardinal principle was: 'A double agent should, as far as possible, actually live the life and go through the motions of a genuine agent.'

So Eddie surreptitiously visited his objective four nights before he was going to 'blow it up'. Personally he stole the high explosive from Sevenoaks quarry. A daylight reconnaissance followed, with Eddie and a case officer, Major Ryde, mingling with the de Havilland workers dressed in overalls and eating in the works canteen.

On 29 January 1943, at midnight when the shifts had just

changed, a third party took over. He was Major Maskelyne, who had played a major part in the 8th Army's deception operations prior to the Battle of El Alamein. Jasper Maskelyne came from a long line of stage illusionists and magicians. Now he was employed to use the tricks of his trade to create a major explosion: Eddie Chapman's destruction of the laminated wood factory.

That night the Major blew off part of the factory's roof. He planted smoke bombs all around which, when ignited, blackened the area as if something had exploded and then burned furiously. As a final touch, he scattered rusty bits of machinery all about the 'destroyed' plant to simulate the explosive force of the stolen gelignite.

By morning and the appearance of the next shift rumours were already spreading that a mysterious explosion had taken place overnight. Thus when Schlichting and Charlie were 'allowed' to fly over the site to photograph the explosion, little did they realize that they were not viewing Fritz's handiwork but that of an even more skilled operator, a major in the British Army, who during the early 1942 'Rommel Crisis' had actually managed to make part of the Suez Canal 'disappear'!

Shortly thereafter Fritz also disappeared, as we have seen. He returned of his own volition to Germany after forwarding several plans to the XX Committee, which, according to Masterman, included the suggestion that he should undertake the assassination of Hitler as a one-man effort. To Major Masterman's disgust it was turned down and left to the OSS. Perhaps the British thought it would be more in the Yanks' line to kill the Führer.*

It would be nearly two years before the XX Committee heard of Eddie again. Then, in May, 1944, Masterman had news of him from Oslo, the capital of Norway. It was of a 'man speaking bad German in a rather loud, high-pitched voice, clad in a pepper-and-salt suit, displaying two gold teeth and enjoying the amenities of a private yacht!'

What Masterman didn't mention was that the man was also

---

* The OSS and, later, the British gave the matter serious consideration, including using hormones, which the OSS boffins thought would turn Hitler into a homosexual. Shades of Mel Brooks's movie *The Producers* and its famous song *Springtime for Hitler!*

sporting the Iron Cross on his civilian jacket in the German fashion, received, so it was said, from the hands of the Führer himself. What Masterman did mention, however, was that 'this we thought must be Zigzag, and so it was'.

Eddie Chapman had always been a born survivor.

BOOK THREE:

END GAME

'Ach, Schellenberg, after one's been in our
profession a while, one begins to see pink
elephants everywhere.'

*Abwehr Colonel Helferich
to Schellenberg 1943.*

ENTER WALTER SCHELLENBERG

'You should not let yourself be lulled to sleep by
him. Seeing the two of you together, one would
take you for bosom friends. You won't get
anywhere by handling him with kid gloves.'

*Heydrich to Walter Schellenberg, early 1942,
speaking about Admiral Canaris.*

On 2 February, 1944, Admiral Canaris motored to the German
General Staff bunker at Hitler's HQ in East Prussia, code-named
'Zeppelin'. Here he would meet the strangely named head of
'Foreign Armies West', *Oberst* Alexis von Roenne.

The aristocratic Chief of Military Intelligence in the West, who
would be executed for treason within the year, having been
implicated in the July 1944 attempt on Hitler's life, was a worried
man. No one, it seemed, would believe his forecast about the
coming Anglo-American invasion of the European mainland.

Hitler himself, knowing Churchill's addiction to indirect
attacks, felt that there might first be a diversionary attack in the
Mediterranean, perhaps through Spain, now that the Western
Allies were bogged down in Italy. It wouldn't be the Allies major
effort. That could be anywhere from Norway to Northern France.
It was a thesis supported by the head of the SS's own spy *apparat*,
the up-and-coming General Schellenberg, head of the *SD*.

Von Roenne thought Hitler's ideas were nonsense. He had
even gone so far as to create thirty fictional divisions in Britain in
order to upset this absurd idea. He told his horrified staff that if
Schellenberg's amateurs had scaled down his imaginary allied
divisions, the *SD* might be closer to the truth. For, as the Colonel

saw it, the Allies had only sufficient strength to launch one all-out invasion.

By late 1943 it seemed that von Roenne was winning the staff battle. But still all was not well. Hitler and the military lackeys who surrounded him believed that the terrain in Normandy was not suitable for a major landing – no infrastructure, road network, major ports, etc. It had to be Brittany or the Pas de Calais.

On this February day, with the Russians pushing hard on the Eastern Front and the Allies waiting in Britain, von Roenne had called a full-day intelligence conference to discuss the potential sites. When he had all the information available he would present his case to the Führer and his generals.

Von Roenne hoped that Canaris would offer him further evidence so that later he could make a more convincing case when he next reported to Hitler, Keitel and Jodl. Personally, he wasn't too impressed by Canaris or his *Abwehr* agents, but he knew the Führer, despite the *Abwehr*'s mistakes in the past, still had some respect for the Admiral.

So he received the invariably carelessly dressed Admiral with guarded optimism. Canaris made an impression that surprised even von Roenne. He told the Chief of Military Intelligence that 'the fact he had any V-men* at all in Britain is undoubtedly the most remarkable feat in the history of espionage'.

The Admiral explained how difficult it was to penetrate the British security arrangements; after all Britain *was* an island and British anti-spy measures had increased tenfold since the Allies had made their decision when and where to invade *Festung Europa*.

All the same the *Abwehr* ran an intact network of agents which went back two or three years and which covered every aspect of British life, from the mood of the people to the activities of the Anglo-American military. In a *tour de force*, he explained that he had nearly a hundred V-men located in major centres now, from Bristol in the south to Aberdeen in the north.

'We have succeeded in sustaining them so well,' Canaris continued, 'that we are receiving, even at this stage, an average

---

* *Vertrauensmanner*, literally 'men of trust', i.e. agents.

of thirty to forty reports a day from inside England, many of them radioed directly on the clandestine radio sets we have working – in defiance of the most intricate and elaborate electronic counter-measures.' In addition, all his main and subsidiary *Abwehr* stations from Berne to Brussels had agents working from without and within the enemy country.

According to the suddenly boastful Canaris – a sign that he was losing his nerve, for he wasn't normally given to boasting – he had a spy at Eisenhower's HQ in London's Grosvenor Square. Another worked from General Bradley's headquarters in nearby Bryanston Square. Both the 'neutral' Spanish and Portuguese embassies in London contained *Abwehr* networks run by fascist Spaniards and Portuguese for the Germans, or by men who had been bought by Canaris' slush fund. There was even a secretary at No 10 Downing Street, who 'could be persuaded to work for the *Abwehr*'.

It was an impressive exposition and von Roenne, initially sceptical, was impressed. He was warm with his congratulations and Canaris, for once, basked in praise and congratulations. He knew that his enormous *apparat* built up over four years, would now play a vital strategic role in this year of decision.

Naturally Canaris did not know that all his agents were 'turned' or compromised and that by then Britain was breaching the rules of diplomatic protocol and secretly searching the diplomatic mail and pouches of those 'neutral' Spaniards and Portuguese. Not that it really mattered. Both Canaris and von Roenne would be absent from the great battle for Europe. Within the year one would be under arrest and the other dead.

Three days later the new German Ambassador in Spain, Hans Heinrich Dieckhoff, heard that Canaris was about to pay another visit to the country he loved and where he seemed able to relax and let down his customary mask. He reacted immediately. He cabled his boss, von Ribbentrop, the German Foreign Minister in Berlin: 'Have just learned confidentially that Admiral Canaris has under consideration a plan to come to Spain next week. As much as I would welcome the opportunity of reviewing with him the *Abwehr* apparatus here, I believe it is incumbent upon me to advise emphatically against such a trip by Admiral Canaris at this time. His visit, which could not be kept secret, would not only

147

give the Anglo-Saxons opportunity to intensify their pressures, but would also embarrass our Spanish friends.'

Dieckhoff's reasoning was sound. Franco, the Spanish dictator, had seen the writing on the wall. The Allies were winning and he didn't want to be too intimately associated with Hitler. But there was something else behind his plea, if it had really originated with him. Von Ribbentrop and the SD wanted to be rid of Canaris. They wanted the *Abwehr* under their control. The Admiral's star was sinking fast. *

One week after that affront, the storm really broke. It had originated five months earlier at what was known to the Schellenberg SD group as 'Frau Solf's Tea Party'. On 10 September, 1943, Frau Solf, a convinced anti-Nazi and widow of a former German ambassador to Japan, had given one of her celebrated afternoon teas for a group of distinguished guests of the same persuasion as herself. They included Elizabeth von Thadden, a famous headmistress, who had brought along with her a pleasant young doctor working as a Swiss volunteer in Berlin's famous La Charité hospital.

The Swiss, a Dr Reckse, expressed some bitter anti-Nazi opinions. The other guests joined in. Particularly outspoken was a certain Otto Kiep, who had been dismissed from his Foreign Office post because he had attended a party given in New York in the honour of the Jewish Professor Einstein.

Before the party was over Dr Reckse had even volunteered to take letters secretly to German anti-Nazis living in Switzerland and, more importantly, to British and American diplomats, presumably Dulles included. Thereafter Dr Reckse, bearing the letters, hurried away, not to La Charité, but to 10 Prinze Albrecht-strasse. Of course the Swiss doctor was a Gestapo spy.

Himmler was overjoyed, but he didn't arrest the anti-Nazi circle at once. He wanted more evidence and had their phones tapped. But Himmler had not reckoned with the convoluted state of upper-class German society in that year of defeat. There was a

* When Dieckhoff had presented his accreditation to Franco, the latter is supposed to have said, 'I am glad that I will be able to deal with a genuine representative of the Third Reich rather than that busybody Canaris.'

spy among Himmler's spies. Dr Reckse's phone was tapped. He was revealed for what he was. The spy passed on his information about Himmler's intention to arrest the traitors and anyone associated with them.

Panic broke out in Berlin. It spread from city to city. It crossed Germany's borders and finally reached Istanbul, where two of Kiep's closest friends had just been ordered back to Berlin for questioning. They were Erich Vermehren and his beautiful aristocratic wife, the former Countess von Plettenberg. Both were *Abwehr* agents.

For a while the two, basically out of the immediate reach of the Gestapo, waited. They wanted to see what would happen to the 'Solf Group'. They soon found out. Most of the protagonists were arrested, tried in secret by one of the new and frightening 'People's Courts' and summarily executed. By 12 January, 1944, it was all over and the young *Abwehr* couple realized they'd be next.

They got in touch with the SIS representative in Istanbul. He jumped at the chance of getting his hands on two major *Abwehr* agents. After all, 'C' in London was only too eager to destroy Canaris' reputation after the North Pole fiasco. They were picked up and, in the same week that Canaris conferred with von Roenne in East Prussia, flown to Cairo and from there to London.

Hitler raged. At first it was mistakenly thought that the Vermehrens had defected with the *Abwehr*'s and the German Diplomatic Service's secret codes. All the same, although they had not, their defection plus the now proven treachery of Canaris' chief-of-staff, General Oster, was the last straw for the Führer. The *Abwehr* was rotten from top to bottom.

On 18 February, 1944, the Führer ordered that the *Abwehr* should be dissolved as a separate institution. It should be taken over by the SD and integrated into the SS's own secret service, headed by young General Schellenberg, now emerging as the key figure in Himmler's SS.

Surprisingly enough, Canaris was not arrested, although Himmler, Schellenberg and 'Gestapo' Muller all believed they had enough evidence to prove that he had been engaged in treacherous activities over the last five years and that in some way he was connected with the plotters against the Führer. He was not even retired, as Himmler had half-expected. Instead he was given a new post. Not a very important one, but an official post all the same. He was made Chief of the Office for Commercial and Economic Warfare.

As an Austrian SD agent, Hoett, pointed out after the war, 'It seems astonishing that Canaris should have succeeded in retaining his position until as late as February, 1944, in spite of the fact that his political views remained by no means unknown and that his organization had been widely discredited in the eyes of the Nazis.'

It was indeed strange. The Gestapo and SD dossier on Canaris ran to ten volumes. The men who hated him had evidence of his double-dealing and treachery. Yet they stayed their hands. No court proceedings were taken against him then or later, when he was finally arrested.

A few months earlier, for example, Dr Kaltenbrunner, who had replaced the murdered Heydrich as the head of the Nazi police *apparat*, had gone to Himmler with evidence of Canaris' double-dealing. He had demanded his dismissal there and then. Himmler had answered that he knew all about Canaris and he had good reasons of his own for not taking any action against the Admiral. 'He's an old fox who you've got to watch,' he said and dismissed Kaltenbrunner.

Since the war there have naturally been historians who maintain that the reason for Canaris remaining free from arrest was that he had something on Hitler and Himmler. He could blackmail them. Usually they claim that he had some kind of sexual information about the two Nazi bosses. Hitler was so degenerate that he liked women to urinate and defecate upon him, hence the suicide of two of his girlfriends. He suffered from a mother complex. He was minus one testicle, and so on. Time and again post-war historians have churned out sexual reasons for the Führer's megalomania which his former 'friends', such as 'Putzi' Hanfstaengel and Otto Strasser, had related to the OSS researchers back in the early forties.* As for Himmler, his young

---

* Thirty years later they were still revealing the same 'dirty secrets' to the author when he interviewed them.

protégé Schellenberg had a secret hold over him because he knew of Himmler's cancer of the rectum.

But how in a totalitarian police state like Nazi Germany, where men like Hitler and Himmler controlled everything, could anyone blackmail them? Anyone daring to publish the least derogatory statement of the private life of these political leaders would be heading straight for the gas chamber.

Hitler and Himmler evidently thought Canaris of so little importance that in February, 1944, when he at last fell from grace, he was given a sinecure which would keep him off centre stage until he proved too much of a nuisance or they needed him no longer.

Thus he wandered off to his new job, which allowed him to spend most of his afternoon reading or playing with his two dogs, while everywhere his agents who were compromised or felt threatened fled abroad, surrendered to the Allies or waited for that early-morning knock on the door which heralded the arrival of the Gestapo. Canaris' celebrated 'dossiers' were moved back into the Gestapo's safes at No 10 Prinz Albrechtstrasse in much-bombed Berlin and the war in the shadows continued much as it had done before.

There was only one significant change, the man at the top: *Brigadiergeneral der SS* Walter Schellenberg.

'An intellectual thug,' Professor Bullock, one of the first and best historians of the Nazi period, called Schellenberg. William Shirer, another reliable authority on the Nazis (the American correspondent-historian had known most of them personally during his years in Berlin), was of the same opinion. For him Schellenberg was a 'university-educated intellectual gangster'. Others who knew Schellenberg personally, when he later became a tool of the SIS,* weren't so convinced.

Squadron-Leader G. Harrison, who interrogated him after his capture – surrender would be a better description – thought differently. He said, 'His demeanour at this camp has not

---

* The SIS probably wrote his memoirs for him and paid him afterwards to keep his mouth shut about operations concerning the UK, especially Operation Willi (1940), dealing with the Duke and Duchess of Windsor.

produced any evidence of outstanding genius as appears to have been generally attributed to him. On the contrary, his incoherence and incapability of producing lucid verbal or written statements have rendered him a much more difficult subject to interrogate than other subjects of inferior education and of humbler status.'

But Schellenberg did have something about him that enabled him to cope with very difficult bosses. First there had been Reinhard Heydrich. He frightened everyone, probably even the Führer. Still Schellenberg managed to work with him. Then there was Himmler, pasty-faced, oily, a sadistic schoolmaster at heart, who half the time never really seemed to know his own mind. Schellenberg managed the *Reichsführer SS* as well.

Perhaps it was his silky, almost feline charm. Perhaps it was the fact that he came from the Saar and was a *'Halbfranzose'*, as Germans called, and still call, people from that region, 'a Half-Frenchman', who had spent some of his life in Luxembourg, where he had learned to accommodate those two powerful neighbours. But whatever the secret of his ability to remain at the top and survive dealing with people who had power of life and death over their subordinates, Schellenberg had now really arrived.

Heydrich was dead. The Führer was dying. Himmler was wavering, wondering if it wasn't time to get rid of the Führer and make peace with the Western Allies and save his own hide. As for Kaltenbrunner and Muller, who ran the internal police forces, including the Gestapo, they were inferior creatures, frightening to the great mass of the German people, but not to Schellenberg.

Perhaps it was fortunate for the Allies that Schellenberg had taken over Germany's intelligence services on the eve of D-Day. He was out for bigger game than planting a spy in obscure Allied HQs or luring some third-rate neutral agent into a honeypot from which he would emerge, chastened but richer, to work for German intelligence. Schellenberg was playing for higher stakes. The game was dangerous, he knew that, but not as dangerous as some people might have thought; after all he and Himmler ran Germany's police force. For it was Schellenberg's intention to ease Germany out of the war before everything was hopelessly lost and, in the course of doing so, ensure that he came out of it smelling of roses.

As Chester Wilmot, one of the earliest historians of the 1944/45 campaign in Western Europe and a distinguished war correspondent, wrote in 1952: 'In trying to estimate Allied intentions, the German High Command was working under a serious handicap, for its Foreign Intelligence Service, now under Himmler's sinister control, was producing information of the most doubtful character. Himmler's absorption of the *Abwehr* in March could not have come at a less opportune time. . . . [they] picked up every canard which British agents spread abroad in neutral capitals, and in the weeks immediately preceding the invasion, Himmler's men were deliberately swamped with "secret information", which they had neither the time nor the wit to sift and appraise.'

According to Wilmot after the war the Allies found a dossier of some 250 individual reports in the German Admiralty archives, all dealing with the time and place of the invasion. 'Of these only one, from a French colonel in Algiers, was correct. . . . But this had been filed away unheeded with the dross. The majority opinion gave July [1944] as the month and the Pas de Calais as the place.'

'C' and his senior officers at Queen Anne's Gate of course knew of Canaris' dismissal and of Schellenberg's appointment. Yet they were probably not as complacent about Canaris' defeat as some post-war experts thought. They were daily concerned that the Ultra operation might be compromised. By now the senior Allied generals who were in on the secret had come to rely upon it in their assessments of German military plans and thinking. As Fred Winterbotham, in charge of Ultra security, told the author, 'Those who dealt with Ultra in the field were armed all the time, kept apart from the rest of the Allied HQ to which they were attached and kept on their toes constantly by the prospect of an immediate court-martial if they slipped up.'

The men at the top in Whitehall also knew that the *Abwehr* and other German intelligence agencies were involved in protecting the Swiss financial transactions on behalf of the Germans. What exactly the Swiss and the German Intelligence Services (for by now they were intimately linked, thanks to Schellenberg) were up to, they didn't quite know. But it was still a vital area that had to be watched, especially now that Morgenthau's representatives in Europe, in particular a certain Colonel 'Bernie' Bernstein, a Jew and a fanatical Germanophobe, attached to Eisenhower's

153

British HQ, were steering a dangerous and different course to the British Treasury, acting under Churchill's directives.

Schellenberg's so-called spy ring in the UK might be a farce, his agents elsewhere fools who could be bought with money or outrageous lies, his *apparat* riddled with anti-Nazis who wanted to get rid of the Führer (one might regard Schellenberg as belonging to this group himself), but in certain key areas it still presented a danger, not only to Allied victory but to their post-war plans for a peaceful Europe under Anglo-American domination, one that was resolutely anti-Soviet.

Thus, while Schellenberg worked on his own secret plans that went beyond the realms of ordinary intelligence, the *Abwehr* old hands, mostly in the field of counter-intelligence, continued to work loyally enough for their doomed Fatherland. At the German listening post at the Dutch plant of Phillips Electric outside Einhoven they were listening to the radio traffic on the main cable between Britain and the USA for example. Soon after Schellenberg took over the experts here hit the jackpot; they managed to overhear a conversation on the scrambler phone between Churchill and Roosevelt. Schellenberg wrote after the war: 'Had the two statesmen known the enemy was listening to their conversation, Roosevelt would hardly have been likely to say goodbye to Churchill with the words: "Well, we'll do our best. Now I'll go fishing."'

Perhaps it was in Switzerland that Schellenberg had become interested in economics (where he had studied law), for now he launched Operation Bernhard, which would trouble the British authorities not only during the war but for some years afterwards.

This was an attempt to undermine the British economy with the mass production of fake white British five pound notes. In those days Britons often had to sign the notes in order to get them accepted as tender in businesses and shops. The fakes were produced by a team of international forgers, all prisoners, in selected German concentration camps.

As Schellenberg explained Operation Bernhard: 'A plan had been worked out to send bombers over Britain which, instead of dropping bombs, were to drop forged notes by the ton. The country was to be flooded with them. One can imagine what the result would have been. The government would have been forced to withdraw all treasury notes . . . and the population would have been entirely confused.'

That part of the plan was withdrawn. It was found too costly to infiltrate the bombers through Britain's air defences. Instead the Germans smuggled the forgeries into neutral countries. One Gestapo man had the audacity to ask a Swiss bank to check whether the notes were fakes or not. He said he suspected they were. The Swiss gave the notes a clean bill of health. In other cases they used them to buy smuggled arms, dropped by the Allies to so-called 'resistance groups' who were only too eager to sell the weapons for hard currency to their supposed oppressors. As Schellenberg commented, 'It seemed ironical that the partisans should have sold us the very weapons which we used against them.'

In the end the Bank of England had to withdraw ten per cent of its notes because of the success of Operation Bernhard and had to start printing a new issue of the five pound notes and withdraw all the old ones from circulation.

While Schellenberg became involved in yet more fanciful and dangerous operations, such as a plan to assassinate Stalin and the despatch of German U-boats to America to bombard New York with V-I rockets, his agents from the old *Abwehr* still soldiered on.

Giskes, now a Lieutenant Colonel, was one such. With the ending of the North Pole operation, he had been relegated to more mundane operations in the Low Countries and Northern France. Once again his agents infiltrated the Dutch resistance, which, according to all accounts, was not too difficult a thing to do. According to Group-Captain Winterbotham Major-General Menzies would not even trust Prince Bernhard of the Netherlands in his HQ when secret operations were being discussed. 'He was German-born, had been a member of the SS and now he was Dutch. That was enough for Menzies,' Winterbotham maintained.

For a while Giskes was worried about the loose contacts he had with the anti-Nazi resistance. The Gestapo had obtained his name and he was called to Berlin for questioning. For a time he talked himself out of any suspicion, but now he was exceedingly careful about his contacts. For instance he dropped Colonel von Roenne because he felt that he was, in the parlance of our own time, a loose cannon.

Besides he was having to adapt to Schellenberg's new measures in the course of integrating the *Abwehr* and *SD*. Now his unit was entitled *'Frontaufklarungskommando 307* (FAK 307) – Front Reconnaissance Unit – which would come directly under the command of German Army Group B once the invasion started. This new outfit would work against the Resistance, enemy infiltrators, reconnaissance groups behind the German lines, and such like. In the event of the Germans being forced to retreat, which the Colonel thought more than likely, then FAK 307 would continue to provide intelligence information in the form of 'sleepers'.

'Sleepers' were local civilians who would let themselves be overrun by the advancing Allies and would remain dormant until they were activated by a secret order given over an *Abwehr* radio set, which most of them possessed hidden in their homes. Then they would set about sabotaging Allied installations, cutting land signal lines and the like, and reporting on enemy troop movements. The British had dreamed up a similar scheme at the height of the 1940 invasion scare: a secret organization of 8-man cells was formed to go to earth (sometimes literally so) and continue fighting the German invaders after the military had departed.*

In the case of the Germans, there were plenty of likely candidates to become sleepers. Along the borders of Holland, France, Belgium and Luxembourg there were many pro-German speakers of that language. Closer to the coast there were Breton and Flemish nationalists prepared to work against the 'Mother' country, France. In addition there were many European businessmen, officials and local fascists who could be blackmailed into carrying out the same task.

From his HQ in Dribergen and then later at the Hotel Metropole in Brussels Giskes had the task of preparing sleepers of varying nationalities to 'take a dive' and wait to welcome their 'liberators'.

He already had a nucleus of tried agents to chose from. Back in 1940/41, before he had been posted to Holland, Giskes had been

---

* The existence of these units was kept secret for decades after the war, due to the fact that the Government felt it might have to use a similar set-up during the Cold War. Only in 1999 did NATO reveal that the Russians had done the same in Western Europe.

stationed in Paris at the Hotel Lutetia, the *Abwehr*'s HQ. In the defeated France of that year there were many who flocked to the offices of the German Occupation Power to offer their services. By the end of the first year of occupation most of French industry was working for the Germans, the French police were already rounding up French Jews by the thousands and delivering them to German concentration camps and Giskes, in a humbler manner, had a whole network of agents, French, Russian and Austrian from every walk of life, under his command.

After the war when the singer Edith Piaf was accused of collaborating with the Germans for having taken a handsome young *Luftwaffe* officer as her lover, she replied scornfully, 'My cunt might have belonged to Germany, but my heart belonged to France!' In a chaster fashion, one might have said this of some of Giskes' agents, and in one case in particular, that of a young agent who would become vitally important to Giskes in this summer of defeat.

The handsome agent had been born an Austrian, a fact that he made much of among his French friends. His country had also been occupied and when the Germans had marched into Austria they had been welcomed with open arms. Not that that meant much to his sophisticated French friends. They probably hated the English more than they did the Germans. Hadn't they betrayed them in 1940? The French were ever great in explaining how their disasters were due to betrayal. They had been doing so since the time of Joan of Arc back in the fifteenth century.

But there was a section of the French aristocracy which had vaguely Jewish and English connections and it was among them that Giskes' agent made the most of his Austrian birth and his anti-Nazism.

Indeed by the time Giskes had left for Holland the Austrian was actively engaged in aristocratic underground activities, naturally of the more genteel kind where one didn't get one's manicured hands dirty. He was helping his titled French friends to send underground mail from Paris to neutral countries. He would travel from the capital through Unoccupied France to Marseilles where the offices of the Savon-Gibbs concern, soap and toothpaste manufacturers, were the last staging post for outgoing clandestine letters and communications. A year later he was aiding his titled *'petite amie'* to smuggle downed Allied fliers to safety. One wonders how many of the French 'ratlines' were unwittingly betrayed in the course of returning a total of sixteen British aviators to duty.

The handsome Austrian with his vague post in the German Occupation Administration was turning out trumps for Giskes. Now, on the eve of the Allied invasion, Giskes must have asked himself if 'Freddi', as he called the Austrian, was ready to relinquish the fleshpots of Paris and really earn his keep.

The time of decision had come.

The Prime Minister, Mr Churchill, was extremely proud of his half American parentage. In his celebrated address to the US joint houses of the Senate and Congress in 1941, he made much of it, pointing out that if the nationality of his parents had been reversed he might have been present 'this day by right of birth'. Probably at the time his few admirers in the chamber might have murmured to themselves, knowing Churchill's ego, 'Yes, as President of the United States'.

Churchill's most important American ancestors were the Jeromes, two of whom had fought against the British in the American War of Independence, serving with the Berkshire County Militia in one case and, in the other, fighting with George Washington's army at Valley Forge. Through Winston's mother Jennie, daughter of Leonard Jerome, sometime proprietor and editor of the *New York Times*, the blood of the Jeromes had helped to revive the Marlborough dynasty, which had been in a state of suspended animation for the seven generations since John Churchill, Queen Anne's great commander, had won his ducal title in battle in the 18th century.

In the late 19th century it had been fashionable for impoverished British and Continental aristocrats to marry wealthy American heiresses. Their families might have been hopelessly parvenu in the eyes of the upper class Continentals, but they did have the money to keep the master and the family pile afloat for another generation.

One such was Isaac Merritt Singer, the American inventor of the Singer Sewing Machine, sold throughout the world in the middle decades of the 19th century. So much so that the American multimillionaire was able to retire from business in 1865 and buy a big house at Torbay in Devon, not very far from where, in the early summer of 1944, the Americans were practising for their landings in Normandy.

Both Isaac's daughters married European aristocrats and in 1918, when the Prince de Broglie, who was the husband of his granddaughter, was killed in action, Daisy, as she was known, married an Englishman, the Hon Reginald Fellowes. Thereafter Daisy and her daughter, Jacqueline, moved between Paris, the Riviera and her English home, Donnington Grove, Berkshire. It was during this period that Daisy Fellowes entertained blue-bloods such as the Windsors, artists like Cecil Beaton and Somerset Maugham, and also her cousin, a politician then in the wilderness, Winston Churchill. Forced to make a living as best he could by writing books and political journalism, Churchill was always glad of a free holiday, especially on Daisy's 250-foot yacht the *Sister Anne*.

But by 1940 that was all over. There were no more parties and no more 'freebies' on the Med.

Daisy sat out the war at the Dorchester Hotel on Park Lane, patronized at the time by such diverse personalities as General Eisenhower and Ernest Hemingway, while her daughter Jacqueline, aged 22 in 1940, remained in Occupied Paris.

Jacqueline, who had been educated in England, at Heathfield School, Ascot, had set up her own little 'court' at a small château in Surenne in 1936. Little Daisy, rich, quite pretty and spoiled rotten, commuted between the château and Paris where the collapse of France caught her in 1940. According to some sources her elder sister Emmeline and her husband Count Alexandre de Castija promptly joined the 'Underground'.

Jacqueline seemingly took another course. In 1941, just after Giskes left for Holland, at the age of 23, she married a certain Freddie Kraus (in the German fashion, Giskes wrote of him as 'Freddi'). Born in Sarajevo, he had been a citizen of the old Austrian-Hungarian Empire. Automatically, when that empire disappeared after the First World War, together with the Hapsburg Monarchy, Freddie became a citizen of the new Austrian Republic. Just over a quarter of a century later he changed his nationality again and became *ein strammer deutscher Staatsburger*, an upright German citizen. By marriage he also became a distant cousin of Winston Churchill. *

One year later Freddie and Jacqueline had a daughter, born on 10 June, 1942, who was promptly farmed out to maids and nannies while the handsome young couple continued their merry round, as if a world war was taking place a million miles away.

Now, as Giskes fled Brussels, leaving his headquarters behind to the Belgian looters, the young couple were fêted by a new crowd, British and American officers who were impressed by their activities with the Resistance during that 'terrible' occupation.

The fact that Freddie was a German and had served in some sort of capacity, official or otherwise, for four years in the French capital didn't seem to worry the new crowd. Why didn't they ask that elementary question, 'Why weren't you called up?' or, even more pointedly, 'What kind of job was it that kept an able-bodied chap like you out of the forces so long?'

Seemingly no one did, a fact that must have made Giskes exceedingly happy, on the run as he was, chased intermittently by Allied fighter-bombers, which fell out of the sky when one least expected them and shot up everything which moved.

Somehow Freddie managed to obtain a British uniform, complete with a captain's pips. Anything was possible in Paris that August of 1944. The newly liberated city was full of crazy types and even crazier happenings. There was Ernest Hemingway maintaining he'd 'liberated' the Hotel Ritz and ordering seventy-odd cocktails to celebrate. He didn't do either. There was a certain Sergeant Robert Maxwell, once known as Jan Hoch, also receiving a mysterious commission and graduating to yet another regiment.

But Freddie, now a British captain, waited for the call. It came indirectly. Mrs Fellowes, the older Daisy, regained contact with her daughter after four years and was surprised to learn that she had acquired a husband, foreign to boot, a daughter aged three and some sort of mysterious bug which didn't allow her to leave

---

* Not so remarkable when one considers that two prominent members of the current British royal family had even closer relatives who were generals in Himmler's SS.

160

Paris. However her husband was prepared to cross the Channel to meet his mother-in-law. There was only one slight hitch. He seemed, despite his British rank and uniform, to be what was called in those days 'an enemy alien'.

Such matters didn't worry Daisy. After all she had slept a floor or so above the Supreme Allied Commander for several months before the invasion and she was related to the Prime Minister. In spite of her new son-in-law's decidedly bourgeois name, she was very eager to give him the once-over. Strings were pulled, some say with help from Churchill himself, and in the last week of August he crossed the Channel to be welcomed with open arms. Giskes had his agent in place.

The Germans had initially retreated in small groups. They were the 'rear echelon stallions', as the frontline squaddies called them contemptuously. They had had their cases packed ever since the invasion three months earlier. Now they drove eastwards, their *gazogenes* (gas-driven vehicles) decked with camouflage and piled high with four years of loot and black-market wheeling and dealing. Behind them came the disorganized rabble of the beaten German Army. In these wretched convoys they streamed back eastwards to the cover of the Siegfried Line, which snaked four hundred-odd miles across the border country from southern Holland to Switzerland.

Behind them came the Americans, British, Canadians and soldiers from half a dozen other Allied nations. They advanced in a line, the British and Canadians in the north, the Americans in the south, heading for a quick victory in the Reich. Already the papers back home were saying they'd be home for Christmas.

Of the four exits from Northern France and into Germany, Giskes chose the one between Maastricht and Ettelbruck, the border crossing between Luxembourg and Germany. Behind him swarmed the mass of General Hodges' US 1st Army. Here Hodges, a softly spoken, slow-moving infantryman, had two ways through the Ardennes-Eifel region which barred any rapid progress across the frontier and the River Rhine. One was to the north in the general area of Liège (Belgium), Maastricht (Holland) and Aachen (Germany); the other was to the south in the region of Metz (France), Luxembourg City and Trier (Germany).

161

Hodges chose the northern route. By the first week of September, despite the difficulty of the area's infrastructure – narrow forest roads difficult for armour, numerous streams and small rivers running from north to south generally, to form easily manned defensive positions – the US First Army was making good progress. On 11 September, 1944, his Fifth Armored Division sent elements across the Our-Sauer* River Line, followed the next day by patrols in company strength of his 4th and 28th Infantry Divisions. By the end of the second week of September, the US First Army had closed up on the German frontier for nearly eighty miles from Aachen to Ettelbruck. Now in front of the Americans lay the only real man-made obstacle to bar their progress to the River Rhine and final victory, the Siegfried Line. Not that that seemed to worry the Top Brass particularly. In the last two months they had become accustomed to victory. Why shouldn't they be able to take the Siegfried Line on the run once they had all the necessary artillery, engineering equipment, fuel and supplies in position? Already the first patrols of the 28th Infantry and the 5th Armored had reported that Hitler's vaunted Line was unmanned. Most of the bunkers and pillboxes had had their cannon removed and had been locked since 1940. Indeed, when the Germans did start to man the Line they couldn't find the keys to the fortifications in many cases. The bunkers were out of date, the Americans concluded, and modern weapons wouldn't fit into the concrete positions which had been built six or seven years before. Anyway, they were manned by old men, boys and invalid soldiers.

The GIs who would fight them thought differently. As one weary GI told the reporter of the US *Yank* magazine that winter when whole divisions were being swallowed up by the border fighting, 'I don't care if the guy behind the gun is a syphilitic prick who is a hundred years old. He's still sitting behind eight feet of concrete and he's still got enough fingers to press triggers and shoot bullets.'

* *Sûre* in French. This was, and is, a German-speaking area. But for political-linguistic reasons most border towns and villages have two names, sometimes three.

BATTLE ON THE BORDER

'Gimme the goods and I'll go through that Wall
like shit through a sieve.'

General Patton, September, 1944.

General Cota's 28th US Infantry Division kicked off General
Hodges' first corps-strong attack on the *Westwall*. The forward
elements of the division crossed the River Our that night. They
soon captured the anti-tank positions to the front of the great
fortifications, but as dawn broke on that unlucky thirteenth, they
ran straight into the German bunker line – and serious trouble.
Heavy mortar and artillery fire fell on the GIs as they ascended
the tree-lined slopes and they went to ground almost at once,
calling to their own artillery over on the other side of the border
river in Luxembourg, but it had little effect.

On the next day the Americans attacked again. This time they
were luckier and started capturing some of the front-line
bunkers. For a while the commanders thought they had been
right after all. They were breaking through the German defences
on the run. One of the Germans captured that day, a 40-year-old
Wehrmacht cook, told his captors he had been in the line exactly
two hours before being captured. Another, a tank captain, had a
wooden leg. A third said he had been in a so-called 'alarm
company', hurriedly assembled from odds and sods in nearby
Trier and thrown into the fight under the command of a Catholic
priest!

But when the American casualties were counted, the mood
changed. The 28th Division had made two small dents in the
Siegfried Line defences at a cost of several hundred men killed,

wounded or taken prisoner. Major James Ford, S-3 of the 110th Infantry Regiment stated: 'It doesn't matter much what training a man may have had when he's placed inside such protection as is afforded by the pillboxes. Even if he merely stuck his weapon through the aperture and fired occasionally, it kept our men from moving ahead freely.'

But the 28th's Corps Commander, General Gerow, was not too unhappy with the division's progress. He reasoned that the first 'punctures' of a fortified position were always the toughest and ordered his 5th Armored Division to stand by for the decisive breakthrough, when it would race through the infantry heading for the Rhine; he encouraged the 28th to redouble its efforts. At least for the Corps Commander, well away from the fighting front at his new headquarters at Eupen in Belgium, things were going according to plan.

By now Colonel Giskes had recovered from his ordeal. He wasn't allowed the time to wallow in the grim details of that flight from Brussels to the German border. He had a new boss, vital, impatient and exceedingly swift in ordering court-martials for officers who didn't follow his instructions smartly enough. He was Field Marshal Walter Model, commander of Army Group B, which held the section of the Westwall running from Trier to Cleves.

Model, who regarded himself as the 'Führer's Fire Brigade' – on occasion he had seized rifle and led individual companies into the attack – might have doubts about the future, but if he did he kept them to himself. He was ready to fight to the last. Indeed, apart from Rommel and von Kluge, who were forced to do so, he was the only German field marshal in the Second World War who committed suicide rather than surrender.

According to Giskes' own account, he thought differently. 'Were those in Berlin and at the headquarters of C-in-C West still not prepared to recognize that the defeat in the West was now complete and decisive? Were they holding on to the chance of a recovery through a battle among the fortifications of the West Wall?' These were the questions he asked at the time.

But in that grim autumn of 1944 there was no one for him to ask these questions and be given a rational answer. He wrote in his memoirs: 'With a clear consciousness of being entangled in the web of a remorseless fate, we went into battle for the last time, a battle which was to cost myriads of victims on both sides, which would lay flourishing provinces and cities in rubble and ashes and whose issue in the long run could never be in doubt.' A little melodramatic, to be sure, but essentially true.

On 9 September, three days before the Americans began their first attack on the Westwall, which would hold them up until the following March, Giskes set up his new HQ at the small town of Dersdorf just outside Bonn on the Rhine. He and his men of FAK 307 would not fight at the front. They would continue their war in the shadows, 'with a new opponent who now faced us – the US Army Secret Service.'

He didn't have long to wait to meet these new opponents. A couple of days after the 28th's first and costly attempts to break through the Siegfried Line, the Americans tried again a little further south. Here, between Wallendorf and Bollendorf on the River Sauer, the 5th Armored Division, supported by a regiment of infantry borrowed from the 28th, crossed the shallow river, pushed through the initial defences easily and, before the surprised Germans could react, were heading for the nearest town, Bitburg, and its important road network. Six months later Patton would start his successful drive for the Rhine from Bitburg, with his Fourth Armored Division reaching Germany's last natural barrier within fifty hours.

One of the reasons for the Fifth's success was that they had unwittingly attacked at the boundaries between two German Army groups. The soldiers from one army might be a matter of metres from those of another, but their orders could be coming from headquarters separated by a hundred kilometres.

Field Marshal von Rundstedt at his HQ near Koblenz on the Rhine was understandably alarmed by this surprise enemy attack at the link between his Army Groups B and G. Addicted to cognac as he now was, the aged field marshal was still shrewd enough to realize the inherent danger in this seemingly minor break-through at divisional strength and ordered an immediate counter-attack at corps strength. Naturally the German divisions at that time, after the débâcle in France, weren't up to full strength, but the two and a half divisions which von Rundstedt sent into the attack did have tanks and some of the most

165

experienced soldiers left in the *Wehrmacht*. A humble American divisional commander, with three or four months' battle experience, was being attacked by a German Field Marshal, whose active military experience went back to the turn of the century. General Oliver, commander of the 5th Armored Division, didn't have a chance in hell.

The Germans attacked from three sides and soon forced the *Amis* out of their hilltop positions, then split them into little pockets, knocking out the Fifth's armour first and then proceeded to drive them back to the River Sauer. Within days the Americans had lost some sixty tanks and were barely managing to hold the bridgehead on the River Sauer at the German-Luxembourg village of Wallendorf. *

Then on 22 September something totally unprecedented in the war in the shadows happened. It shouldn't have happened, but it did. On that Friday, as General Gerow at Eupen decided to call off his attack – he had already lost 1,500 men – and pull back the survivors across the Sauer, three civilians masquerading as army officers arrived at Wallendorf. They had driven from Bradley's HQ at Luxembourg City some 20-odd miles away on what could only be called a 'sight-seeing tour', despite the fact that they knew they were contravening the strict instructions given them before they had come to the battle zone: never to put themselves in a position where they might be captured by the enemy.

They were a Major Maxwell J. Papurt, X2 Head at Patton's HQ in Nancy, Gertrude Legendre, an American society woman, who was on leave from her job as supervisor of the OSS message centre in Paris, and one of those rich Republicans who were particularly attracted to the OSS, Lieutenant-Commander Robert Jennings, a Texan oilman in civilian life. It goes without saying that he had once worked for that notorious Captain Rieber, of the Texas Oil Company, who had been so helpful to the Germans back in the summer of 1940.

All three were in possession of Allied Intelligence's greatest secret of the Second World War; each of them knew about Ultra. Now they had ventured to have a look at the front and as the

---

* The village straddles the river's banks on both sides of the frontier.

Germans came out of the low hills of the Ferschweiler Plateau just behind Wallendorf and barrelled through the flaming village heading for the river they took them all prisoner! For the very first time Americans who knew about the great decoding operation had fallen into the hands of the Germans. As the OSS report on their capture stated later, 'Both Legendre and Jennings are in a position to give away extremely damaging information.' As was Major Papurt, in charge of Patton's counter-intelligence, for there was a British Ultra unit stationed permanently with Patton, and Fred Winterbotham, who often delivered top secret information personally to the General, had routinely warned Ultra personnel about loose security and the vital importance of their work by having an officer with a drawn pistol standing next to the person in question while he issued his warning.*

Within a short time the three prisoners were shipped back first to Trier and then to Koblenz. From there they were despatched under heavy guard to Army HQ for more detailed interrogation. One can guess who was behind that detailed interrogation, the star of the *Abwehr's* counter-intelligence, now under the command of General Schellenberg, Lieutenant-Colonel Hermann Giskes.

According to the *Abwehr* records captured after the war by the Allies, the Germans soon ascertained that the three officers were from the American 'secret service', as Giskes persisted in calling the SOS.** Soon thereafter their interrogators learned that there was an Allied organization they had never heard of before: a special SHAEF outfit, the SCI (Special Counter-Intelligence), which operated on tips it received from Ultra decodes and information collected by double agents.

The Germans' interest grew apace. Papurt, who hadn't long to

* According to one of the author's correspondents, the designer of the US Seventh Army's flag and just a humble GI, Patton himself was decidedly lax with the Ultra decodes, often reading them in his presence and making comments on the top secret information therein.
** Throughout the war the Germans had difficulty in realizing that there wasn't an American secret service as such. There were military intelligence organizations, naturally, but the US Secret Service was primarily concerned with guarding the President.

live, apparently tried to mislead the enemy. He said that the SCI was concerned with psychological warfare, making a play of the fact that Radio Luxembourg, just up the road from Wallendorf, had been taken over by the group of German emigres, working for the Americans, who broadcast psychological warfare from there. Naturally the Germans knew of the broadcasts. Indeed from their bunker positions on the top of the Ferschweiler Plateau they could see the nearest three masts of Radio Luxembourg. But during this feint Papurt revealed the real names and tasks of thirty key SCI double-agents. What happened to them, if anything, is discreetly glossed over in the post-war US report.

But what of Ultra? If Papurt betrayed his agents, presumably because he was scared, did he also betray one of the greatest secrets of the war? Giskes' memoir, written long before Fred Winterbotham first revealed the Ultra secret to the world, one that would necessitate a re-writing of the history of the Allied efforts in the Second World War (a reassessment that is not yet complete), says nothing of what transpired at Army HQ that last week in September. So did the Germans, at any rate Giskes and his team from the old *Abwehr*, penetrate that tremendous secret?

The only clue that we have is this. The *Abwehr*'s own code used in the Enigma machine transmissions upon which the Ultra team in Bletchley worked, called 'ISK', vanished abruptly. The British and later the Americans had been using the information gained from the 'ISK' ever since it had first been penetrated in December, 1941. Now, suddenly, the *Abwehr* began using a totally new code.

Why? Was it because, under Schellenberg's new measures, the old code had been changed? Had, on the other hand, Colonel Papurt been forced to reveal the secret of Ultra? In either case it seems that German Intelligence had realized that their code had been compromised and there was a necessity for a change.

There is one thing that gives one pause for thought, however. Although the new *Abwehr-SD* apparat changed its code, the Enigma machine remained in service. Can we therefore conclude that Papurt had spilled the beans, namely that the Allies could read the *Abwehr*'s code, but had limited the amount of information that he was prepared to reveal? Thus, in the time-honoured manner of captured spies, he appeared to be telling all he knew in order to appease his captors, while in reality he was giving them the little finger and *not* the whole hand.

We shall never know the truth. For on the eve of the great offensive in the Ardennes in December, 1944, Colonel Papurt was killed in an Allied bombing attack on his POW cage at Diez just outside that great castle on the Rhine, a score of miles away from Giskes' own HQ. Papurt was the second person who knew about Ultra who was killed while in German captivity. Accident or design?

'I don't want a man from the OSS, not a dwarf, nor a pygmy, nor a goddamned soul from the OSS,' Colonel 'Monk' Dickson, Hodges' Chief-of-Intelligence, raged that winter as the fighting died away in the Ardennes and the area along the Our-Sauer Line settled down in what had become known as the 'Ghost Front'. The bespectacled ex-college professor had had bad experiences with the OSS in Normandy and the capture of the three 'tourists' at Wallendorf had not encouraged him to change his attitude.

So while Giskes had time to ponder over what he had discovered and waited for some sign of life from 'Freddi', both sides slumped into a kind of lethargy: the Germans knowing that orders would come soon for the final battle in the west; the Americans waiting for the Germans' inevitable collapse.

In Washington General Donovan, who led the OSS, seemed to pass his time dreaming up schemes to speed up that process. He knew that once Hitler was out of the way the final collapse of Germany would take place. Already he knew that not only Goering and Ribbentrop were making peace overtures to the Allies, but even Himmler, the 'most feared man in Europe', was taking his first tentative steps in that direction through Schellenberg. All that was stopping the 1,000 Year Reich's rush for peace was the Führer. In Donovan's opinion, the solution was simple. Eliminate Hitler and there'd be peace talks the day after his death was announced.

Learning, for instance, that Hitler might meet Mussolini, his puppet now, at the Brenner Pass, the representative of the SO (the OSS's Subversive Operations) in Washington suggested, 'Let's parachute a cadre of our toughest men into the area and

169

shoot up the bastards. Sure it'll be suicide, but that's what we're organized to carry out.'

Donovan, a former infantry colonel who had won America's highest award, the Congressional Medal of Honor, turned to his chief scientific adviser, Dr Lovell, and asked, 'How would Professor Moriarty capitalize on this situation?'

The scientific adviser, who was used to Donovan's heavy-handed Irish 'jokes', answered, 'I propose an attack which they can't anticipate. They'll meet in the conference room of an inn or at a hotel. [The reference to an inn or hotel shows how hopelessly out of touch the OSS bosses in Washington were with the realities of how Hitler was guarded.] If we can have one operator for five minutes or less in that room, just before they gather there, that is really all we need.'

There was a buzz of scepticism among the OSS brass present, but Lovell was not put out. He explained further, 'I suggest that he brings a vase filled with cut flowers in water and that he places it on the conference table or nearby.' He indicated the janitor who had just entered as if he had been waiting behind the door all the time for his cue. 'In this janitor's hand is a capsule containing liquid nitrogen – mustard gas. It's a new chemical derivative which has no odour whatsoever. It is colourless and floats on water. I have it available at my lab.'

He looked directly at Donovan and said, 'As our man places the bouquet on the conference table he crushes the capsule and drops it among the flowers. An invisible, oily film spreads over the water in the dish and starts vaporizing. Our man is safely out and I think he should disappear into Switzerland as soon as possible.'

'What happens to the men in the conference room?' Donovan asked.

Lovell smiled. 'Well, if they are in the room for twenty minutes, the invisible gas will have the peculiar property of affecting their bodies through the naked eyeballs. Everyone in that room will be permanently blinded. The optic nerve will be atrophied and never function again. A blind leader can't continue the war, at least I don't believe he can.'

As Lovell had anticipated, his murderous suggestion aroused a great deal of excited controversy. But he was not finished yet. 'There's a big pay-off possible, gentlemen, if it is done. If the Pope would issue a Papal Bull, or whatever is appropriate, it might read something like this: "My children, God, in his infinite wisdom, has stricken your leaders blind. His Sixth Commandment is Thou Shalt Not Kill. This blindness of your leaders is a warning that you should lay down your arms and return to the ways of peace."'

Donovan, a strict Catholic, seemed slightly bemused, which he should have been if he had known the thinking of Pope Pius, who had turned a blind eye whenever he had been confronted with Nazi wrongdoing. After all, for the Pope, Hitler's anti-communist 'crusade' was more important. Lovell went on, 'General, this may appear to be a suggestion of hypocrisy that the Pope is asked to practise. But a great number of the German and Italian fighting forces are Roman Catholics. They will heed Pius XII. If he can use his high office to stop this killing, isn't he advancing the cause of Christianity more than any man on earth?'

Donovan promised he would discuss the matter with a friend of his, a member of the American Catholic hierarchy, probably Cardinal Spellman, but nothing came of it.

Undismayed, Lovell tried another tack. He thought he might attack the Führer 'through his glands'. Lovell agreed with the top-secret study of Hitler's emotional life. He and the 'experts' felt that Hitler's 'poor emotional control, his violent passions, his selection of companions like Roehm*,' indicated that the Führer was on the sexual borderline between male and female. Now Lovell felt it might be possible to nudge Hitler over that border-line on to the female side so that 'his moustache would fall off and his voice become soprano'.

Again Lovell had designed an impossible scenario that owed more to Tinseltown than the harsh realities of a world war. His plan envisaged 'smuggling in' a gardener. (To *where*? Hitler was on the move back and forth between east and west all the time.) The latter would doctor Hitler's vegetables for his personal vege-tarian diet with the female hormone. This would upset the Führer's hormonal balance and radically affect his future direc-tion of the war. As Lovell commented in his book *Of Spies and Stratagems*: 'Since he [Hitler] survived, I can assume that the

* Homosexual SA Leader.

171

gardener took our money and threw the syringes and medications into the nearest thicket.' One wonders if Doctor Lovell didn't do something similar.

In Britain the SOE, the rival of Menzies' SIS, also plotted. Now under the command of tough, outspoken General Templer, a fighting soldier who had broken his back when a piano had fallen off a truck in front of him and smashed into him*, the British agents had already broken their own unspoken rule and had decided to eliminate Hitler by force.

Back in 1939 Colonel Mason-Macfarlane, the British military attaché in Berlin, had worked out a plan to assassinate the Führer. He was going to use a telescopic rifle and 'knock the Führer off' from the balcony of his flat in Berlin's Charlottenburg Chaussee. (The plot was strangely reminiscent of Geoffrey Household's famous 1939 thriller *Rogue Male*, later made into a film by Fritz Lang. Curiously, Household was also an SIS agent.) The powers-that-be turned the project down because, as Macfarlane commented in disgust, 'They said it was unsportsmanlike.'

By late 1944 the British sense of fair play had gone out of the window. They had had enough of the Führer. Get rid of him and the whole Nazi house of cards would collapse. Thus it was that after Templer took over active consideration was given, as in Washington, to eradicating Hitler. Captured generals were quizzed on the layout of his headquarters in the West, in particular the 'Eagle's Nest'. SS men who had once worked there were asked to detail the daily routine. For instance they discovered that an SS Guard was always posted outside the Führer's bedroom *day* and night (in case the Leader had a siesta) with a loaded pistol in his hand.

While all this was going on Sefton Delmer, once chief reporter on the *Daily Express* and now in charge of 'black radio' operations against Germany, in particular the notorious *Soldartensender Calais*, approached Templer and discussed with him one of the

---

* Templer had a saving grace of humour despite his frightening manner. Years ago when the author asked him warily for some information, he said cheerfully, 'Of course it's better in your files than slung away in my wastepaper basket as useless rubbish.'

General's pet schemes. It was to release pigeons over the occupied countries and ask the locals to forward details via the birds of German military operations. Sefton Delmer, who had lived in Germany and spoke fluent German, thought it a splendid idea. 'I suggest,' he added to Templer, 'that in addition to parachuting live birds with questionnaires in their boxes, we should also drop dead ones without boxes but with questionnaires attached to their legs which have already been completed – *by ourselves*.'

Templer got it at once, laughed uproariously and approved the scheme immediately. He knew where it would lead. A massive Gestapo search for 'traitors'.

The pigeons were duly dropped and resulted in quite a few questionnaires being returned by Germans who were dissatisfied with Hitler's regime. One day, however, a tired pigeon returned to the SOE London lofts with a polite message scrawled over the customary questionnaire. It read, 'I had the sister of this one for supper. Delicious! Please send us some more.'

The pigeon ploy was over and the plot to kill Hitler was put on hold for a while. At least, it is supposed it was. But then, with victory in sight, politicians on both sides of the front were becoming even more reluctant to become involved in the nasty business of killing a national leader.

In this way some of the Allied chiefs of intelligence spent the early winter of 1944. Giskes, for his part, had more immediate problems on his hands. Freddi had now disappeared on the other side of the Channel. We do not know how Giskes was supposed to keep in touch with his agent. It is hardly likely that the creator of Operation North Pole would use the compromised system of double agents in the UK, run by the Double Cross Committee. More than likely contact would be maintained through one of the neutral embassies.

At all events, Giskes had a much more difficult espionage assignment to carry out in the Ardennes-Eifel border country, where seemingly nothing ever happened of a warlike nature, though to north and south of that sixty-mile front the war continued in its full ferocity.

In early November, 1944, he was summoned by the Army Group B Commander, Field Marshal Walter Model, to his HQ at Munster-Eifel. To his surprise there seemed to be very few troops in the villages he passed through, despite the fact that the Allies were only fifty kilometres away.

In due course he arrived at the well-camouflaged hunting lodge outside the little town which housed the notorious general with a very short fuse. For 'the boy marshal', as von Rundstedt called him, would sack an inefficient officer at the snap of a finger. Fortunately Giskes had not been summoned to meet the Field Marshal himself. Instead he had a good lunch with Model's Chief-of-Intelligence, where he was asked if 'I could think up any scheme to fool the *Amis*, using Allied nationals.'

Giskes was confused by the questions, but he was a realist enough to answer the Chief-of-Intelligence that 'at this stage of the war' it would be virtually impossible for Allied Nationals to work for the Germans, 'even as sleepers'. Giskes didn't mention, of course, that their reluctance was understandable: they knew Germany had lost the war.

But Model's Intelligence Chief didn't seem put off by Giskes' straightforward answer. Whatever he thought of the war situation, he still had the Field Marshal breathing down his neck. Obviously he thought it wiser to carry on with his brief. He told Giskes that he had to try to find a scheme which would fool the enemy on the Western Front to Germany's strategic intentions and that he had four hours to consider the matter.

Giskes raised no more objections. Since the Army plot to kill Hitler the previous July even the *Wehrmacht* was not safe from the Gestapo. He thought it better to try to carry out the Intelligence Chief's wishes without further objections; it would be safer that way.

All that November afternoon, with the distant rumble of the guns from the fighting in the Hurtgen Forest reminding him that he was probably dabbling in the fate of many honest and humble German soldiers, Giskes pondered the problem.

As it was starting to grow dark outside and the orderlies began to close the blackout shutters of the former hunting lodge, dusty animal heads still decorating its walls, Giskes came up with a rough-and-ready idea. He was summoned to the senior officers' table and after 'an excellent dinner' he and the Chief-of-Intelligence discussed his plan for a 'camouflage operation' on the Western Front.

The colonel absorbed Giskes' plan, occasionally making suggestions, as if they were two staff officers planning a real offensive. Then Giskes asked a question. Was the fake operation he was planning, one that somehow or other he was to leak to the Allies, in any way close to a real op – Giskes had guessed that one was planned – currently being worked out at Army Group B HQ? Model's staff officer didn't give him a chance to pursue that line of inquiry. He said Giskes had been given all the information he needed. All he would tell him was that a great new operation in the West was already well beyond the planning stage and eventually would 'shake the enemy out of his self-satisfied complacency'.

That was that. Giskes returned to his HQ puzzled and worried. What if he had come up an offensive that was similar to the one already planned by Model? If he had, then the fat would really be in the fire and he might well end up behind bars, like his poor old ex-chief, the man they'd mocked as 'High C' (a play on Canaris' name and a popular German vitamin drink, full of that vitamin). Not that Canaris would be needing vitamins, for Admiral Canaris wasn't going to live much longer.

On the first Sunday in August that year Schellenberg was working in his Berlin office, equipped with twin machine guns built into his big desk that could be fired by a button at his feet – Schellenberg had a touch of the James Bond in his make-up – when he received a call from 'Gestapo' Muller.

Fully aware that he had the backing of Heydrich's successor, Dr Kaltenbrunner, Muller laid it on the line. He told Schellenberg to go to Canaris' home and arrest him in connection with 'Landesverrat', treachery. He was then to take his prisoner to the castle of Furstenberg.

According to Schellenberg's post-war recollections he protested that he 'would not dream of carrying out such an assignment'. Furthermore he told the head of the Gestapo, 'I shall telephone Himmler at once. This is an imposition.' That, at least, is what he said he said. But by then Muller had vanished and Kaltenbrunner had been executed.

Muller wasn't impressed. 'You know,' he replied, 'that Kaltenbrunner has been put in charge of the July 20 Plot investigation, *not* Himmler! If you refuse to comply with the order, which I herewith repeat, you will have to suffer the consequences.'

That settled it. Schellenberg wasn't one to stick his neck out for anyone. Without another word, he hung up and went off to carry out the order. Just to be on the safe side, he borrowed the adjutant of Colonel Skorzeny's *Jagdkommando*, the German equivalent of the SAS. He was a Baltic-German aristocrat, Baron von Voelkersam, who would also be dead soon. Together they set off for Canaris' home at Berlin-Schlachtensee. Schellenberg knew it well. In better times he had met Canaris there each morning and they had gone for a ride.

Canaris received the two SS officers calmly. When he heard their mission, he dismissed his guests, had Voelkersam remain outside, while he remained closeted with his young rival.

'Somehow, I felt it would be you,' Canaris said to Schellenberg. 'Please tell me first, have they found anything in writing from that fool Colonel Hansen?' He was referring to one of his senior *Abwehr* officers involved in the plot to kill Hitler.

'Yes,' Schellenberg answered. 'A notebook in which there was, among other things, a list of those who were to be killed. But there was nothing on you or your participation.'

'Those dolts on the General Staff can't live without their scribblings,' Canaris snapped. He shook his head, as if he couldn't believe his own ears.

Then Schellenberg revealed the complete details of his mission. Canaris didn't seem too surprised. 'It's too bad,' he commented, 'but we'll get over it. Promise me faithfully that within a few days you will get me an opportunity to talk to Himmler personally. All the others, Kaltenbrunner and Muller, are filthy butchers out for my blood.'

Schellenberg promised. If we are to believe his own written statement he said, 'Herr Admiral, if he wishes to make arrangements then I beg him to consider me at his disposal.' As a sign of his respect, he used the 18th century fashion of indirect address, customary to subordinates when speaking to superiors. 'I shall wait in this room for an hour and in that time you may do whatever you wish. My report will say that you went to your bedroom in order to change.'

Schellenberg was offering Canaris' the officer's way-out – suicide. It was very generous of him. It also would dispense with awkward questions afterwards. But Canaris wasn't falling for that old trick. He wasn't going to be swept under the carpet like that. There was still life in him and while there was life there was hope. 'No, my dear Schellenberg,' he said, 'flight is out of the question for me. And I won't kill myself either. I am sure of my case and I have faith in the promise you have given me.'

Schellenberg doesn't record his feelings at that moment, but we can guess at his anger and frustration.

Half an hour later Canaris came down from his bedroom carrying a small bag. He shook his head at Schellenberg. 'Those devils! They had to draw you into this too. But be on your guard. I've known for a long time that they're after you as well.' With tears in his eyes he embraced the younger man and said thickly, 'When I talk to Himmler I'll tell him about your case as well. Let's go.'

One can guess that Canaris was again playing one of his subtle little games. He was drawing Schellenberg ever deeper into the murky post-July plot by showing apparent concern for the younger man's predicament, while at the same time making sure that Schellenberg remembered that it was vital for him, *for both of them*, that he talked to the SD General's chief, Heinrich Himmler.

They drove through the flat darkened countryside to the castle where Canaris was to be imprisoned. Both men were preoccupied with their own apprehensions. Once Canaris broke the silence to remark that he hoped fate would be kinder to Schellenberg and that he 'would not be hunted down as he had been.'

They arrived at the castle, which housed a training school for border guards. Here Canaris begged Schellenberg to stay with him a little longer. The General obliged and they dined together, for the last time as it turned out. Over dinner Canaris gave Schellenberg instructions on how he should inform Himmler of his arrest and asked him to tell other important people he knew.

It was nearly eleven that Sunday night when Schellenberg said he had to get back to Berlin. Once again Canaris made him promise that he would inform Himmler. Schellenberg gave his word, though he knew he wouldn't, not for the moment. Himmler, at Schellenberg's insistence, had dabbled with the July's plotters as well. Now he had to be seen as merciless towards them. He daren't show any leniency, even to Canaris, whom he respected for reasons known only to himself.

So Canaris embraced him for the last time. 'You are my only hope,' he whispered. 'Goodbye, young friend.'

Schellenberg walked away to where Voelkersam was waiting. He did not look back. He knew that Canaris was as good as dead already.

Just after midnight he was back in his office with its concealed microphones, machine guns and steel shutters of which he was so inordinately proud. He glanced through the pile of red and buff-coloured official files which had come in during his absence, then he ordered an immediate message to be sent to Muller. It read: 'I have carried out the order which you transmitted to me by telephone today. Further details will come to you from *Reichsführer SS* Himmler.' Then he dismissed the Admiral from his life for good.

For the fourth time in his long career Canaris found himself in prison. Three times, as we have seen, he had been able to talk his way out. But this time his luck had run out for good.

While his ex-chief languished in jail Giskes got on with his plan, although almost to the end he didn't know what exactly he was supposed to conceal. First he recruited a reliable German engineer, who got on well with the forced labourers he employed from German-speaking France, Belgium and Luxembourg, along with a few Italians. The engineer was running a work camp for men who laboured on the frontier defences between the border and the Rhine. Originally there had been a *levée en masse* of Germans to do the work, but only three-quarters of a million of the expected one and a half million anticipated by the Party had turned up the previous September. Now the shortfall had been made up by conscripted foreign labour, willing or otherwise.

Giskes told the engineer that he wanted some of his men to escape. The engineer was horrified. Why should he make it easy for his charges to escape? He could be punished. Giskes explained that the escapees could unwittingly help Germany if they managed to reach the US lines, which were some thirty kilometres away from the camp. He improvised a cover story for the engineer. The latter was to pretend to be a covert communist from East Germany and wanted to allow some of his charges to escape so that they could contact the *Amis* in 'liberated' territory, taking with them secret messages which the engineer thought would help the Americans in their efforts to beat the Nazis.

Once the engineer, and naturally Giskes, who remained discreetly in the background, had gained the would-be escapees' confidence and promise that they would do what was expected of them, Giskes dreamed up his own German 'offensive' in the West. It was a two-pronged attack on Aachen, which had been captured by the Americans the previous month.

The 'Giskes offensive' envisaged some ten German divisions, led by armour, sweeping on both flanks into Belgium as far as the River Meuse, splitting the British Army from the American and then squeezing out the subsequent salient. In essence, the 'Giskes Plan' was quite similar to the 'small solution' that some of Germany's top generals, including Field Marshal Model, had suggested as an alternative to the Führer's own grander scheme.

When Giskes finally learned of the Ardennes offensive, 'I felt a sense of intense relief,' he told the author many years later, 'because I thought that by chance I might have hit upon the *real* plan. After all Aachen was the old German Imperial City, of symbolic value to the nation, and Goebbels had promised it would soon be back in our hands.'

In mid-November Giskes proceeded apace with his deception. The first two 'escapers' were let loose from a sub-camp where they were felling trees to make corduroy roads through the forests for military traffic. With them one of the escapers carried a 'secret' message written in milk on a scrap of paper. According to Giskes' devious mind, milk would be the only substance available to conscripted labourers to use for invisible writing. The message was hidden in an old tobacco pouch and the escaper carrying it was to hand it and the message to the first US officer he met when he felt himself in safety.

Just as he had done in the days of Operation North Pole, Giskes wanted confirmation that his plan was working. The 'feedback' was to be for American-controlled Radio Luxembourg, the most powerful transmitter in Europe in those days, to broadcast a

179

statement that someone was sending 'Regards to Otto from Saxony' (the supposed communist engineer who had allowed the labourer to 'escape'). When that message was received the engineer would send further details of a new Nazi plan for a strike westwards.

Ten days after the man escaped it gave Giskes pleasure to hear one of the 'German Jews' who operated the Luxembourg propaganda broadcasts to the Reich under the command of Hans Habe, the German novelist, now transformed into Captain Habe, repeating that message, 'And tonight we sent regards to Otto from Saxony.'

Thereafter Giskes managed to smuggle ten 'escapees' through the 'Ghost Front', each one carrying a new piece of information from the communist 'Otto from Saxony'. They all indicated that the 'enemy' would launch a small-scale 'spoiling attack' in the general area of Aachen. By the end of November 'Operation Heinrich', as the deception plan was called, was going full swing.

Whether it affected Allied thinking in the field of battle is now difficult to assess. The failure of the mainly American command to spot the coming Ardennes Offensive, 'America's Gettysburg of the 20th Century', as it has been called, had become the most discussed intelligence issue of the Second World War. It seems to have caught Eisenhower and *some* of the US Top Brass with their pants down. Others, including Patton for instance, appear to have known that the attack was coming, ordering his staff to plan a counter-operation for the 3rd US Army *four* days before the enemy assault and *seven* days before Eisenhower ordered him to do something to help. Indeed, Patton had at least two counter-intelligence detachments in the First Army area, quite contrary to military etiquette, nearly a month before that fateful Saturday, 16 December when the offensive started and so many American military reputations were ruined, including that of General Hodges, 1st Army commander.

Ultra was blamed for the American failure to see what was coming, though Eisenhower had the equally informative Magic to give him details of the coming attack. General Marshall defended Eisenhower by stating later, 'Ike was let down by his English Chief-of-Intelligence'. But that Englishman (he was actually a Scot) Sir Kenneth Strong, Ike's senior intelligence officer, only learned a quarter of a century later, as he wrote to the author, that the two copies of the highly classified 'Top Secret' intelligence digests for the critical period of that winter had been destroyed after the war 'for security reasons'. Why? We don't know, though we can guess.

Giskes' contribution to the *Abwehr* deception plan, which on the face of it seems to have worked perfectly, if we are to accept the conventional account of the Allies being caught completely by surprise in the Ardennes, must, therefore, remain unassessed. Were the details of Operation Heinrich burned in the 'Top Secret' intelligence reports after the war? Had Giskes' escapers been fooled by Allied intelligence? Had Giskes himself blown up a minor deception ploy into a major operation in order to protect himself at a time when all senior *Abwehr* officers were in danger of being arrested as party to the July plot to kill the Führer? Too many questions with too few answers.

Not that Colonel Giskes had much time now for games of question-and-answer. In January, 1945, after the defeat in the Ardennes, he was on the run like the rest of the *Wehrmacht*. For Germany it was five minutes to midnight. Time was running out fast and the cry was a panicked *sauve qui peut*!

DEATH COMES TO THE ADMIRAL

'An intelligence service is the ideal vehicle for a conspiracy. Its members can travel about at home and abroad under secret orders and no questions asked.'

Allen Dulles, 1945.

By 1945 Schellenberg had been dealing with the Swiss Secret Service for three years, during which time Germany had become Switzerland's most important customer. Sixty per cent of all Swiss exports went to the Reich and Switzerland was Germany's main source of foreign currency. It was therefore vital that both Intelligence services, German and Swiss, should liaise in order to protect this vital inter-state trade from any threat.

In the case of Switzerland the most important player was middle-aged, rather dull-looking Colonel Roger Masson, wartime head of Swiss military intelligence. After his first (of three) meetings with Schellenberg in September, 1942, he became what can be seen today as the perfect symbol of Switzerland's compromised wartime 'neutrality'.

This Swiss-Nazi economic and intelligence collaboration which had the approval of the Swiss Federal Government (the two intelligence chiefs met twice on Swiss soil in 1943) had other not so important spin-offs. Schellenberg convinced the Swiss to close their borders to any further Jewish refugees. In return he told Masson that he had nothing to fear from a German invasion. Why should the Germans kill the goose that laid the golden eggs, despite Hitler's well-known and recorded scorn for the 'money-grabbing Swiss'?

But as far as Schellenberg was concerned, having learned from Masson of Dulles's operations in Switzerland, he began to wonder, as Germany's fortunes started to turn for the worse, whether he could use this contact to open a channel to the West for a separate peace with the Allies. As a contemporary Swiss revisionist historian has written, 'He [Schellenberg] was a very complicated personality, playing the game and looking out for his future after the war. Schellenberg was a careerist and he would do anything for his career. He wanted to make connections and the place to do that was Switzerland.'

By 1944, as time started to run out for Nazi Germany, Schellenberg knew all he needed to know about Dulles and his operations. After all he had the *Abwehr* records at his disposal. He had learned that Dulles had represented German big business, including some of those who belonged to the *Freundeskreis des Reichsfuhrers SS Himmler* (the Friends of Himmler), who yearly voted the head of the SS a huge sum of money running into millions of reichsmark. These 'friends' from big business were making fortunes from the concentration camps with their cheap labour, which could work a seven-day week on a starvation diet for a handful of concentration camp marks to be used in shops owned by themselves.

He knew, too, that Dulles was supposedly no friend of the Jews and, more importantly, that he was definitely anti-communist. Indeed Dulles seemed genuinely to *like* Germans – he surrounded himself with them – and often he appeared more intent on building up an anti-Russian post-war Europe than defeating Germany.

As another contemporary Swiss historian has summed him up: 'He was an egomaniac; he wanted to run the war out of Berne. He was a very successful corporate lawyer and he had a tremendous number of friends in the German business and legal community. He was not pro-Nazi, but he was pro-German. He supported the conservative resistance very heavily. . . . He was setting up deep-penetration operations all over Europe; he was lobbying and setting up networks of people everywhere with a very clear antenna out for the Russians, paving the way for the post-war, Cold War era. . . . He was devious and condescending and as far as he was concerned anything that was good for international business was good for him and vice-versa.'*

By the end of 1944 he had worked out a ploy which might start the ball rolling. His aim was to bring about a peace approach made through Dulles to the US government. But there was one major catch: the Jewish lobby. By now it was known that the Nazis – Nazis and SS were already becoming the alibi of the German nation, for it wasn't the ordinary German who was the criminal, but the Nazi and SS man – were persecuting the Jews. What if a senior SS officer made an offer to free a large number of Jews? How would that go down with America, especially their most powerful representative in Roosevelt's administration, the author of the plan to reduce Germany to the level of an agricultural state, Henry Morgenthau?

As Schellenberg himself wrote after the war, 'It was at this time that my Swiss contacts brought me in touch with Herr Musy, a former President of Switzerland. He was an utterly selfless man, highly intelligent and knowledgeable, who had but one aim, the saving of as many as possible of the hundreds of thousands in concentration camps.'

Others didn't have such a high opinion of the 75-year-old Jean-Marie Musy. They thought this friend of Himmler was pro-Nazi and, now that the Germans were losing the war, Musy was attempting to restore his tattered reputation by helping the Jews inside Occupied Europe. At a price, naturally. After all, he was Swiss.

Towards the end of 1944, after weeks of preparation, Schellenberg persuaded Himmler to talk to this Swiss paragon. Himmler said he'd agree to a mass evacuation of certain Jewish concentration camp inmates in return for tractors, cars and medicine for Germany. Musy made a counter-suggestion. Himmler should accept foreign currency instead. The Americans, the Swiss statesman maintained, would never accept a deal in which vehicles to be used in the German war effort (paid for, incidentally, by Jews outside the Reich) were bartered for Jewish lives. If the Germans wanted to establish some sort of bridge to the US

* It must be remembered that ever since the Swiss Gold scandal started, and other money-laundering operations that might have taken place in Switzerland in our own decade, the Swiss have gone over from the defensive to the attack. After all, their existence depends upon it.

administration it would have to be Jews for money, the foreign currency being used for the swap to be kept in Switzerland which would be used as a 'place of transit' for these Jews who would emigrate from there to the USA.

It was horse-trading of the worst kind: *money for lives*. But the 'package' was cunningly designed. Himmler would have his first contact with the Americans at the top. Switzerland would retain the money, for a while at least, and be shown in its usual, customary humanitarian fashion, but wouldn't have the problem of supporting the Jews in transit. As for the USA, if Roosevelt turned the package down, he'd be shown by the US Jewish-owned media as being a hard-hearted bastard who was sticking to that uncompromising 'unconditional surrender' edict of his, leaving himself no room to save the lives of these pathetic victims of Nazi cruelty. In essence, the Swiss must have told themselves, as 1944 gave way to 1945 and the Allied Chiefs-of-Staff were making their first tentative plans to invade Switzerland, if anyone was going to come out of this barter deal smelling of roses, it was going to be the much-maligned neutral Swiss.

So the ground was prepared. Now the time had come to lure Dulles to the conference table. For time was running out for both the Germans and their bankers. On both frontiers, East and West, the Allies were attacking all out, pushing back the *Wehrmacht* all the time. At Eisenhower's Headquarters, Colonel Bernie Bernstein, Morgenthau's man in Europe, was urging ever more stringent measures to block the outflow of capital from Germany via Switzerland. And Colonel Bernstein didn't hesitate about not using 'channels', going over the Supreme Commander's head to report to Morgenthau, who had the ear of the dying President Roosevelt. In Switzerland itself the secret communist agent, Currie, head of the inquiry commission set up by Morgenthau, was putting on the pressure to make the Swiss disclose, among other things, the amount of Nazi assets currently being held by Swiss banks and their branches overseas. Now, if the Swiss gave way and lifted their much-prized 'Swiss Bank Secret', then they would lose the confidence of foreign customers for all time.

On Sunday, 25 February, 1945, a cold and sunless day in Alsace, the visit of Dulles and his assistant, von Gævernitz, to the

US Sixth Army Group's HQ in that part of embattled France was rudely disturbed by an urgent message from Switzerland. The message came at a very inopportune time. General Devers' Sixth Army Group had just lost a safe full of Ultra documents. It was, potentially, a major disaster. Eisenhower had blown up when he had heard the news; he didn't like General Devers as it was. He ordered a 'theaterwise' search. If the safe, with its war-winning secret, was not found, heads would roll and Devers must have wondered if one of them would be his.

All the same the message from Major Waibl of Swiss Intelligence made him forget the Ultra mystery.* Waibl was Dulles's most important contact within Swiss Intelligence and the former's message that he needed to see the two OSS men that very night in Lucerne got Dulles and von Gævernitz on the road immediately. They drove to Strasbourg and from there took the first train to Lucerne.

Major Waibl and his companion, Professor Husmann, who was a Pole who had become a Swiss citizen and was now the head-master of a fashionable boys' school at Montane am Zugerberg and probably a spy of some sort, dined at a discreet restaurant near Lake Lucerne. Here he informed his American guests that he had a strange visitor, a garrulous Italian baron named Parilli. The Baron, who had political aspirations, had come to Switzerland to ask the Swiss to use their good offices to open a channel for peace talks with the German commanders of the Northern Italian front. They still had a million soldiers under their orders and were preventing the Allies from advancing into the Po Valley and driving for the Austrian frontier. Dulles, who was now asked by Waibl if he would help, must have realized that his finest hour had arrived. With a bit of luck, if everything went well, he was about to be instrumental in bringing the war in the south to an end. It was a golden opportunity to win the kudos of victory and at the same time prepare an important section of Western

---

* The mystery of who took the truck with the safe was never cleared up. The truck and the safe, apparently untouched, were found half-submerged in a stream. It remains one of the minor intelligence mysteries of the Second World War.

Europe for the kind of right-wing, anti-communist future he envisaged for the Old Continent.

Perhaps he didn't know it at the time, at least he never mentioned the fact in his post-war book on his 'unique victory', but Dulles was beginning his deals with European big business. They would ensure that the Morgenthau Plan was never put into force and that the post-war governments of Western Europe were mainly right-wing, dependent on and supported by the United States, by armed force if necessary.

For Baron Parilli was not just some stage dago with a taste for fancy clothes and tall blondes, he was also the son-in-law of the enormously rich Milan industrialist, Posch. Not only that, Parilli was himself a captain of industry with a large stake in the fate of industry in the Po Valley, threatened as it was now by the left-wing Italian partisans, who might well take over, once the *Tedeschi* fled.

Naturally Dulles checked on Parilli with his friends in Washington and was delighted to learn that he had once been the 'competent sales representative in Italy of an American appliance firm', as Dulles's latest biographer has described him. That must have clinched the deal. Operation Sunrise, as it was later code-named, was on.

Things now started to move and for a totalitarian state, where the slightest wrong move, the merest hint of treachery, resulted in the person concerned being attached to a meat hook or having a chicken wire noose placed around his neck pretty smartish, a handful of high-ranking Germans moved with a great deal of apparent freedom.

Within days of that meeting in Lucerne Parilli, a former salesman for the American Nash-Kelvinator Corporation, manufacturers of refrigerators, was meeting SS General Wolff in Italy. The commander of all SS troops and allied German police forces in that theatre was himself a former businessman, admittedly a failed one. Yet, after a long career in the SS, Wolff had still managed to keep up his business contacts. He was an acquaintance of Baron von Schroeder, a long-time Nazi and one of the leading members of that group of German bankers, industrialists and businessmen who formed the *Freundeskreis des Reichsführers SS Heinrich Himmler* (The Circle of Friends of

Reichsführer SS Heinrich Himmler). This group annually paid in a large sum to Himmler for any purpose he wished to use it. Naturally, in return, they expected certain favours and over the years they had received them and had become very rich indeed.

So when, in March, 1945 Dulles, Woolf and Parilli met to discuss the surrender of Italo-German forces in Northern Italy, they were like three businessmen sitting down at a table to hammer out the fine details of some business transaction, not whether young men of twenty different nationalities should live or die. For while they deliberated, Allied generals sent their troops into the final attack in the Po Valley, in which thousands were killed and wounded unnecessarily, including one young American, a future presidential hopeful, Senator Dole, who was severely wounded as an officer of the US 10th Mountain Division.

And in the wings hovered Walter Schellenberg, waiting to produce no less a personality than Himmler himself, who was now desperately searching for someone to negotiate a peace with before the Thousand Year Reich collapsed in total ruin.

But that wasn't to be. Within two months Himmler would be dead by his own hand and Schellenberg would be beginning his three-year 'tour' of Allied interrogation centres bartering his life as a potential war criminal for the tangled mess of lies and half-truths which masqueraded as intelligence. Seven years later Walter Schellenberg would be dead and forgotten.

Behind him, however, he left a muddying of the waters that is with us to this day, that of the Melmer Shipments and the role the Swiss had played in their use, not to forget those businessmen-bankers and supposed spymasters who in 1945 and afterwards contributed to the great cover-up.

Fifty years later the anniversary of VE Day seems to have re-opened the door to that murky past. Senator Alfonso D'Amato, representing New York with its vital Jewish vote, set the ball rolling. He was followed by others, making their claims for redress and retribution, not only for the Jews, but those forgotten masses of slave labourers from the German-occupied countries, in particular in the East, whose claims had been fobbed off for decades because they had had the misfortune to live under another totalitarian regime.

President Clinton naturally got in on the act, as did, predictably,

Labour Member of Parliament and chairman of the Holocaust Educational Trust, Greville Janner. Both demanded some sort of final solution, a release of the still hidden 'Nazi Gold' and compensation for those who had suffered at Nazi hands.

President Clinton's representative, Mr Eizenstat, who was to negotiate with the representatives of the current German government and those of German firms such as Mercedes, Siemens and Volkswagen which had survived the war, declared, 'As the leader of the Allied effort during the war, as the liberator of many of the concentration camps, we have a personal interest in seeing that the last sad chapter of World War II is closed in a just and fair manner.'

It was easier said than done. President Clinton wanted the whole business wound up by September, 1999, the sixtieth anniversary of the outbreak of the war. But the Germans and the Swiss refused to play to America's tune. Negotiations broke down and remain unresolved. It seems that, in the end, time alone will solve the problem. There will be no survivors left to be compensated.

But what of Canaris?

By the time General Wolff was talking with Dulles, Canaris' luck had finally run out. Kaltenbrunner had interrogated him and found the Admiral to be 'a masochist, a sadist and a homosexual of both active and passive character at the same time'. If that wasn't enough to have him incarcerated under Paragraph 175 of the German Legal Code (Paragraph 175 was the one dealing with homosexuals), Canaris was also a traitor with links to the 20 July plotters.

After lengthy cross-examination at Gestapo HQ in Berlin, Canaris and other 'traitors' were taken by bus to the remote Flossenburg Concentration Camp. Perhaps Kaltenbrunner thought it far enough from Berlin to get rid of prominent prisoners of the Reich without too much fuss. In the death throes of the Reich Hitler intended that none of those who had betrayed him would survive. Indeed, from his last will and testament, it seems that he would have liked to have seen the whole German people perish for having failed him.

Flossenburg had originally been built for 16,000 prisoners, but by that spring its population had expanded to 60,000. The most important of these were imprisoned in the so-called 'bunker'. There they were held in forty cells, the threat of death hanging constantly over their shaven heads. For Kaltenbrunner and Hitler had both decreed that they would die before they were liberated by Patton's Third Army. Right to the end that malicious German streak was to operate.

By April Patton was getting close. His divisions had already reached Buchenwald and released the surviving 50,000 inmates. He was now closing on Flossenburg.

In Berlin Kaltenbrunner ordered the execution of the 'July conspirators'. On 8 April, 1945, one of them, a Bavarian nicknamed 'Ox-Jo', was led out to the gallows and told, 'The last act is about to begin. You will be hanged right after Canaris.' Surprisingly, nothing happened. The confusion was too great. We must assume that the SS guards were not very happy about executing important Germans with the *Amis* perhaps only a day's march away. 'Ox-Jo' was left standing in the yard in front of the gallows, wondering what to do next, when one of the guards gestured back to the cells and said, 'We'll have to forget you for today.' Bewildered, 'Ox-Jo' was led back to his cell.

Most of them waiting that April morning were to survive to tell their tale. Soon they'd be part of a fleeing SS convoy which would be taken over by a resolute *Wehrmacht* officer and end their ordeal in, of all places, the island of Capri.

One of them, however, *had* to die!

Colonel Lunding tried to sleep, but to no avail. It had been a strange night. At four he had fallen asleep, but had been woken almost immediately by the cry of a child. Perhaps it was the daughter of the ex-Chancellor of Austria, Kurt von Schuschnigg. He didn't know. He crept in his stockinged feet to a crack in the wooden door. He peered down the ill-lit corridor. It was empty. Behind the SS office at the far end there was a window. Through it he could just make out the six nooses of the gallows, swaying slightly in the dawn breeze. They were waiting for someone.

At six he heard the stamp of heavy boots. Names were called. Again Lunding crept to the door and peered through the crack. The lights in the yard had been turned on. The nooses were clearly outlined. Behind them the metal plates used to stop the bullets of the *coup de grace* if the victim was still alive after the hanging gleamed.

The stamp of boots had stopped at the next cell. Canaris had been right. That had been his last interrogation. There was the clatter of the prisoner's chains falling to the stone floor. He had been freed from them, but release meant death.

Lunding could see the prisoner quite clearly. He was dressed in a neat grey suit and grey tweed overcoat. As he recorded afterwards, 'the prisoner's face showed no fear'. They moved off. Down below there was the order, *'Alles ausziehen'* – everything off.

Lunding gasped. Canaris' body, when he pulled off his white shirt, was a mass of bruises and bloody wounds. He had been badly beaten.

The naked prisoners shuffled forward in single file to their personal Golgotha. Lunding hoped they wouldn't hang the old man. After all, he *had* been a patriot, an admiral in the German Navy. Perhaps they'd shoot him. That would be more fitting for an officer with over thirty years of service behind him; he shouldn't die like a common criminal at the end of a rope.

But it wasn't to be. The prisoner was strung up at the end of a piece of chicken wire. There he kicked and writhed in agony until it was over.

Time passed. 'Ox-Jo' sat slumped on his three-legged stool. The slide of the Judas Hole was opened slowly. A voice, speaking English, asked, 'Do you understand me?'

'Yes,' Ox-Jo answered. 'I speak English.'

'I am an English officer,' the voice said. 'Do you belong to the officers going to be executed?'

'Yes, I appear to belong to them.'

There was a moment's silence. Then he gave 'Ox-Jo' a message that made him feel that God himself was watching over him. 'Well,' the Englishman breathed, 'it's not going to happen. It's all over. They're burning your friends now, behind the hut.'

The wheel had come full circle. The little spymaster was dead at last. The man who had played such a strange role in the life of his nation had died the way that Italian jailer had predicted so long before. *Dopodomani* had arrived at last.

191

ENVOI

'There is not, there was not and there never will
be any romance about the spy trade. The silent
war of the spy is mean, cold and bitter. It is the
dirtiest side of war. And I hate war as I hated the
trade of the spy. *For always!*

Erich Gimpel, Agent 146, the last
Abwehr spy to be released from US captivity in
1955.

Much to Colonel Ritter's surprise, British Intelligence arrested
him in Hamburg in the summer of 1945. In the last year of the
war, when it had become obvious that his *Abwehr* cover was
blown, he had been transferred to the command of a *Luftwaffe*
flak regiment. After the *Kapitulation*, as the Germans call it to this
day, never the surrender, he returned to the scene of his great
days as the spymaster in charge of operations against the Anglo-
Americans. Here he had attached himself to the staff of a flak
division. The staff was in the process of being interrogated by a
bunch of American civilians masquerading as soldiers on the
effect of American bombing on German cities. Naturally the
Germans told the *Amis* what they wanted to hear: bombing had
been the US's decisive weapon. 'They were very nice people,
very generous,' Ritter recalled three decades later, 'but they did
warn us against the Liemies' (*sic* – limeys).

But unlike the Germans and the Americans, the British have
long memories. Some maintain they always live in the past. Be
that as it may, British Intelligence finally caught up with
Colonel Ritter. He wasn't exactly in the first league of espionage

by now, so the gentlemen of the Intelligence Corps had plenty of time. Ritter wasn't going anywhere that summer save eventually to the former Nazi concentration camp at nearby Neuengamme.

Ritter didn't like the English. Surprisingly, the spymaster who had run virtually all the early operations against Britain had never been to that country. Now his illusions about the English quickly vanished.

A certain Captain Bell, who first interrogated him, didn't waste too much time on Ritter. He told him that all his agents from 'Johnny' onwards had really been double agents, with the British controlling them all, including the one who won the Iron Cross and was transmitting to Germany until 3 May, 1945, the day the British Seventh Armoured Division rolled into Hamburg.

Ritter didn't believe him, but the clincher came when the Intelligence Corps officer told him as much as the German needed to know about what Ritter later called the 'Erickson Group'. Casually Bell asked about 'Vera' or 'Viola', as Ritter had called her. The Colonel steadfastly refused to answer. He felt 'the need to protect my agent'.

Vera had not been *his* agent from the start. Another British officer named 'Cook' took over. Again he asked about Vera. Ritter refused to speak. He was shown photos. According to Ritter he spotted Druegge in one and when he said he knew the man Cook said, 'He was a brave man. We had to shoot him because he pointed his pistol at one of our people as he was being arrested.'

That pleased Ritter. In later years he would never admit that the British officer had obviously lied to him in order to gain his confidence and answer any questions posed about the mysterious Vera. Cook then told Ritter that Vera had been working for them since 1937. She had come to England for a brief visit and MI5 had arrested her 'because she'd been a communist'. Something which seems hardly likely in those far-off days.

But in the end Ritter had to accept the fact that Vera, Lady May and the Duchess of Château-Thierry had all been working for the British and that he had been set up. The full extent of how greatly he had been fooled never dawned upon him until in his old age he read Masterman's book on the Double-Cross System.

But even the fact that he had sent some sixteen agents to death and imprisonment did not seem to worry him. Almost to the end in his little flat in Gross Flottbek, not far from the River Elbe, outside Hamburg, he would shrug his shoulders and say, 'It was war, I suppose.'

Colonel Giskes proved to be a tougher nut than Ritter. Both Britain and Holland were gunning for him. But the British got him first and, perhaps because the British secret services, MI6 and the SOE, now allegedly disbanding, had something to hide, Giskes was whisked off smartish to Latchmere House, a three-storey manor house hidden behind a high wall in the Surrey village of Ham Common.

Here, under the command of a monocled Rhodesian colonel, nicknamed 'Tin-Eye' Stephens, a skilled staff put Giskes and his last major agent 'Freddy' through their paces.

Giskes, according to his own story, was subjected to harsh and humiliating treatment. Held in the place's 'centre cage', he was routinely stripped naked and faced with hour-long interrogations by relays of intelligence men. (From which service they came he never discovered.)

At first the interrogators were only concerned with the North Pole operation. The Dutch government were establishing a team to enquire into how nearly fifty agents, all Dutch, could fall into German hands so easily, especially after the captured radio operators had transmitted their secret distress signals back to London. Giskes, who felt that he had a clear conscience (it had been war and it had been his duty as an *Abwehr* officer to fight it as efficiently as he could), answered readily enough. It was easier to co-operate, even if one didn't want to. He'd learnt that after Canaris' dismissal and the take-over of his service by the SS and SD.

For a while there was an unwelcome change of direction. The interrogators started asking Giskes about the 'King Kong' affair, the possibility that his Dutch double agent Lindemann might have betrayed the Arnhem Operation of September, 1944, to the Germans. Giskes denied the allegation strenuously. He didn't want to be sent to Holland on account of what had happened at Arnhem.

Once Giskes heard a voice that he'd last heard six years

194

before. He took a careful look over the balcony to the courtyard below and nearly fell over. There was the double-traitor Jack Hooper, dressed in the khaki uniform of a British captain. Back in the '30s, the naturalized Englishman Hooper, who had been born Dutch, had worked for the SIS in Holland. He had also betrayed the SIS's secrets to the *Abwehr* for the currency of his land of birth.

Back in October, 1939, Hooper had phoned him from the Hague to his room at the Dom Hotel in Cologne and asked Giskes to come to Holland immediately. He had a vital message for him.

Giskes had set off on the next train from Cologne via Aachen, bound for Holland. But at Aachen, just before the express to Holland crossed the frontier, Giskes had received a 'train telegramme' warning him 'with the utmost urgency' not to venture any further. His chief had discovered that Hooper had been turned yet again. Now he was working for the British once more. He was luring Giskes to his death, for as he told the author, 'undoubtedly he would have plunged me there into the nearest *graacht* to keep me silent for good'.

Years later he recalled, 'I was not prepared to betray anyone. But Hooper was different. I was still angry with him. After all, he had tried to murder me.' Duly he reported to his interrogator what he knew of Hooper's double-dealing. Immediately he was taken out under escort to confront the man, who was strolling about with a number of other men in khaki. Giskes identified the traitor and would-be killer and that was that. Some time later he asked his interrogator what had happened to the man. The answer was a laconic: 'We've hanged him!'

In due course Giskes was released and, like Ritter, he joined the German-led Gehlen Organization, named after the Intelligence General of that name, which was financed by the newly emerging CIA which Allen Dulles had encouraged to enlist the Germans' support.

Not that Dulles had been offered control of the CIA by President Truman as he had expected. He had powerful friends in Washington, but powerful enemies as well. Just before his death General Donovan, the wartime head of the OSS, told 'Moriarty', aka Dr Lovell: 'The other day Allen Dulles came in here and said he had been offered the job of head of the CIA. What did I advise?

I told him, "Al, you were a great performer as a lone operator, but this CIA job needs an expert organizer and you're no good whatever at that." He left damned mad at me, but God help America if he heads up the CIA.'

Naturally Dulles had been flying a kite at the time, but in the end he did 'head up the CIA'. With the help of his ex-*Abwehr* agents, he fought the good fight until President Kennedy had had enough of him and sacked him after the Bay of Pigs fiasco. But by then America and the West were so deeply involved in the Cold War that it would take another quarter of a century before that even greater war in the shadows finally came to an end.

So, in one of the many ironies of post-war Europe, both Ritter and Giskes, who had fought long and hard against Dulles and his fellow 'spooks', became their most trusted and reliable comrades-in-arms in yet another war in the shadows.

But what about 'Freddi', Giskes' last and most ambitious project? What had happened to him and why had he been sent to Britain on such a risky premise in the first place? Was he there to spy or had he been given a more sinister mission, the murder of Winston Churchill?

Even before America entered the war in 1941 Edgar Hoover, the head of the FBI, kept a record of all assassination attempts on Churchill's life, and there were plenty of them. They came from Irish-Americans, America Firsters, and the general run of crackpots and anti-British nut cases. Hoover collected such threats, basically an expression of deep-rooted anglophobia in certain sections of US society, by the bundle. We can assume that there were similar threats assembled by the Special Branch and MI5 in Britain too. Churchill, guarded by a single middle-aged bodyguard, Inspector Thompson of the 'Yard', must have been subjected to such threats on his life throughout his political career.

Hitler, surprisingly enough, ordered that no attempt should be carried out to assassinate his most determined adversary. It was suggested during the war that, despite the Führer's orders, a British plane from North Africa to England had been shot down by the *Luftwaffe* over the Bay of Biscay because one of the passengers was supposed to be Churchill. Indeed, there was a

British businessman on board who did have some resemblance to the Prime Minister. Another passenger who died in that crash was Leslie Howard, the famous actor, but the charge was never proven.

Had Hitler rescinded the order by the time of the Allied invasion of France? Was 'Freddi' sent to Britain as part of a plot to kill Churchill? At that time, any rupture of the Anglo-American alliance by whatever means could only benefit Germany. We don't know. For Giskes refused to talk on the matter (to the author at least) and whatever documentation that survives concerning Freddi's presence here has disappeared or is still securely under official lock and key. However, we *do* know that the Austrian agent was in Britain till at least the summer of 1945 and that, thereafter, he was quietly got rid of by the British authorities, presumably to return to his native Austria.

On 8 April, 1945, the Independent Member of Parliament for Eye, Edgar Granville, raised a question in the House. Tipped off by the war correspondent of the now defunct *News Chronicle*, he asked about a 'handsome German officer named Captain Klause (sic)' who had parachuted into 'a country area about a month ago'. From there he had made his way to London, where disguised as a refugee, he hoped 'to use information he gained in Paris during the German occupation as his bargaining point to enable him to change sides at this late stage of the war'. Granville then addressed a question to the Home Secretary, Herbert Morrison. It was: 'Did this man bring various proposals with him and did he make certain contacts in this country?' He added pointedly that perhaps this was the reason why 'Captain Klause' was receiving 'special treatment not usually afforded to Nazi prisoners.'

'Red Ellen', the ultra left-wing Parliamentary Under-Secretary to the Home Office, Miss Ellen Wilkinson, answered for her chief. She set Mr Granville to right without any fussing about. He'd got most of his story wrong. The man was not a German, but an Austrian. He was not a captain in the German Army, but a civilian who had been an employee of a German firm in Occupied Paris. And, he wasn't even called 'Klause'; his real name was Alfred Ignatz Maria Kraus! That 'Ignatz Maria' clinched her case.

Anyone who knew anything about Catholic Austria knew that those two names could only mean the man in question was not a German but a God-fearing Austrian.

With Granville on the run, she relaxed and conceded that Herr Kraus wasn't all he seemed to be when he had arrived 'through friends' in London. In 1944, after the liberation of Paris, he claimed to have rendered assistance during the occupation to the Allied cause and offered to join the British Army. In September, 1944, he was brought to this country on insufficient information about him and without proper authority. She didn't say on whose authority he was brought from France, but ended her answer with the statement that the authorities had decided Kraus was a person 'who should not be at liberty' and 'he was accordingly interned. . . . Herr Kraus was not receiving any preferential treatment.' And that was that, it appeared.

But Granville was not satisfied with the explanation. On 24 April, with the war in Europe entering its final week of real fighting, Mr Granville asked more questions in the House. This time the Home Secretary answered personally. He revealed, according to *Hansard*, that Kraus had been brought to London 'without explicit permission to leave France' and that he had been given British uniform 'which he was not entitled to wear'. Morrison went on to state that the British officer responsible had been court-martialled. Who that British officer was, Morrison didn't say.

Granville persisted at Question Time: 'How had Kraus been allowed to run about for a whole month without being apprehended,' he asked. Morrison said, 'There were irregularities in his arrival. We got track of him as quickly as we could and put him inside.'

'But is my Right Honourable Friend quite sure that he has the fullest information about this man?'

Morrison answered Granville's question with his head bent characteristically to one side, one eye twinkling behind his old-fashioned spectacles. 'I think,' he said confidently, 'we know all about him. In fact, the honourable Member would be surprised how much we know about all sorts of things.' And that was that. Freddi Kraus disappeared into the obscurity from whence he had come.

Not a mile away from where the Home Secretary assured the House of Commons that its members would be surprised if they knew 'how much we know about all sorts of things', Blunt, Philby and all the rest of those upper class traitors were already geared up, ready to start the new 'war in the shadows'. One secret war had been won; another was about to begin.

BIBLIOGRAPHY

N. Ritter: *Deckname Dr Rantzau*. Hoffmann & Campe. 1972.

H. Hoehne: *Canaris*. Hoffmann & Campe. 1974.

C. Whiting: *Canaris*. Ballantine. 1973.

C. Whiting: The Spymaster. Saturday Review Press. (Dutton Inc) 1976.

A. Lebor: *Hitler's Secret Bankers*. Birch Lane Press. 1997.

P. Grose: *The Gentleman* Spy. Houghton Mifflin. 1997.

K. Abshagen: *Canaris: Patriot und Weltburger*. Deutsche Verlagsgesellschaft. 1960.

R. Accoce and P. Quest: *La Guerre a été gagné en Suisse*. Gallimard.

P. Dourlein: *Inside North Pole*. Kimber. 1956.

G. Buchheit: *Der Deutsche Geheimdienst*. Econ Verlag. 1956.

G. Peis: *So ging Deutschland in die Falle*. Econ. 1976.

W. Hagen: *Die Geheime Front*. Wiener Verlagshaus. 1967.

D. Kahn: *The Codebreakers*. Macmillan. 1963.

J. Peikalkiewicz: *Spione, Agenten, Soldaten*. Berthelsmann. 1970.

L. Farago: *The Game of Foxes*. Hodder & Stoughton. 1971.

INDEX

202

Kaltenbrunner, Ernst, xii, 108, 150, 175–76, 189–90
Kennedy, Joseph, 44, 94
Kent, Tyler, 94
Kiep, Otto, 148, 149
Kolbe, Fritz, 96
Kopper, Colonel, 128
Kostring, General, 23
Kraus, Freddie, 157–58, 159–61, 169, 173, 196–98
Krohn, *Kapitain zur See* von, German naval attaché, 8, 10

Landing, Alfred, 33
Lang, Hermann, 36–38
Lauwers, Hubertus, 115
Leahy, Admiral William D., 96
Lee, Duncan, xiii
Legendre, Gertrude, 166, 167
Lend-Lease agreements, 99
Liebknecht, Karl, 15
Lindemann, Professor Frederick, 38, 40
Lindner, *Kapitanleutnant*, 130–31
Liss, General Ulrich, 63
Local Defence Volunteers, 57
London, City of, 26, 104–5
Long Range Desert Group, 76–77
Lonkowski, William, 28–29, 33
Lovell, Dr, 170–72, 195
Lowenthal, Herr, 51
Luedecke, *Kapitanleutnant*, 6–7
Luftwaffe
    122nd Reconnaissance Squadron, 127, 128
    need for US technology, 28, 31–37
Lunding, Colonel, 3–5, 190–91
Luxemburg, Rosa, 15, 16

McCarthy, J.R., 99
Mackenzie, Compton, 9
McKittrick, Thomas, 93, 103
Marshall, General George, 180

Maskelyne, Major Jasper, 140
Mason-Macfarlane, Colonel, 172
Masri Pasha (Egyptian Army), 67–69
Masson, Colonel Roger, 182
Masterman, Major John, 139, 140–41
Maugham, Somerset, 9
Maxwell, Sgt Robert, 160
May, Herr, 118
Melmer Shipments, 90–92, 101, 106–7, 134, 188
Mendelsohn, Erich, 39–40, 41
Menzies, General Stewart, 122, 155
Mercedes-Benz, 189
Merriless, Chief Constable, 60–61
Military intelligence, German *see* *Abwehr*
Model, Field Marshal Walter, 164, 173–75, 179
Monkaster, Peter (Sandberg), 74, 81, 83–84
Montabelli di Condo, Countess ('Duchess'), 53, 54
Montgomery, General Bernard, 71–72, 85
Mooney, James, 44
Morgenthau, Henry, US Treasury Secretary, 41, 47, 95, 184, 185
Morgenthau Plan for Germany, 99–102, 103–5, 106–7, 187
Morrison, Herbert, MP, 197, 198
Muller, General, head of Gestapo, 108, 149, 175
Musy, Jean-Marie, 184

Nasser, Gamal Abdel, 68
Nationalist movements, 83, 156
Naval Intelligence (British), 8
Navy, German, 14–15
    Hitler's view of, 24
Netherlands
    Abwehr operations in, 112–25
    double agents in, 194–95

US Army
  1st Army, 161–62
  5th Armored Div, 162, 164
  28th Infantry Div, 162, 163–64
  and Ardennes offensive, 180–81
  Sixth Army Group, 186
US Communist Party, 97
USA
  Abwehr activity in, 45–47
  anti-British views, 105
  and communist threat, 97–98
  German-American agents in,
    28–31, 46–47
  Hitler's view of, 23
  industrial sabotage, 130–34
  isolationism, 24–25, 47
  Jewish lobby in, 184, 188
  leaks from cabinet meetings,
    94–95
  liberal pro-communist faction, 25
  and OSS, 169–70
  and Pearl Harbor, 81
  pro-German interests in, 24–26,
    43–46
  Rieber-Westrick dinner at Waldorf,
    43–46
  and Russia, 95

USAAF
  Eighth Air Force, 41
  strategic bombing, 131

Venona decodes (US), 25, 102
'Vera' *see* Schalburg, Vera von
Vermehren, Erich, 149
Voelkersam, Baron von, 176, 178
Vogel, Lieutenant, 16
Volkswagen, 26, 90, 189
Vought Aviation, 28

Waibl, Major, 186
Waldberg, Jose, 49
Wallace, Henry, US Vice President,
  94–96, 105
Walti, Werner, 49, 55, 58, 60–61, 62
Welsh nationalists, 48, 65
Westrick, Dr, 43, 46
White, Harry Dexter, 25, 99–100, 102
Wichmann, Captain, 51
Wilhelmshaven, 18
Wilkinson, Ellen, MP, 197–98
Wilmot, Chester, 153
Winterbotham, Gp Capt Fred, x,
  124, 153, 155, 167
Wolff, General, 88, 187–88, 189
World Bank, 100